International Standards for Automatic Exchange of Information in Tax Matters

CRYPTO-ASSET REPORTING FRAMEWORK AND 2023 UPDATE TO THE COMMON REPORTING STANDARD

OECD
BETTER POLICIES FOR BETTER LIVES

The Crypto-Asset Reporting Framework (CARF) and a set of amendments to the Common Reporting Standard (CRS), along with associated Commentaries and exchange of information frameworks (collectively referred to as the International Standards for Automatic Exchange of Information in Tax Matters), were approved by the OECD Committee on Fiscal Affairs over the course of 2022/2023 [CTPA/CFA(2022)16 and CTPA/CFA(2023)5].

The OECD Recommendation on the International Standards for Automatic Exchange of Information in Tax Matters [OECD/LEGAL/0407] was adopted by the OECD Council on 15 July 2014 and revised on 8 June 2023. For access to the official and up-to-date text of the Recommendation, as well as other related information, please consult the Compendium of OECD Legal Instruments at http://legalinstruments.oecd.org.

This document, as well as any data and map included herein, are without prejudice to the status of or sovereignty over any territory, to the delimitation of international frontiers and boundaries and to the name of any territory, city or area.

The statistical data for Israel are supplied by and under the responsibility of the relevant Israeli authorities. The use of such data by the OECD is without prejudice to the status of the Golan Heights, East Jerusalem and Israeli settlements in the West Bank under the terms of international law.

Note by the Republic of Türkiye
The information in this document with reference to "Cyprus" relates to the southern part of the Island. There is no single authority representing both Turkish and Greek Cypriot people on the Island. Türkiye recognises the Turkish Republic of Northern Cyprus (TRNC). Until a lasting and equitable solution is found within the context of the United Nations, Türkiye shall preserve its position concerning the "Cyprus issue".

Note by all the European Union Member States of the OECD and the European Union
The Republic of Cyprus is recognised by all members of the United Nations with the exception of Türkiye. The information in this document relates to the area under the effective control of the Government of the Republic of Cyprus.

Please cite this publication as:
OECD (2023), *International Standards for Automatic Exchange of Information in Tax Matters: Crypto-Asset Reporting Framework and 2023 update to the Common Reporting Standard*, OECD Publishing, Paris, https://doi.org/10.1787/896d79d1-en.

ISBN 978-92-64-41061-9 (print)
ISBN 978-92-64-89395-5 (pdf)
ISBN 978-92-64-48115-2 (HTML)
ISBN 978-92-64-32841-9 (epub)

Revised version, October 2023
Details of revisions available at: https://www.oecd.org/about/publishing/Corrigendum_International-Standards-for-Automatic-Exchange-of-Information-in-Tax-Matters.pdf

Corrigenda to OECD publications may be found on line at: www.oecd.org/about/publishing/corrigenda.htm.

Foreword

This publication contains the Crypto-Asset Reporting Framework (CARF) and a set of amendments to the Common Reporting Standard (CRS), along with associated Commentaries and exchange of information frameworks (collectively referred to as the International Standards for Automatic Exchange of Information in Tax Matters), as approved by the OECD's Committee on Fiscal Affairs over the course of 2022/2023.

Both the CARF and the amendments to the CRS were adopted as part of a comprehensive review of the Standard for Automatic Exchange of Financial Account Information in Tax Matters. This Standard, initially developed in response to a G20 request, was embodied in the OECD Recommendation on the Standard for Automatic Exchange of Financial Account Information in Tax Matters [OECD/LEGAL/0407] (the Recommendation), and adopted by the OECD Council on 15 July 2014 and calls on jurisdictions to obtain information from their financial institutions and automatically exchange that information with other jurisdictions annually.

The CARF provides for the automatic exchange of tax relevant-information on Crypto-Assets and was developed to address the rapid development and growth of the Crypto-Asset market and to ensure that recent gains in global tax transparency will not be gradually eroded. Part I of this publication contains the Rules of the CARF, the Multilateral Competent Authority Agreement on Automatic Exchange of Information pursuant to the CARF (CARF MCAA), as well as the related Commentaries.

The CRS was amended to bring certain electronic money products and Central Bank Digital Currencies in scope. Changes have also been made to ensure that indirect investments in Crypto-Assets through derivatives and investment vehicles are now covered by the CRS. In addition, amendments have been made to strengthen the due diligence and reporting requirements (including the reporting of the role of each Controlling Person) and to foresee a carve-out for genuine non-profit organisations. Part II of this publication contains both the amendments to the CRS and an Addendum to the Multilateral Competent Authority Agreement on Automatic Exchange of Financial Account Information (CRS MCAA), as well as the related Commentaries.

Finally, the Recommendation, revised by the Council on 8 June 2023 under the new name OECD Recommendation on the International Standards for Automatic Exchange of Information in Tax Matters, is contained in an annex to this document.

Additional work is ongoing on the development of a dedicated XML Schema to support the exchange of information pursuant to the CARF as well as an updated version of the CRS XML schema to facilitate exchanges under the amended CRS. These schemas will be published separately.

Table of contents

Abbreviations and acronyms

AML	Anti-Money Laundering
API	Application Programming Interface
ATM	Automated Teller Machine
CARF	Crypto-Asset Reporting Framework
CARF MCAA	Multilateral Competent Authority Agreement on Automatic Exchange of Information pursuant to the Crypto-Asset Reporting Framework
CBDC	Central Bank Digital Currency
CBI	Citizenship by Investment
CRS	Common Reporting Standard
CRS MCAA	Multilateral Competent Authority Agreement on Automatic Exchange of Financial Account Information
FATCA	Foreign Account Tax Compliance Act
FATF	Financial Action Task Force
IT	Information Technology
KYC	Know Your Customer
LEI	Legal Entity Identifier
NFE	Non-Financial Entity
NFT	Non-Fungible Token
OECD	Organisation for Economic Co-operation and Development
RBI	Residence by Investment
TIN	Taxpayer Identification Number
XML	Extensible Mark-up Language

Executive summary

The Common Reporting Standard (CRS) was designed to promote tax transparency with respect to financial accounts held abroad. Since the CRS was adopted in 2014, over seven years have passed, in which over 100 jurisdictions have implemented the CRS and financial markets have continued to evolve, giving rise to new investment and payment practices. The OECD, working together with G20 countries, has therefore conducted the first comprehensive review of the CRS in consultation with participating jurisdictions, financial institutions and other stakeholders.

This has resulted in two outcomes:

I. a new tax transparency framework which provides for the automatic exchange of tax information on transactions in Crypto-Assets in a standardised manner with the jurisdictions of residence of taxpayers (referred to as the "Crypto-Asset Reporting Framework" or "CARF"); and
II. a set of amendments to the CRS.

Crypto-Asset Reporting Framework

One major development that the OECD has sought to address is the emergence of Crypto-Assets, which can be transferred and held without interacting with traditional financial intermediaries and without any central administrator having full visibility on either the transactions carried out, or the location of Crypto-Asset holdings.

These developments have reduced tax administrations' visibility on tax-relevant activities carried out within the sector, increasing the difficulty of verifying whether associated tax liabilities are appropriately reported and assessed, which poses a significant risk that recent gains in global tax transparency will be gradually eroded. In light of the specific features of the Crypto-Asset markets, the OECD, working with G20 countries, has developed the CARF, a dedicated global tax transparency framework which provides for the automatic exchange of tax information on transactions in Crypto-Assets in a standardised manner with the jurisdictions of residence of taxpayers on an annual basis.

The CARF consists of three distinct components:

- Rules and related Commentary that can be transposed into domestic law to collect information from Reporting Crypto-Asset Service Providers with a relevant nexus to the jurisdiction implementing the CARF. These Rules and Commentary have been designed around four key building blocks: i) the scope of Crypto-Assets to be covered; ii) the Entities and individuals subject to data collection and reporting requirements; iii) the transactions subject to reporting, as well as the information to be reported in respect of such transactions; and iv) the due diligence procedures to identify Crypto-Asset Users and Controlling Persons and to determine the relevant tax jurisdictions for reporting and exchange purposes.

- a Multilateral Competent Authority Agreement on Automatic Exchange of Information pursuant to the CARF (CARF MCAA) and related Commentary (or bilateral agreements or arrangements); and
- an electronic format (XML schema) to be used by Competent Authorities for purposes of exchanging the CARF information, as well as by Reporting Crypto-Asset Service Providers to report CARF information to tax administrations (as permitted by domestic law).

Part I of this publication contains the Rules and Multilateral Competent Authority Agreement on Automatic Exchange of Information pursuant to the CARF and their related Commentaries. The XML schema to support the exchange of information pursuant to the CARF will be published separately.

Amendments to the Common Reporting Standard

Developed alongside the CARF, the first comprehensive review of the CRS has resulted in amendments to bring new financial assets, products, and intermediaries within its scope, because they are potential alternatives to traditional financial products, while avoiding duplicative reporting with that foreseen in the CARF. Additional amendments have also been made to enhance the reporting outcomes under the CRS, including through the introduction of more detailed reporting requirements, the strengthening of the due diligence procedures, the introduction of a new, optional Non-Reporting Financial Institution category for Investment Entities that are genuine non-profit organisations and the creation of a new Excluded Account category for capital contribution accounts. In addition, further details have been included in the Commentary to the CRS in a number of locations to increase consistency in the application of the CRS and to incorporate previously released Frequently Asked Questions and interpretative guidance.

Part II of this publication contains:

- the amendments to the CRS Rules and related Commentary; and
- an Addendum to the CRS Multilateral Competent Authority Agreement and related Commentary, which provides an updated legal basis for participating jurisdictions to exchange the broadened scope of information contained in the amended CRS.

The amended CRS XML schema to support the exchange of information pursuant to the amended CRS will be published separately.

Part I Crypto-Asset Reporting Framework

1 Introduction

Crypto-Assets: The impact on financial markets

1. The market for Crypto-Assets (including cryptocurrencies, as well as cryptography-based tokens) is growing rapidly. This is also affecting tax administrations, which must adapt to the growing role of Crypto-Assets. In particular, several characteristics of Crypto-Assets are likely to pose novel challenges in tax administrations' efforts to ensure taxpayer compliance.

2. Firstly, Crypto-Assets' reliance on cryptography and distributed ledger technology, in particular blockchain technology, means that they can be issued, recorded, transferred and stored in a decentralised manner, without the need to rely on traditional financial intermediaries or central administrators.

3. In addition, the Crypto-Asset market has given rise to a new set of intermediaries and other service providers, such as Crypto-Asset exchanges and wallet providers, which may currently only be subject to limited regulatory oversight. Crypto-Asset exchanges typically facilitate the purchase, sale and exchange of Crypto-Assets for other Crypto-Assets or Fiat Currencies. Wallet providers offer digital "wallets", which individuals can use to store their Crypto-Assets via authorisation through public and private keys. These services may either be provided in online (i.e. "hot") wallets, or via service providers offering products allowing individuals to store their Crypto-Assets offline on downloaded (i.e. "cold") wallets. Both types of products are relevant for tax authorities.

Repercussions of Crypto-Assets on global tax transparency

4. The Crypto-Asset market, including both the Crypto-Assets offered, as well as the intermediaries and other service providers involved, poses a significant risk that recent gains in global tax transparency will be gradually eroded. In particular, the Crypto-Asset market is characterised by a shift away from traditional financial intermediaries, the typical information providers in third-party tax reporting regimes, such as the Common Reporting Standard (CRS), to a new set of intermediaries and other service providers which only recently became subject to financial regulation and are frequently not yet subject to tax reporting requirements with respect to their users. Furthermore, the ability of individuals to hold Relevant Crypto-Assets in wallets unaffiliated with any service provider and transfer such Relevant Crypto-Assets across jurisdictions, presents the risk that Relevant Crypto-Assets are used for illicit activities or to evade tax obligations. Overall, the characteristics of the Crypto-Asset sector have reduced tax administrations' visibility on tax-relevant activities carried out within the sector, increasing the difficulty of verifying whether associated tax liabilities are appropriately reported and assessed.

5. The CRS, published by the OECD in 2014, is a key tool in ensuring transparency on cross-border financial investments and in fighting offshore tax evasion. The CRS has improved international tax transparency by requiring committed jurisdictions to obtain information on offshore accounts held with Financial Institutions and automatically exchange that information with the jurisdictions of residence of taxpayers on an annual basis. However, Relevant Crypto-Assets will in most instances not fall within the scope of the CRS, which applies to traditional Financial Assets and Fiat Currencies held in accounts with

Financial Institutions. Even where Relevant Crypto-Assets do fall within the definition of Financial Assets for purposes of the definition of Custodial Account, they can be owned either directly by individuals in cold wallets or via Crypto-Asset exchanges that do not have reporting obligations under the CRS (if they are not Financial Institutions) and are therefore unlikely to be reported to tax authorities in a reliable manner.

6. Therefore, the current scope of assets, as well as the scope of obliged entities covered by the CRS, do not provide tax administrations with adequate visibility on when taxpayers engage in tax-relevant transactions in, or hold, Relevant Crypto-Assets.

Increasing global tax transparency with respect to Crypto-Assets

7. Recognising the importance of addressing the above-mentioned tax compliance risks with respect to Relevant Crypto-Assets, the OECD has developed the Crypto-Asset Reporting Framework (CARF), designed to ensure the collection and automatic exchange of information on transactions in Relevant Crypto-Assets.

8. The CARF consists of three distinct components:

- Rules and related Commentary that can be transposed into domestic law to collect information from Reporting Crypto-Asset Service Providers with a relevant nexus to the jurisdiction implementing the CARF;
- a Multilateral Competent Authority Agreement on Automatic Exchange of Information pursuant to the CARF (CARF MCAA) and related Commentary (or bilateral agreements or arrangements); and
- an electronic format (XML schema) to be used by Competent Authorities for purposes of exchanging the CARF information, as well as by Reporting Crypto-Asset Service Providers to report CARF information to tax administrations (as permitted by domestic law).

9. It is acknowledged that Crypto-Asset markets, including the types of Crypto-Assets offered, the Entities and individuals active in, and the technology supporting the markets, are evolving rapidly. In this context, the OECD will continue to monitor Crypto-Asset markets and consider whether further technical work to elaborate the rules will be necessary to ensure adequate tax reporting on Relevant Crypto-Assets. It is also anticipated that the OECD will continue developing guidance to support the consistent application of the CARF, including on the definition of Relevant Crypto-Assets and in particular the criteria for adequately determining that a Crypto-Asset can or cannot be used for payment or investment purposes. Furthermore, the OECD stands ready to proceed with future amendments to the CARF, in case this is needed to ensure adequate tax reporting with respect to Relevant Crypto-Assets, as well as sufficient global coverage of the CARF. In this respect, particular attention will be given to the development of decentralised finance.

The Rules and Commentary of the Crypto-Asset Reporting Framework

10. The Rules and Commentary of the CARF have been designed around four key building blocks: i) the scope of Crypto-Assets to be covered; ii) the Entities and individuals subject to data collection and reporting requirements; iii) the transactions subject to reporting as well as the information to be reported in respect of such transactions; and iv) the due diligence procedures to identify Crypto-Asset Users and the relevant tax jurisdictions for reporting and exchange purposes.

Scope of Crypto-Assets to be covered

11. The definition of Crypto-Assets under the CARF focuses on the use of cryptographically secured distributed ledger technology, as this is a distinguishing factor underpinning the creation, holding and transferability of Crypto-Assets. The definition also includes a reference to "similar technology" to ensure it can include new technological developments that emerge in the future and that operate in a functionally similar manner to Crypto-Assets and raise similar tax risks. The definition of Crypto-Assets thereby targets those assets that can be held and transferred in a decentralised manner, without the intervention of traditional financial intermediaries, including stablecoins, derivatives issued in the form of a Crypto-Asset and certain non-fungible tokens (NFTs).

12. The term Relevant Crypto-Assets (i.e. Crypto-Assets that give rise to reporting on Relevant Transactions) excludes from reporting requirements three categories of Crypto-Assets that pose limited tax compliance risks. The first category are those Crypto-Assets which the Reporting Crypto-Asset Service Provider has adequately determined cannot be used for payment or investment purposes. This exclusion builds on the scope of the virtual asset definition of the Financial Action Task Force (FATF) and seeks to exclude Crypto-Assets that do not have the capacity of being used for payment or investment purposes. The second category are Central Bank Digital Currencies, representing a claim in Fiat Currency on an issuing Central Bank, or monetary authority, which function similar to money held in a traditional bank account. The third category covers Specified Electronic Money Products that represent a single Fiat Currency and are redeemable at any time in the same Fiat Currency at par value as a regulatory matter, in addition to meeting certain other requirements. Reporting on Central Bank Digital Currencies and certain Specified Electronic Money Products held in Financial Accounts will be included within the scope of the CRS.

13. With the above-mentioned considerations in mind, the definition of Relevant Crypto-Assets means that in most cases Relevant Crypto-Assets covered under the CARF also fall within the scope of the FATF Recommendations, ensuring the due diligence requirements can, as far as possible, build on existing AML/KYC obligations.

Intermediaries and other service providers in scope

14. As noted above, intermediaries and other service providers facilitating exchanges between Relevant Crypto-Assets, as well as between Relevant Crypto-Assets and Fiat Currencies, play a central role in the Crypto-Asset market. As such, those Entities or individuals that as a business provide services effectuating Exchange Transactions in Relevant Crypto-Assets, for or on behalf of customers, are considered Reporting Crypto-Asset Service Providers under the CARF.

15. Such intermediaries and other service providers are expected to have the best and most comprehensive access to the value of the Relevant Crypto-Assets and the Exchange Transactions carried out. These intermediaries and other service providers also fall within the scope of obliged entities for FATF purposes (i.e. virtual asset service providers). As such, they are in a position to collect and review the required documentation of their customers, including on the basis of AML/KYC documentation.

16. The above functional definition covers not only exchanges, but also other intermediaries and other service providers providing exchange services such as brokers and dealers in Relevant Crypto-Assets and operators of Relevant Crypto-Asset ATMs. Further, taking into account the October 2021 updated guidance of the FATF on virtual asset service providers, the Commentary clarifies the scope of application of the CARF to certain decentralised exchanges.

17. With respect to the reporting nexus, Reporting Crypto-Asset Service Providers will be subject to the rules when they are (i) tax resident in, (ii) both incorporated in, or organised under the laws of, and have legal personality or are subject to tax reporting requirements in, (iii) managed from, (iv) having a regular place of business in, or (v) effectuating Relevant Transactions through a branch based in, a

jurisdiction adopting the rules. The CARF also contains rules to avoid duplicative reporting in case a Reporting Crypto-Asset Service Provider has nexus with more than one jurisdiction by creating a hierarchy of nexus rules and including a rule for cases where a Reporting Crypto-Asset Service Provider has nexus in two jurisdictions based on the same type of nexus.

Reporting requirements

18. The following three types of transactions are Relevant Transactions that are reportable under the CARF:

- exchanges between Relevant Crypto-Assets and Fiat Currencies;
- exchanges between one or more forms of Relevant Crypto-Assets; and
- Transfers (including Reportable Retail Payment Transactions) of Relevant Crypto-Assets.

19. Transactions will be reported on an aggregate basis by type of Relevant Crypto-Asset and distinguishing outward and inward transactions. In order to enhance the usability of the data for tax administrations, the reporting on Exchange Transactions is to be distinguished between Crypto-Asset-to-Crypto-Asset and Crypto-Asset-to-Fiat Currency transactions. Reporting Crypto-Asset Service Providers will also categorise Transfers by Transfer type (e.g. airdrops, income derived from staking, or a loan), in instances where they have such knowledge.

20. The CARF foresees that for Crypto-Asset-to-Fiat Currency transactions, the fiat amount paid or received is reported as the acquisition amount or gross proceeds. For Crypto-Asset-to-Crypto-Asset transactions the value of the Crypto-Asset (at acquisition) and the gross proceeds (upon disposal) must (also) be reported in Fiat Currency. In line with this approach, in respect of Crypto-Asset-to-Crypto-Asset transactions, the transaction is split into two reportable elements, i.e.: (i) a disposal of Crypto-Asset A (the reportable gross proceeds based on the market value at the time of disposal); and (ii) an acquisition of Crypto-Asset B (the reportable acquisition value based on the market value at the time of acquisition). The Commentary to the CARF furthermore contains detailed valuation rules for Relevant Crypto-Assets subject to reporting on the basis of a Transfer.

21. Taxpayers' holdings and transfers of Relevant Crypto-Assets outside the scope of Reporting Crypto-Asset Service Providers subject to reporting are also relevant to tax authorities. In order to increase visibility on these, the CARF requires reporting of the number of units and the total value of Transfers of Relevant Crypto-Assets effectuated by a Reporting Crypto-Asset Service Provider, on behalf of a Crypto-Asset User, to wallets not associated with a virtual asset service provider or a financial institution. In case this information gives rise to compliance concerns, tax administrations could then request more detailed information on the wallet addresses associated with a Crypto-Asset User through existing exchange of information channels.

22. Finally, the CARF also applies to certain instances where a Reporting Crypto-Asset Service Provider processes payments on behalf of a merchant accepting Relevant Crypto-Assets in payment for goods or services, focussing on high-value transactions (i.e. Reportable Retail Payment Transactions). In such instances, the Reporting Crypto-Asset Service Provider is required to also treat the customer of the merchant as a Crypto-Asset User (provided the Reporting Crypto-Asset Service Provider is required to verify the identity of the customer on the basis of domestic anti-money laundering rules and by virtue of effectuating the Reportable Retail Payment Transaction), and report with respect to the value of the transaction on that basis. This information is expected to provide tax administrations with information on cases where Relevant Crypto-Assets are used to purchase goods or services, therewith realising a capital gain on the disposal of such Relevant Crypto-Assets.

Due diligence procedures

23. The CARF contains the due diligence procedures to be followed by Reporting Crypto-Asset Service Providers in identifying their Crypto-Asset Users, determining the relevant tax jurisdictions for reporting purposes and collecting relevant information needed to comply with the reporting requirements under the CARF. The due diligence requirements are designed to allow Reporting Crypto-Asset Service Providers to efficiently and reliably determine the identity and tax residence of their Individual and Entity Crypto-Asset Users, as well as of the natural persons controlling certain Entity Crypto-Asset Users.

24. The due diligence procedures build on the self-certification-based process of the CRS, as well as existing AML/KYC obligations enshrined in the 2012 FATF Recommendations, including updates in June 2019 with respect to obligations applicable to virtual asset service providers.

Effective implementation

25. The effective implementation requirements of the CARF are set out in the Commentary on Section V. Similar to Section IX of the CRS, these requirements aim to ensure effective implementation by Reporting Crypto-Asset Service Providers and participating jurisdictions.

Multilateral Competent Authority Agreement on Automatic Exchange of information pursuant to the CARF (CARF MCAA) and related Commentary

26. The CARF MCAA provides for the automatic exchange of information collected under the CARF with jurisdiction(s) or residence of Crypto-Asset Users and is based on Article 6 of the Convention on Mutual Administrative Assistance in Tax Matters.

27. As an alternative to the CARF MCAA, jurisdictions can also establish automatic exchange relationships through bilateral competent authority agreements based on bilateral double tax treaties or tax information exchange agreements that permit the automatic exchange of information, or the Convention on Mutual Administrative Assistance in Tax Matters. Jurisdictions could also enter into a self-standing intergovernmental agreement or rely on regional legislation covering both the reporting obligations and due diligence procedures coupled with the exchange of information modalities.

Interaction between the Crypto-Asset Reporting Framework and the CRS

28. As the CARF is a separate and complementary framework, there will be some Entities reporting under both the CRS and the CARF. The CARF was designed to report information on Crypto-Assets to address tax compliance risks. Nonetheless, to reduce reporting burdens, particular attention was given to the efficient and frictionless interaction of the CARF with the CRS, as reflected in the following features:

- The definition of Relevant Crypto-Assets excludes Specified Electronic Money Products and Central Bank Digital Currencies from the scope of the CARF, as reporting on these assets is ensured under the CRS;
- As there are certain assets that qualify both as Relevant Crypto-Assets under the CARF and as Financial Assets under the CRS (e.g. shares issued in crypto form), the CRS contains an optional provision to switch-off gross proceeds reporting under the CRS if such information is reported under the CARF;
- Indirect investments in Relevant Crypto-Assets through traditional financial products, such as derivatives or interests in investment vehicles, are covered by the CRS; and
- To the extent possible and appropriate, the due diligence procedures are consistent with the CRS due diligence rules, to minimise burdens on Reporting Crypto-Asset Service Providers, in particular when they are also subject to CRS obligations as Reporting Financial Institutions. In

particular, the CARF allows Reporting Crypto-Asset Service Providers that are also subject to the CRS to rely on the due diligence procedures for New Accounts performed for CRS purposes.

2 Rules

Section I: Obligations of Reporting Crypto-Asset Service Providers

A. A Reporting Crypto-Asset Service Provider is subject to the reporting and due diligence requirements in Sections II and III in [Jurisdiction], if it is:

1. an Entity or individual resident for tax purposes in [Jurisdiction];
2. an Entity that (a) is incorporated or organised under the laws of [Jurisdiction] and (b) either has legal personality in [Jurisdiction] or has an obligation to file tax returns or tax information returns to the tax authorities in [Jurisdiction] with respect to the income of the Entity;
3. an Entity managed from [Jurisdiction]; or
4. an Entity or individual that has a regular place of business in [Jurisdiction].

B. A Reporting Crypto-Asset Service Provider is subject to the reporting and due diligence requirements in Sections II and III in [Jurisdiction] with respect to Relevant Transactions effectuated through a Branch based in [Jurisdiction].

C. A Reporting Crypto-Asset Service Provider that is an Entity is not required to complete the reporting and due diligence requirements in Sections II and III it is subject to in [Jurisdiction] pursuant to subparagraphs A(2), (3) or (4), if such requirements are completed by such Reporting Crypto-Asset Service Provider in a Partner Jurisdiction by virtue of it being resident for tax purposes in such Partner Jurisdiction.

D. A Reporting Crypto-Asset Service Provider that is an Entity is not required to complete the reporting and due diligence requirements in Sections II and III it is subject to in [Jurisdiction] pursuant to subparagraphs A(3) or (4), if such requirements are completed by such Reporting Crypto-Asset Service Provider in a Partner Jurisdiction by virtue of it being an Entity that (a) is incorporated or organised under the laws of such Partner Jurisdiction and (b) either has legal personality in the Partner Jurisdiction or has an obligation to file tax returns or tax information returns to the tax authorities in the Partner Jurisdiction with respect to the income of the Entity.

E. A Reporting Crypto-Asset Service Provider that is an Entity is not required to complete the reporting and due diligence requirements in Sections II and III it is subject to in [Jurisdiction] pursuant to subparagraph A(4), if such requirements are completed by such Reporting Crypto-Asset Service Provider in a Partner Jurisdiction by virtue of it being managed from such Partner Jurisdiction.

F. A Reporting Crypto-Asset Service Provider that is an individual is not required to complete the reporting and due diligence requirements in Sections II and III it is subject to in [Jurisdiction] pursuant to subparagraph A(4), if such requirements are completed by such Reporting Crypto-Asset Service Provider in a Partner Jurisdiction by virtue of it being resident for tax purposes in such Partner Jurisdiction.

G. A Reporting Crypto-Asset Service Provider is not required to complete the reporting and due diligence requirements in Sections II and III in [Jurisdiction] with respect to Relevant Transactions it effectuates through a Branch in a Partner Jurisdiction, if such requirements are completed by such Branch in such Partner Jurisdiction.

H. A Reporting Crypto-Asset Service Provider is not required to complete the reporting and due diligence requirements in Sections II and III it is subject to in [Jurisdiction] pursuant to subparagraphs A(1), (2), (3) or (4), if it has lodged a notification with [Jurisdiction] in a format specified by [Jurisdiction] confirming that such requirements are completed by such Reporting Crypto-Asset Service Provider under the rules of a Partner Jurisdiction pursuant a substantially similar nexus that it is subject to in [Jurisdiction].

Section II: Reporting requirements

A. For each relevant calendar year or other appropriate reporting period, and subject to the obligations of Reporting Crypto-Asset Service Providers in Section I and the due diligence procedures in Section III, a Reporting Crypto-Asset Service Provider must report the following information with respect to its Crypto-Asset Users that are Reportable Users or that have Controlling Persons that are Reportable Persons:

1. the name, address, jurisdiction(s) of residence, TIN(s) and date and place of birth (in the case of an individual) of each Reportable User and, in the case of any Entity that, after application of the due diligence procedures, is identified as having one or more Controlling Persons that is a Reportable Person, the name, address, jurisdiction(s) of residence and TIN(s) of the Entity and the name, address, jurisdiction(s) of residence, TIN(s) and date and place of birth of each Reportable Person, as well as the role(s) by virtue of which each Reportable Person is a Controlling Person of the Entity;
2. the name, address and identifying number (if any) of the Reporting Crypto-Asset Service Provider;
3. for each type of Relevant Crypto-Asset with respect to which it has effectuated Relevant Transactions during the relevant calendar year or other appropriate reporting period:
    a) the full name of the type of Relevant Crypto-Asset;
    b) the aggregate gross amount paid, the aggregate number of units and the number of Relevant Transactions in respect of acquisitions against Fiat Currency;
    c) the aggregate gross amount received, the aggregate number of units and the number of Relevant Transactions in respect of disposals against Fiat Currency;
    d) the aggregate fair market value, the aggregate number of units and the number of Relevant Transactions in respect of acquisitions against other Relevant Crypto-Assets;
    e) the aggregate fair market value, the aggregate number of units and the number of Relevant Transactions in respect of disposals against other Relevant Crypto-Assets;
    f) the aggregate fair market value, the aggregate number of units and the number of Reportable Retail Payment Transactions;
    g) the aggregate fair market value, the aggregate number of units and the number of Relevant Transactions, and subdivided by Transfer type where known by the Reporting Crypto-Asset Service Provider, in respect of Transfers to the Reportable User not covered by subparagraphs A(3)(b) and (d);
    h) the aggregate fair market value, the aggregate number of units and the number of Relevant Transactions, and subdivided by Transfer type where known by the Reporting Crypto-Asset Service Provider, in respect of Transfers by the Reportable User not covered by subparagraphs A(3)(c), (e) and (f); and
    i) the aggregate fair market value, as well as the aggregate number of units in respect of Transfers by the Reportable Crypto-Asset User effectuated by the Reporting Crypto-Asset Service Provider to wallet addresses not known by the Reporting Crypto-Asset

Service Provider to be associated with a virtual asset service provider or financial institution.

B. Notwithstanding subparagraph A(1), the TIN is not required to be reported if (i) a TIN is not issued by the relevant Reportable Jurisdiction or (ii) the domestic law of the relevant Reportable Jurisdiction does not require the collection of the TIN issued by such Reportable Jurisdiction.

C. Notwithstanding subparagraph A(1), the place of birth is not required to be reported unless the Reporting Crypto-Asset Service Provider is otherwise required to obtain and report it under domestic law.

D. For the purposes of subparagraphs A(3)(b) and (c), the amount paid or received must be reported in the Fiat Currency in which it was paid or received. In case the amounts were paid or received in multiple Fiat Currencies, the amounts must be reported in a single Fiat Currency, converted at the time of each Relevant Transaction in a manner that is consistently applied by the Reporting Crypto-Asset Service Provider.

E. For the purposes of subparagraphs A(3)(d) through (i), the fair market value must be determined and reported in a single Fiat Currency, valued at the time of each Relevant Transaction in a manner that is consistently applied by the Reporting Crypto-Asset Service Provider.

F. The information reported must identify the Fiat Currency in which each amount is reported.

G. The information pursuant to paragraph A must be reported by xx/xx of the calendar year following the year to which the information relates.

Section III: Due diligence procedures

A Crypto-Asset User is treated as a Reportable User beginning as of the date it is identified as such pursuant to the due diligence procedures described in this Section.

A. Due diligence procedures for Individual Crypto-Asset Users

The following procedures apply for purposes of determining whether the Individual Crypto-Asset User is a Reportable User.

1. When establishing the relationship with the Individual Crypto-Asset User, or with respect to Preexisting Individual Crypto-Asset Users by 12 months after the effective date of these rules, the Reporting Crypto-Asset Service Provider must obtain a self-certification that allows the Reporting Crypto-Asset Service Provider to determine the Individual Crypto-Asset User's residence(s) for tax purposes and confirm the reasonableness of such self-certification based on the information obtained by the Reporting Crypto-Asset Service Provider, including any documentation collected pursuant to AML/KYC Procedures.
2. If at any point there is a change of circumstances with respect to an Individual Crypto-Asset User that causes the Reporting Crypto-Asset Service Provider to know, or have reason to know, that the original self-certification is incorrect or unreliable, the Reporting Crypto-Asset Service Provider cannot rely on the original self-certification and must obtain a valid self-certification, or a reasonable explanation and, where appropriate, documentation supporting the validity of the original self-certification.

B. Due diligence procedures for Entity Crypto-Asset Users

The following procedures apply for purposes of determining whether the Entity Crypto-Asset User is a Reportable User or an Entity, other than an Excluded Person or an Active Entity, with one or more Controlling Persons who are Reportable Persons.

1. **Determine whether the Entity Crypto-Asset User is a Reportable User.**
    a) When establishing the relationship with the Entity Crypto-Asset User, or with respect to Preexisting Entity Crypto-Assets Users by 12 months after the effective date of these rules, the Reporting Crypto-Asset Service Provider must obtain a self-certification that allows the Reporting Crypto-Asset Service Provider to determine the Entity Crypto-Asset User's residence(s) for tax purposes and confirm the reasonableness of such self-certification based on the information obtained by the Reporting Crypto-Asset Service Provider, including any documentation collected pursuant to AML/KYC Procedures. If the Entity Crypto-Asset User certifies that it has no residence for tax purposes, the Reporting Crypto-Asset Service Provider may rely on the place of effective management or on the address of the principal office to determine the residence of the Entity Crypto-Asset User.
    b) If the self-certification indicates that the Entity Crypto-Asset User is resident in a Reportable Jurisdiction, the Reporting Crypto-Asset Service Provider must treat the Entity Crypto-Asset User as a Reportable User, unless it reasonably determines based on the self-certification or on information in its possession or that is publicly available, that the Entity Crypto-Asset User is an Excluded Person.
2. **Determine whether the Entity has one or more Controlling Persons who are Reportable Persons.** With respect to an Entity Crypto-Asset User, other than an Excluded Person, the Reporting Crypto-Asset Service Provider must determine whether it has one or more Controlling Persons who are Reportable Persons, unless it determines that the Entity Crypto-Asset User is an Active Entity, based on a self-certification from the Entity Crypto-Asset User.
    a) **Determining the Controlling Persons of the Entity Crypto-Asset User**. For the purposes of determining the Controlling Persons of the Entity Crypto-Asset User, a Reporting Crypto-Asset Service Provider may rely on information collected and maintained pursuant to AML/KYC Procedures, provided that such procedures are consistent with the 2012 FATF Recommendations (as updated in June 2019 pertaining to virtual asset service providers). If the Reporting Crypto-Asset Service Provider is not legally required to apply AML/KYC Procedures that are consistent with the 2012 FATF Recommendations (as updated in June 2019 pertaining to virtual asset service providers), it must apply substantially similar procedures for the purposes of determining the Controlling Persons.
    b) **Determining whether a Controlling Person of an Entity Crypto-Asset User is a Reportable Person**. For the purposes of determining whether a Controlling Person is a Reportable Person, a Reporting Crypto-Asset Service Provider must rely on a self-certification from the Entity Crypto-Asset User or such Controlling Person that allows the Reporting Crypto-Asset Service Provider to determine the Controlling Person's residence(s) for tax purposes and confirm the reasonableness of such self-certification based on the information obtained by the Reporting Crypto-Asset Service Provider, including any documentation collected pursuant to AML/KYC Procedures.
3. If at any point there is a change of circumstances with respect to an Entity Crypto-Asset User or its Controlling Persons that causes the Reporting Crypto-Asset Service Provider to know, or have reason to know, that the original self-certification is incorrect or unreliable, the Reporting Crypto-Asset Service Provider cannot rely on the original self-certification and must obtain a valid self-certification, or a reasonable explanation and, where appropriate, documentation supporting the validity of the original self-certification.

C. Requirements for validity of self-certifications

1. A self-certification provided by an Individual Crypto-Asset User or Controlling Person is valid only if it is signed or otherwise positively affirmed by the Individual Crypto-Asset User or Controlling Person, it is

dated at the latest at the date of receipt and it contains the following information with respect to the Individual Crypto-Asset User or Controlling Person:

a) first and last name;

b) residence address;

c) jurisdiction(s) of residence for tax purposes;

d) with respect to each Reportable Person, the TIN with respect to each Reportable Jurisdiction; and

e) date of birth.

2. A self-certification provided by an Entity Crypto-Asset User is valid only if it is signed or otherwise positively affirmed by the Crypto-Asset User, it is dated at the latest at the date of receipt and it contains the following information with respect to the Entity Crypto-Asset User:

   a) legal name;

   b) address;

   c) jurisdiction(s) of residence for tax purposes;

   d) with respect to each Reportable Person, the TIN with respect to each Reportable Jurisdiction;

   e) in case of an Entity Crypto-Asset User other than an Active Entity or an Excluded Person, the information described in subparagraph C(1) with respect to each Controlling Person of the Entity Crypto-Asset User, unless such Controlling Person has provided a self-certification pursuant to subparagraph C(1), as well as the role(s) by virtue of which each Reportable Person is a Controlling Person of the Entity, if not already determined on the basis of AML/KYC Procedures; and

   f) if applicable, information as to the criteria it meets to be treated as an Active Entity or Excluded Person.

3. Notwithstanding subparagraphs C(1) and (2), the TIN is not required to be collected if the jurisdiction of residence of the Reportable Person does not issue a TIN to the Reportable Person, or the domestic law of the relevant Reportable Jurisdiction does not require the collection of the TIN issued by such Reportable Jurisdiction.

D. General due diligence requirements

1. A Reporting Crypto-Asset Service Provider that is also a Financial Institution for the purposes of the Common Reporting Standard may rely on the due diligence procedures completed pursuant to Sections IV and VI of the Common Reporting Standard for the purpose of the due diligence procedures pursuant to this Section. A Reporting Crypto-Asset Service Provider may also rely on a self-certification already collected for other tax purposes, provided such self-certification meets the requirements of paragraph C of this Section.

2. A Reporting Crypto-Asset Service Provider may rely on a third party to fulfil the due diligence obligations set out in this Section III, but such obligations remain the responsibility of the Reporting Crypto-Asset Service Provider.

3. A Reporting Crypto-Asset Service Provider is required to maintain all documentation and data for a period of not less than five years after the end of the period within which the Reporting Crypto-Asset Service Provider must report the information required to be reported pursuant to Section II.

Section IV: Defined terms

A. Relevant Crypto-Asset

1. The term **"Crypto-Asset"** means a digital representation of value that relies on a cryptographically secured distributed ledger or a similar technology to validate and secure transactions.
2. The term **"Relevant Crypto-Asset"** means any Crypto-Asset that is not a Central Bank Digital Currency, a Specified Electronic Money Product or any Crypto-Asset for which the Reporting Crypto-Asset Service Provider has adequately determined that it cannot be used for payment or investment purposes.
3. The term **"Central Bank Digital Currency"** means any digital Fiat Currency issued by a Central Bank.
4. The term **"Specified Electronic Money Product"** means any Crypto-Asset that is:
    a) a digital representation of a single Fiat Currency;
    b) issued on receipt of funds for the purpose of making payment transactions;
    c) represented by a claim on the issuer denominated in the same Fiat Currency;
    d) accepted in payment by a natural or legal person other than the issuer; and
    e) by virtue of regulatory requirements to which the issuer is subject, redeemable at any time and at par value for the same Fiat Currency upon request of the holder of the product.

    The term "Specified Electronic Money Product" does not include a product created for the sole purpose of facilitating the transfer of funds from a customer to another person pursuant to instructions of the customer. A product is not created for the sole purpose of facilitating the transfer of funds if, in the ordinary course of business of the transferring Entity, either the funds connected with such product are held longer than 60 days after receipt of instructions to facilitate the transfer, or, if no instructions are received, the funds connected with such product are held longer than 60 days after receipt of the funds.

B. Reporting Crypto-Asset Service Provider

1. The term **"Reporting Crypto-Asset Service Provider"** means any individual or Entity that, as a business, provides a service effectuating Exchange Transactions for or on behalf of customers, including by acting as a counterparty, or as an intermediary, to such Exchange Transactions, or by making available a trading platform.

C. Relevant Transaction

1. The term **"Relevant Transaction"** means any:
    a) Exchange Transaction; and
    b) Transfer of Relevant Crypto-Assets.
2. The term **"Exchange Transaction"** means any:
    a) exchange between Relevant Crypto-Assets and Fiat Currencies; and
    b) exchange between one or more forms of Relevant Crypto-Assets.
3. The term **"Reportable Retail Payment Transaction"** means a Transfer of Relevant Crypto-Assets in consideration of goods or services for a value exceeding USD 50 000.
4. The term **"Transfer"** means a transaction that moves a Relevant Crypto-Asset from or to the Crypto-Asset address or account of one Crypto-Asset User, other than one maintained by the Reporting Crypto-Asset Service Provider on behalf of the same Crypto-Asset User, where, based on the

knowledge available to the Reporting Crypto-Asset Service Provider at the time of transaction, the Reporting Crypto-Asset Service Provider cannot determine that the transaction is an Exchange Transaction.

5. The term **"Fiat Currency"** means the official currency of a jurisdiction, issued by a jurisdiction or by a jurisdiction's designated Central Bank or monetary authority, as represented by physical banknotes or coins or by money in different digital forms, including bank reserves and Central Bank Digital Currencies. The term also includes commercial bank money and electronic money products (including Specified Electronic Money Products).

D. Reportable User

1. The term **"Reportable User"** means a Crypto-Asset User that is a Reportable Person.
2. The term **"Crypto-Asset User"** means an individual or Entity that is a customer of a Reporting Crypto-Asset Service Provider for purposes of carrying out Relevant Transactions. An individual or Entity, other than a Financial Institution or a Reporting Crypto-Asset Service Provider, acting as a Crypto-Asset User for the benefit or account of another individual or Entity as agent, custodian, nominee, signatory, investment advisor, or intermediary, is not treated as a Crypto-Asset User, and such other individual or Entity is treated as the Crypto-Asset User. Where a Reporting Crypto-Asset Service Provider provides a service effectuating Reportable Retail Payment Transactions for or on behalf of a merchant, the Reporting Crypto-Asset Service Provider must also treat the customer that is the counterparty to the merchant for such Reportable Retail Payment Transaction as the Crypto-Asset User with respect to such Reportable Retail Payment Transaction, provided that the Reporting Crypto-Asset Service Provider is required to verify the identity of such customer by virtue of the Reportable Retail Payment Transaction pursuant to domestic anti-money laundering rules.
3. The term **"Individual Crypto-Asset User"** means a Crypto-Asset User that is an individual.
4. The term **"Preexisting Individual Crypto-Asset User"** means an Individual Crypto-Asset User that has established a relationship with the Reporting Crypto-Asset Service Provider as of [xx/xx/xxxx].
5. The term **"Entity Crypto-Asset User"** means a Crypto-Asset User that is an Entity.
6. The term **"Preexisting Entity Crypto-Asset User"** means an Entity Crypto-Asset User that has established a relationship with the Reporting Crypto-Asset Service Provider as of [xx/xx/xxxx].
7. The term **"Reportable Person"** means a Reportable Jurisdiction Person other than an Excluded Person.
8. The term **"Reportable Jurisdiction Person"** means an Entity or individual that is resident in a Reportable Jurisdiction under the tax laws of such jurisdiction, or an estate of a decedent that was a resident of a Reportable Jurisdiction. For this purpose, an Entity such as a partnership, limited liability partnership or similar legal arrangement that has no residence for tax purposes shall be treated as resident in the jurisdiction in which its place of effective management is situated.
9. The term **"Reportable Jurisdiction"** means any jurisdiction (a) with which an agreement or arrangement is in effect pursuant to which [Jurisdiction] is obligated to provide the information specified in Section II with respect to Reportable Persons resident in such jurisdiction, and (b) which is identified as such in a list published by [Jurisdiction].
10. The term **"Controlling Persons"** means the natural persons who exercise control over an Entity. In the case of a trust, such term means the settlor(s), the trustee(s), the protector(s) (if any), the beneficiary(ies) or class(es) of beneficiaries, and any other natural person(s) exercising ultimate effective control over the trust, and in the case of a legal arrangement other than a trust, such term means persons in equivalent or similar positions. The term "Controlling Persons" must be interpreted in a manner consistent with the 2012 Financial Action Task Force Recommendations, as updated in June 2019 pertaining to virtual asset service providers.

11. The term **"Active Entity"** means any Entity that meets any of the following criteria:
    a) less than 50% of the Entity's gross income for the preceding calendar year or other appropriate reporting period is passive income and less than 50% of the assets held by the Entity during the preceding calendar year or other appropriate reporting period are assets that produce or are held for the production of passive income;
    b) substantially all of the activities of the Entity consist of holding (in whole or in part) the outstanding stock of, or providing financing and services to, one or more subsidiaries that engage in trades or businesses other than the business of a Financial Institution, except that an Entity does not qualify for this status if the Entity functions (or holds itself out) as an investment fund, such as a private equity fund, venture capital fund, leveraged buyout fund, or any investment vehicle whose purpose is to acquire or fund companies and then hold interests in those companies as capital assets for investment purposes;
    c) the Entity is not yet operating a business and has no prior operating history, but is investing capital into assets with the intent to operate a business other than that of a Financial Institution, provided that the Entity does not qualify for this exception after the date that is 24 months after the date of the initial organisation of the Entity;
    d) the Entity was not a Financial Institution in the past five years, and is in the process of liquidating its assets or is reorganising with the intent to continue or recommence operations in a business other than that of a Financial Institution;
    e) the Entity primarily engages in financing and hedging transactions with, or for, Related Entities that are not Financial Institutions, and does not provide financing or hedging services to any Entity that is not a Related Entity, provided that the group of any such Related Entities is primarily engaged in a business other than that of a Financial Institution; or
    f) the Entity meets all of the following requirements:
        i. it is established and operated in its jurisdiction of residence exclusively for religious, charitable, scientific, artistic, cultural, athletic, or educational purposes; or it is established and operated in its jurisdiction of residence and it is a professional organisation, business league, chamber of commerce, labour organisation, agricultural or horticultural organisation, civic league or an organisation operated exclusively for the promotion of social welfare;
        ii. it is exempt from income tax in its jurisdiction of residence;
        iii. it has no shareholders or members who have a proprietary or beneficial interest in its income or assets;
        iv. the applicable laws of the Entity's jurisdiction of residence or the Entity's formation documents do not permit any income or assets of the Entity to be distributed to, or applied for the benefit of, a private person or non-charitable Entity other than pursuant to the conduct of the Entity's charitable activities, or as payment of reasonable compensation for services rendered, or as payment representing the fair market value of property which the Entity has purchased; and
        v. the applicable laws of the Entity's jurisdiction of residence or the Entity's formation documents require that, upon the Entity's liquidation or dissolution, all of its assets be distributed to a Governmental Entity or other non-profit organisation, or escheat to the government of the Entity's jurisdiction of residence or any political subdivision thereof.

E. Excluded Person

1. The term **"Excluded Person"** means (a) an Entity the stock of which is regularly traded on one or more established securities markets; (b) any Entity that is a Related Entity of an Entity described in clause

(a); (c) a Governmental Entity; (d) an International Organisation; (e) a Central Bank; or (f) a Financial Institution other than an Investment Entity described in Section IV E(5)(b).

2. The term **"Financial Institution"** means a Custodial Institution, a Depository Institution, an Investment Entity, or a Specified Insurance Company.
3. The term **"Custodial Institution"** means any Entity that holds, as a substantial portion of its business, Financial Assets for the account of others. An Entity holds Financial Assets for the account of others as a substantial portion of its business if the Entity's gross income attributable to the holding of Financial Assets and related financial services equals or exceeds 20% of the Entity's gross income during the shorter of: (i) the three-year period that ends on 31 December (or the final day of a non-calendar year accounting period) prior to the year in which the determination is being made; or (ii) the period during which the Entity has been in existence.
4. The term **"Depository Institution"** means any Entity that:
   a) accepts deposits in the ordinary course of a banking or similar business; or
   b) holds Specified Electronic Money Products or Central Bank Digital Currencies for the benefit of customers.
5. The term **"Investment Entity"** means any Entity:
   a) that primarily conducts as a business one or more of the following activities or operations for or on behalf of a customer:
      i. trading in money market instruments (cheques, bills, certificates of deposit, derivatives, etc.); foreign exchange; exchange, interest rate and index instruments; transferable securities; or commodity futures trading;
      ii. individual and collective portfolio management; or
      iii. otherwise investing, administering, or managing Financial Assets, money, or Relevant Crypto-Assets on behalf of other persons; or
   b) the gross income of which is primarily attributable to investing, reinvesting, or trading in Financial Assets or Relevant Crypto-Assets, if the Entity is managed by another Entity that is a Depository Institution, a Custodial Institution, a Specified Insurance Company, or an Investment Entity described in subparagraph E(5)(a).

   An Entity is treated as primarily conducting as a business one or more of the activities described in subparagraph E(5)(a), or an Entity's gross income is primarily attributable to investing, reinvesting, or trading in Financial Assets or Relevant Crypto-Assets for purposes of subparagraph E(5)(b), if the Entity's gross income attributable to the relevant activities equals or exceeds 50% of the Entity's gross income during the shorter of: (i) the three-year period ending on 31 December of the year preceding the year in which the determination is made; or (ii) the period during which the Entity has been in existence. For the purposes of subparagraph E(5)(a)(iii), the term "otherwise investing, administering, or managing Financial Assets, money, or Relevant Crypto-Assets on behalf of other persons" does not include the provision of services effectuating Exchange Transactions for or on behalf of customers. The term "Investment Entity" does not include an Entity that is an Active Entity because it meets any of the criteria in subparagraphs D(11)(b) through (e).

   This paragraph shall be interpreted in a manner consistent with similar language set forth in the definition of "financial institution" in the Financial Action Task Force Recommendations.
6. The term **"Specified Insurance Company"** means any Entity that is an insurance company (or the holding company of an insurance company) that issues, or is obligated to make payments with respect to, a Cash Value Insurance Contract or an Annuity Contract.
7. The term **"Governmental Entity"** means the government of a jurisdiction, any political subdivision of a jurisdiction (which, for the avoidance of doubt, includes a state, province, county, or municipality), or

any wholly owned agency or instrumentality of a jurisdiction or of any one or more of the foregoing. This category is comprised of the integral parts, controlled entities, and political subdivisions of a jurisdiction.

a) An "integral part" of a jurisdiction means any person, organisation, agency, bureau, fund, instrumentality, or other body, however designated, that constitutes a governing authority of a jurisdiction. The net earnings of the governing authority must be credited to its own account or to other accounts of the jurisdiction, with no portion inuring to the benefit of any private person. An integral part does not include any individual who is a sovereign, official, or administrator acting in a private or personal capacity.

b) A controlled entity means an Entity that is separate in form from the jurisdiction or that otherwise constitutes a separate juridical entity, provided that:

i. the Entity is wholly owned and controlled by one or more Governmental Entities directly or through one or more controlled entities;

ii. the Entity's net earnings are credited to its own account or to the accounts of one or more Governmental Entities, with no portion of its income inuring to the benefit of any private person; and

iii. the Entity's assets vest in one or more Governmental Entities upon dissolution.

c) Income does not inure to the benefit of private persons if such persons are the intended beneficiaries of a governmental programme, and the programme activities are performed for the general public with respect to the common welfare or relate to the administration of some phase of government. Notwithstanding the foregoing, however, income is considered to inure to the benefit of private persons if the income is derived from the use of a governmental entity to conduct a commercial business, such as a commercial banking business, that provides financial services to private persons.

8. The term **"International Organisation"** means any international organisation or wholly owned agency or instrumentality thereof. This category includes any intergovernmental organisation (including a supranational organisation) (a) that is comprised primarily of governments; (b) that has in effect a headquarters or substantially similar agreement with the jurisdiction; and (c) the income of which does not inure to the benefit of private persons.

9. The term **"Central Bank"** means an institution that is by law or government sanction the principal authority, other than the government of the jurisdiction itself, issuing instruments intended to circulate as currency. Such an institution may include an instrumentality that is separate from the government of the jurisdiction, whether or not owned in whole or in part by the jurisdiction.

10. The term **"Financial Asset"** includes a security (for example, a share of stock in a corporation; partnership or beneficial ownership interest in a widely held or publicly traded partnership or trust; note, bond, debenture, or other evidence of indebtedness), partnership interest, commodity, swap (for example, interest rate swaps, currency swaps, basis swaps, interest rate caps, interest rate floors, commodity swaps, equity swaps, equity index swaps, and similar agreements), Insurance Contract or Annuity Contract, or any interest (including a futures or forward contract or option) in a security, Relevant Crypto-Asset, partnership interest, commodity, swap, Insurance Contract, or Annuity Contract. The term "Financial Asset" does not include a non-debt, direct interest in real property.

11. The term **"Equity Interest"** means, in the case of a partnership that is a Financial Institution, either a capital or profits interest in the partnership. In the case of a trust that is a Financial Institution, an Equity Interest is considered to be held by any person treated as a settlor or beneficiary of all or a portion of the trust, or any other natural person exercising ultimate effective control over the trust. A Reportable Person will be treated as being a beneficiary of a trust if such Reportable Person has the right to receive directly or indirectly (for example, through a nominee) a mandatory distribution or may receive, directly or indirectly, a discretionary distribution from the trust.

12. The term **"Insurance Contract"** means a contract (other than an Annuity Contract) under which the issuer agrees to pay an amount upon the occurrence of a specified contingency involving mortality, morbidity, accident, liability, or property risk.
13. The term **"Annuity Contract"** means a contract under which the issuer agrees to make payments for a period of time determined in whole or in part by reference to the life expectancy of one or more individuals. The term also includes a contract that is considered to be an Annuity Contract in accordance with the law, regulation, or practice of the jurisdiction in which the contract was issued, and under which the issuer agrees to make payments for a term of years.
14. The term **"Cash Value Insurance Contract"** means an Insurance Contract (other than an indemnity reinsurance contract between two insurance companies) that has a Cash Value.
15. The term **"Cash Value"** means the greater of (i) the amount that the policyholder is entitled to receive upon surrender or termination of the contract (determined without reduction for any surrender charge or policy loan), and (ii) the amount the policyholder can borrow under or with regard to the contract. Notwithstanding the foregoing, the term "Cash Value" does not include an amount payable under an Insurance Contract:
    a) solely by reason of the death of an individual insured under a life insurance contract;
    b) as a personal injury or sickness benefit or other benefit providing indemnification of an economic loss incurred upon the occurrence of the event insured against;
    c) as a refund of a previously paid premium (less cost of insurance charges whether or not actually imposed) under an Insurance Contract (other than an investment-linked life insurance or annuity contract) due to cancellation or termination of the contract, decrease in risk exposure during the effective period of the contract, or arising from the correction of a posting or similar error with regard to the premium for the contract;
    d) as a policyholder dividend (other than a termination dividend) provided that the dividend relates to an Insurance Contract under which the only benefits payable are described in subparagraph E(15)(b); or
    e) as a return of an advance premium or premium deposit for an Insurance Contract for which the premium is payable at least annually if the amount of the advance premium or premium deposit does not exceed the next annual premium that will be payable under the contract.

F. Miscellaneous

1. The term **"Partner Jurisdiction"** means any jurisdiction that has put in place equivalent legal requirements and that is included in a list published by [Jurisdiction].
2. The term **"AML/KYC Procedures"** means the customer due diligence procedures of a Reporting Crypto-Asset Service Provider pursuant to the anti-money laundering or similar requirements to which such Reporting Crypto-Asset Service Provider is subject.
3. The term **"Entity"** means a legal person or a legal arrangement, such as a corporation, partnership, trust, or foundation.
4. An Entity is a **"Related Entity"** of another Entity if either Entity controls the other Entity, or the two Entities are under common control. For this purpose control includes direct or indirect ownership of more than 50% of the vote and value in an Entity.
5. The term **"TIN"** means Taxpayer Identification Number (or functional equivalent in the absence of a Taxpayer Identification Number).
6. The term **"Branch"** means a unit, business or office of a Reporting Crypto-Asset Service Provider that is treated as a branch under the regulatory regime of a jurisdiction or that is otherwise regulated under the laws of a jurisdiction as separate from other offices, units, or branches of the Reporting Crypto-

Asset Service Provider. All units, businesses, or offices of a Reporting Crypto-Asset Service Provider in a single jurisdiction shall be treated as a single branch.

Section V: Effective implementation

A jurisdiction must have rules and administrative procedures in place to ensure effective implementation of, and compliance with, the reporting and due diligence procedures set out above.

3 Commentary to the Rules

Commentary on Section I: Obligations of Reporting Crypto-Asset Service Providers

1. This Section sets out the criteria pursuant to which a Reporting Crypto-Asset Service Provider is subject to the reporting and due diligence requirements in Sections II and III in [Jurisdiction].

2. Paragraph A contains four distinct criteria that link a Reporting Crypto-Asset Service Provider to [Jurisdiction]:

- the Entity or individual is resident for tax purposes in [Jurisdiction];
- the Entity is (a) incorporated or organised under the laws of [Jurisdiction], and (b) either has legal personality in [Jurisdiction] or has an obligation to file tax returns or tax information returns to the tax authorities in [Jurisdiction] with respect to the income of the Entity. As such, this criterion captures situations where an Entity Reporting Crypto-Asset Service Provider selects the law of a certain jurisdiction for purposes of establishing its organisation, including through the act of incorporation. However, in addition to being incorporated or organised under the laws of [Jurisdiction], the Entity must also either have legal personality in [Jurisdiction] or be subject to an obligation to file tax returns or tax information returns to the tax authorities in [Jurisdiction] with respect to its income. This condition is intended to ensure that [Jurisdiction]'s tax administration will be able to enforce the reporting requirements. For the purposes of subparagraph A(2), a tax information return is any filing used to notify the tax administration regarding part or all of the income of the Entity, but which does not necessarily state a pursuant tax liability of the Entity;
- the Entity is managed from [Jurisdiction]. This criterion includes situations where a trust (or a functionally similar Entity) that is a Reporting Crypto-Asset Service Provider is managed by a trustee (or functionally similar representative) that is tax resident in [Jurisdiction]. This criterion captures the place of effective management, as well as any other place of management of the Entity; or
- the Entity or individual has a regular place of business in [Jurisdiction]. In this respect, any Branch is to be considered a regular place of business. This criterion captures the principal, as well as other regular places of business.

3. Paragraph B provides that an Entity also has due diligence and reporting obligations in [Jurisdiction] with respect to Relevant Transactions effectuated through a Branch based in [Jurisdiction].

4. A Reporting Crypto-Asset Service Provider must report the information to each jurisdiction for which it fulfils the criteria of paragraphs A and B, subject to the rules in paragraphs C through H to prevent duplicative reporting. For that purpose, paragraphs C through F introduce a hierarchy among the four criteria in paragraph A that link a Reporting Crypto-Asset Service Provider to [Jurisdiction]. This hierarchy ensures that the due diligence and reporting requirements in [Jurisdiction] do not apply in instances where there is a stronger link with another jurisdiction.

5. As such, paragraph C foresees that an Entity that is a Reporting Crypto-Asset Service Provider which is linked to [Jurisdiction] on the basis of the criteria set out in subparagraphs A(2), (3) or (4) (i.e. it is incorporated, or organised under the laws of [Jurisdiction] and has either legal personality or has an obligation to file tax returns or tax information returns to the tax authorities in [Jurisdiction] with respect to the income of the Entity, or is managed from [Jurisdiction], or it has a regular place of business in [Jurisdiction]), is not required to complete the reporting and due diligence requirements in Sections II and III in [Jurisdiction] if it is tax resident in a Partner Jurisdiction and completes the due diligence and reporting requirements in such Partner Jurisdiction.

6. In addition, paragraph D foresees that an Entity that is a Reporting Crypto-Asset Service Provider is not required to complete the reporting and due diligence requirements in Sections II and III in [Jurisdiction] it is subject to pursuant to subparagraphs A(3) or (4) (i.e. it is managed from [Jurisdiction], or has a regular place of business in [Jurisdiction]), to the extent it has legal personality or has an obligation to file tax returns or tax information returns to the tax authorities in [Jurisdiction] with respect to the income of the Entity and is incorporated, or organised under the laws of such Partner Jurisdiction and completes the due diligence and reporting requirements in such Partner Jurisdiction.

7. Paragraph E foresees that an Entity that is a Reporting Crypto-Asset Service Provider is not required to complete the reporting and due diligence requirements in Sections II and III in [Jurisdiction] it is subject to pursuant to subparagraph A(4) (i.e. its regular place of business is in [Jurisdiction]), to the extent such reporting and due diligence requirements are completed by such Reporting Crypto-Asset Service Provider in a Partner Jurisdiction, by virtue of it being managed from such Partner Jurisdiction.

8. Paragraph F foresees that an individual that is a Reporting Crypto-Asset Service Provider is not required to complete the reporting and due diligence requirements in Sections II and III in [Jurisdiction] it is subject to pursuant to subparagraph A(4) (i.e. its regular place of business is in [Jurisdiction]), to the extent such reporting and due diligence requirements are completed in a Partner Jurisdiction, where the individual Reporting Crypto-Asset Service Provider is resident for tax purposes.

9. Paragraph G foresees that a Reporting Crypto-Asset Service Provider is not subject to the reporting and due diligence requirements in Sections II and III in [Jurisdiction], to the extent these are completed in a Partner Jurisdiction, by virtue of effectuating Relevant Transactions for Crypto-Asset Users through a Branch in such Partner Jurisdiction. A Reporting Crypto-Asset Service Provider that maintains one or more Branches fulfils the due diligence and reporting requirements with respect to a Crypto-Asset User, if any one of its Branches in [Jurisdiction] or a Partner Jurisdiction fulfils such requirements.

10. Finally, paragraph H foresees that a Reporting Crypto-Asset Service Provider is not required to complete the reporting and due diligence requirements in Section II and III in [Jurisdiction] it is subject to pursuant to subparagraphs A(1), (2), (3) or (4), to the extent it has a lodged a notification with [Jurisdiction] in a format specified by [Jurisdiction] confirming that such reporting and due diligence requirements are completed by such Reporting Crypto-Asset Service Provider under the rules of a Partner Jurisdiction pursuant to a substantially similar nexus that it is subject to in [Jurisdiction].

11. Paragraph H only applies to instances where a Reporting Crypto-Asset Service Provider is subject to the same nexus in two or more jurisdictions. For example, a Reporting Crypto-Asset Service Provider that is tax resident in two or more jurisdictions, may rely on paragraph H to select one of the two jurisdictions of tax residence where it complies with the due diligence and reporting requirements. Similarly, a Reporting Crypto-Asset Service Provider that has a regular place of business in two or more jurisdictions may rely on paragraph H to select one of these jurisdictions where it complies with the due diligence and reporting requirements; however, such reliance is not permitted if the Reporting Crypto-Asset Service Provider has nexus in a jurisdiction pursuant to subparagraphs A(1), (2), or (3).

Commentary on Section II: Reporting requirements

1. Section II describes the general reporting requirements applicable to Reporting Crypto-Asset Service Providers. Paragraph A specifies the information to be reported with respect to Crypto-Asset Users and Controlling Persons as a general rule, and subject to the due diligence procedures in Section III, while paragraphs B and C provide for exceptions in connection with TIN and place of birth. Paragraphs D and E contain the valuation and currency translation rules. Paragraph F specifies the requirement to identify the Fiat Currency in which the amount of a Relevant Transaction is reported. Paragraph G specifies the timing of the reporting by the Reporting Crypto-Asset Service Provider.

Paragraph II (A) – Information to be reported

Subparagraph A(1) – Information on Reportable Persons

Jurisdiction(s) of residence

2. The jurisdiction(s) of residence to be reported with respect to a Reportable Person is (are) the jurisdiction(s) of residence identified by the Reporting Crypto-Asset Service Provider pursuant to the due diligence procedures in Section III. In the case of a Reportable Person that is identified as having more than one jurisdiction of residence, the jurisdictions of residence to be reported are all the jurisdictions of residence identified by the Reporting Crypto-Asset Service Provider for the Reportable Person.

Taxpayer Identification Number

3. The TIN to be reported is the TIN assigned to the Reportable Person by its jurisdiction of residence (i.e. not by a jurisdiction of source). In the case of a Reportable Person that is identified as having more than one jurisdiction of residence, the TIN to be reported is the Reportable Person's TIN with respect to each Reportable Jurisdiction. In this respect, the term "TIN" includes a functional equivalent in the absence of a Taxpayer Identification Number.

Subparagraph A(2) – Information on the Reporting Crypto-Asset Service Provider

4. Subparagraph A(2) requires that the Reporting Crypto-Asset Service Provider must report its name, address and identifying number (if any). Identifying information on the Reporting Crypto-Asset Service Provider is intended to allow the identification of the source of the information reported and subsequently exchanged in order to allow the providing jurisdiction to, e.g. follow-up on an error that may have led to incorrect or incomplete information reporting. The "identifying number" of a Reporting Crypto-Asset Service Provider is one of the following types of numbers assigned to a Reporting Crypto-Asset Service Provider for identification purposes: a TIN, or in the absence thereof, a business/company registration code/number, or a Global Legal Entity Identifier (LEI). If no identifying number is assigned to the Reporting Crypto-Asset Service Provider, then only the name and address of the Reporting Crypto-Asset Service Provider are required to be reported.

Subparagraph A(3) – Information on Relevant Transactions

5. Subparagraph A(3) contains the financial reporting requirements applicable to Reporting Crypto-Asset Service Providers, whereby Reporting Crypto-Asset Service Providers must report certain information items with respect to Relevant Transactions effectuated for each relevant calendar year or other appropriate reporting period and in relation to each Reportable User. In this respect, subparagraph A(3) specifies the information to be reported, while paragraphs D and E contain the applicable valuation and currency translation rules.

6. Reflecting the different categories of Relevant Transactions, Reporting Crypto-Asset Service Providers must, for each type of Relevant Crypto-Asset, report on:

- the full name of the type of Relevant Crypto-Asset under subparagraph A(3)(a);
- acquisitions and disposals of Relevant Crypto-Assets against Fiat Currency under subparagraphs A(3)(b) and A(3)(c), respectively;
- acquisitions and disposals of Relevant Crypto-Assets against other Relevant Crypto-Assets, under subparagraphs A(3)(d) and A(3)(e), respectively;
- Reportable Retail Payment Transactions, under subparagraph A(3)(f); and
- other Transfers of Relevant Crypto-Assets to and by the Reportable User, under subparagraphs A(3)(g), A(3)(h) and A(3)(i) respectively.

7. Transfers to and by Reportable Users, reported upon under subparagraphs A(3)(g), A(3)(h) and A(3)(i), include acquisitions and disposals in respect of which the Reporting Crypto-Asset Service Provider has no actual knowledge of the consideration paid or received, as well as Transfers that are not acquisitions or disposals (e.g. a Transfer of Crypto-Assets by a user to its private wallet or to its account with another Reporting Crypto-Asset Service Provider).

8. The applicable valuation rules vary between the reporting categories. In the case of Crypto-Asset-to-Fiat Currency transactions under subparagraphs A(3)(b) and A(3)(c), Reporting Crypto-Asset Service Providers must report the amount paid or received by the Reportable User net of transaction fees. Paragraph D provides that such amounts must be reported in the Fiat Currency in which they were paid or received. However, in case amounts were paid or received in multiple Fiat Currencies, they must be reported in a single currency, converted at the time of each Relevant Transaction in a manner that is consistently applied by the Reporting Crypto-Asset Service Provider.

9. For Crypto-Asset-to-Crypto-Asset transactions under subparagraphs A(3)(d) and A(3)(e), Reportable Retail Payment Transactions under subparagraph A(3)(f), other Transfers under subparagraphs A(3)(g) and A(3)(h), as well as reporting on Transfers to wallets not known by the Reporting Crypto-Asset Service Provider to be associated with virtual asset service providers or financial institutions (as such terms are defined in the Financial Action Task Force Recommendations updated in June 2019 pertaining to virtual asset service providers) under A(3)(i), in light of the absence of (known) consideration, Reporting Crypto-Asset Service Providers must report the fair market value of the Relevant Crypto-Assets acquired and disposed or transferred, net of transaction fees. Paragraph E provides that such amounts must be determined and reported in a Fiat Currency, valued at the time of each Relevant Transaction in a manner that is consistently applied by the Reporting Crypto-Asset Service Provider. For the purposes of paragraphs D and E, a jurisdiction may require reporting in a particular Fiat Currency, for example its local currency.

10. For all reporting categories under subparagraphs A(3)(b) through A(3)(i), the rules require the aggregation, i.e. summing up, of all transactions attributable to each reporting category for each type of Relevant Crypto-Asset, as converted and valued pursuant to paragraphs D and E. For example, if units of a Relevant Crypto-Asset can be mutually substituted for corresponding units of the same Relevant Crypto-Asset, then they should all be treated as the same type of Relevant Crypto-Asset for aggregation purposes. If, however, a Relevant Crypto-Asset is non-fungible, and different variations of the Relevant Crypto-Asset do not have the same value among fixed units, each unit should be treated as a separate type of Relevant Crypto-Asset.

Type of Relevant Crypto-Asset

11. The information under subparagraphs A(3)(b) through A(3)(i) must be reported by type of Relevant Crypto-Asset. For these purposes, the full name of the type of Relevant Crypto-Asset is required to be

reported under subparagraph A(3)(a), rather than a Relevant Crypto-Asset's "ticker" or abbreviated symbol that a Reporting Crypto-Asset Service Provider uses to identify a specific type of Relevant Crypto-Asset.

Crypto-Asset-to-Fiat Currency transactions

12. Subparagraph A(3)(b) requires that, in the case of acquisitions of Relevant Crypto-Assets against Fiat Currency, Reporting Crypto-Asset Service Providers must report the aggregate amount paid net of transaction fees by the Reportable User for each type of Relevant Crypto-Assets acquired by the Reportable User.

13. An acquisition is any transaction effectuated by the Reporting Crypto-Asset Service Provider where the Reportable User obtains a Relevant Crypto-Asset, irrespective of whether such asset is obtained from a third-party seller, or from the Reporting Crypto-Asset Service Provider itself.

14. In the case of disposals of Relevant Crypto-Assets against Fiat Currency, subparagraph A(3)(c) requires that the Reporting Crypto-Asset Service Provider must report the aggregate amount received in Fiat Currency net of transaction fees for any Relevant Crypto-Assets alienated by the Reportable User.

15. A disposal is any transaction effectuated by the Reporting Crypto-Asset Service Provider where the Reportable User alienates a Relevant Crypto-Asset, irrespective of whether such asset is delivered to a third-party purchaser, or to the Reporting Crypto-Asset Service Provider itself.

16. There may be instances where a Reportable User acquires or disposes of a Relevant Crypto-Asset against Fiat Currency, although the Reporting Crypto-Asset Service Provider does not have actual knowledge of the underlying Fiat Currency consideration. This would, for example, be the case if the Reporting Crypto-Asset Service Provider only conducted the Transfer of the Relevant Crypto-Assets to and from the Reportable User, without actual knowledge of the Fiat Currency leg of the transaction. Such transactions should be reported upon as Transfers sent to or by a Reportable User under subparagraphs A(3)(g) and A(3)(h), respectively.

Crypto-Asset-to-Crypto-Asset transactions

17. A Crypto-Asset-to-Crypto-Asset transaction that is effectuated by a Reporting Crypto-Asset Service Provider will give rise to reporting under both subparagraphs A(3)(d) and A(3)(e). In this respect, subparagraph A(3)(d) provides that in the case of acquisitions against other Relevant Crypto-Assets, the Reporting Crypto-Asset Service Provider must report the fair market value of the Relevant Crypto-Assets acquired net of transaction fees. Similarly, subparagraph A(3)(e) requires that in the case of disposals against other Relevant Crypto-Assets, the Reporting Crypto-Asset Service Provider must report the fair market value of the Relevant Crypto-Assets disposed net of transaction fees.

18. By way of an example, in respect of an exchange of Relevant Crypto-Asset A for Relevant Crypto-Asset B, the Reporting Crypto-Asset Service Provider must report both the fair market value of Relevant Crypto-Asset A, i.e. the Relevant Crypto-Asset disposed, under subparagraph A(3)(e) and the fair market value of Relevant Crypto-Asset B, i.e. the Relevant Crypto-Asset acquired, under subparagraph A(3)(d), valued at the time of the Relevant Transaction and both net of transaction fees.

19. All Crypto-Asset-to-Crypto-Asset transactions conducted by the same Reporting Crypto-Asset Service Provider are subject to reporting under both subparagraphs A(3)(d) and A(3)(e). As for Crypto-Asset-to-Fiat Currency transactions, there may be instances where a Reportable User effectuates a Crypto-Asset-to-Crypto-Asset transaction, although the Reporting Crypto-Asset Service Provider does not have actual knowledge of the Relevant Crypto-Asset acquired or disposed. This would, for example, be the case when the Reporting Crypto-Asset Service Provider only effectuates the Transfer of either the Relevant Crypto-Assets disposed or acquired, without actual knowledge of the other leg of the transaction. Depending on which leg of the transaction the Reporting Crypto-Asset Service Provider has actual

knowledge of, such transactions should be reported upon as Transfers sent to or by a Reportable User under subparagraphs A(3)(g) and A(3)(h), respectively.

20. **Example**: A Reportable User acquires Relevant Crypto-Asset D in exchange for Relevant Crypto-Asset C. The Reporting Crypto-Asset Service Provider effectuates the Transfer of Relevant Crypto-Asset C to the wallet of the seller of Relevant Crypto-Asset D. In exchange, the seller of Relevant Crypto-Asset D transfers Relevant Crypto-Asset D directly to a cold wallet controlled by the Reportable User. Unless the Reporting Crypto-Asset Service Provider has actual knowledge of the consideration, i.e. the Relevant Crypto-Asset D Transfer, it should report the transaction as a Transfer by a Reportable User of Relevant Crypto-Asset C under subparagraph A(3)(h).

Reportable Retail Payment Transactions

21. Pursuant to subparagraph A(3)(f), aggregate information on Transfers that constitute Reportable Retail Payment Transactions is required to be reported as a separate category of Relevant Transactions. With respect to such Reportable Retail Payments Transactions, the customer of the merchant for, or on behalf of, whom the Reporting Crypto-Asset Service Provider is providing a service effectuating Reportable Retail Payment Transactions must be treated as the Crypto-Asset User (subject to the conditions specified in the definition of Crypto-Asset User), and therefore as the Reportable User, in addition to the merchant. Aggregate information with respect to Reportable Retail Payment Transactions by the customer of the merchant must not be included in the aggregate information reported with respect to Transfers under subparagraph A(3)(h). Aggregate information with respect to Transfers that do not constitute Reportable Retail Payment Transactions solely by virtue of not meeting the de minimis threshold, should be included in the aggregate information reported with respect to Transfers under A(3)(g) and (h). The following examples illustrate the application of subparagraphs A(3)(f) and A(3)(g).

22. **Example 1**: (Reportable Retail Payment Transaction): To facilitate the use of Crypto-Assets by customers to purchase goods, a merchant has entered into an agreement with a Reporting Crypto-Asset Service Provider to process payments to the merchant made in Crypto-Assets by the merchant's customers. The Reporting Crypto-Asset Service Provider does not maintain a separate relationship with the merchant's customers.

The customer makes a payment in Relevant Crypto-Assets for goods acquired from the merchant for a value exceeding USD 50,000. This transaction is a Reportable Retail Payment Transaction. The Reporting Crypto-Asset Service Provider should treat the customer of the merchant as the Crypto-Asset User, and report the payment in Relevant Crypto-Assets as specified under subparagraph A(3)(f) (Reportable Retail Payment Transactions), provided that the Reporting Crypto-Asset Service Provider is required to verify the identity of such customer pursuant to domestic anti-money laundering rules, by virtue of the Reportable Retail Payment Transaction. The Reporting Crypto-Asset Service Provider should also treat the merchant as the Crypto-Asset User of this transaction, and the transaction is reportable as a Transfer to the merchant under subparagraph A(3)(g).

23. **Example 2**: (transaction that is not a Reportable Retail Payment Transaction by virtue of de minimis threshold): The customer engages in another transaction with the merchant that is identical to the transaction described in Example 1, except that the transaction amount is less than USD 50,000. The transaction is not a Reportable Retail Payment Transaction. The Reporting Crypto-Asset Service Provider should therefore treat the merchant as the Crypto-Asset User of this transaction, and the transaction is reportable as a Transfer to the merchant under subparagraph A(3)(g).

Transfers other than Reportable Retail Payment Transactions

24. Subparagraphs A(3)(g) and A(3)(h) require that Reporting Crypto-Asset Service Providers must report the fair market value of other Transfers sent to, and by, a Reportable User, respectively.

Furthermore, the Reporting Crypto-Asset Service Provider should subdivide the aggregate fair market value, aggregate number of units and number of Transfers effectuated on behalf of a Reportable User, during the reporting period, per underlying transfer type, where such transfer type is known by the Reporting Crypto-Asset Service Provider. For instance, where a Reporting Crypto-Asset Service Provider is aware that Transfers effectuated on behalf of a Reportable User are due to an airdrop (resulting from a hard-fork), an airdrop (for reasons other than a hard-fork), income derived from staking, the disbursement, reimbursement or associated return on a loan, or an exchange for goods or services, it should indicate the aggregate fair market value, aggregate number of units and number of Transfers effectuated for each transfer type.

Transfers to external wallet addresses

25. Subparagraph A(3)(i) requires the Reporting Crypto-Asset Service Provider to report, by type of Relevant Crypto-Asset, the aggregate number of units, as well as the aggregate fair market value, in Fiat Currency, of Transfers it effectuates on behalf of a Reportable User to any wallet addresses (including other equivalent identifiers used to describe the destination of a Transfer) not known to be associated with a virtual asset service provider or financial institution, as defined in the FATF Recommendations. The Reporting Crypto-Asset Service Provider is not required to report the aggregate number of units or the aggregate fair market value of Transfers, under subparagraph A(3)(i), in case the Reporting Crypto-Asset Service Provider knows that the wallet address to which the Relevant Crypto-Asset is transferred is associated with a virtual asset service provider or financial institution, as defined in the FATF Recommendations.

26. This rule does not require the reporting of wallet addresses associated with Transfers of Relevant Crypto-Assets. However, pursuant to subparagraph D(3) of Section III and to ensure that necessary information is available to tax administrations in the context of follow up requests, a Reporting Crypto-Asset Service Provider is required to collect and retain within its records, for a period not less than five years, any external wallet addresses (including other equivalent identifiers) associated with Transfers of Relevant Crypto-Assets that are subject to reporting under subparagraph A(3)(i).

Appropriate reporting period

27. The information to be reported under paragraphs A(1) through A(3) must be that in respect of the end of the relevant calendar year or other appropriate reporting period. In determining what is meant by "appropriate reporting period", reference must be made to the meaning that the term has at that time under each jurisdiction's reporting rules.

Paragraphs II (B) and (C) – Exceptions

Taxpayer Identification Number

28. Paragraph B contains an exception pursuant to which a TIN is not required to be reported if either:

- a TIN is not issued by the relevant Reportable Jurisdiction; or
- the domestic law of the relevant Reportable Jurisdiction does not require the collection of the TIN issued by such Reportable Jurisdiction.

29. A TIN is considered not to be issued by a Reportable Jurisdiction (i) where the jurisdiction does not issue a TIN nor a functional equivalent in the absence of a TIN, or (ii) where the jurisdiction has not issued a TIN to a particular individual or Entity. As a consequence, a TIN is not required to be reported with respect to a Reportable Person that is resident in such a Reportable Jurisdiction, or with respect to whom a TIN has not been issued. However, if and when a Reportable Jurisdiction starts issuing TINs and issues a TIN to a particular Reportable Person, the exception contained in paragraph B no longer applies

and the Reportable Person's TIN would be required to be reported if the Reporting Crypto-Asset Service Provider obtains a self-certification that contains such TIN, or otherwise obtains such TIN.

30. The exception described in clause (ii) of paragraph B focuses on the domestic law of the Reportable Person's jurisdiction. Where a Reportable Jurisdiction has issued a TIN to a Reportable Person and the collection of such TIN cannot be required under such jurisdiction's domestic law (e.g. because under such law the provision of the TIN by a taxpayer is on a voluntary basis), the Reporting Crypto-Asset Service Provider is not required to obtain and report the TIN. However, the Reporting Crypto-Asset Service Provider is not prevented from asking for, and collecting the Reportable Person's TIN for reporting purposes if the Reportable Person chooses to provide it. In this case, the Reporting Crypto-Asset Service Provider must report the TIN. In practice, there may be only a few jurisdictions where this is the case (e.g. Australia).

31. Jurisdictions are expected to provide Reporting Crypto-Asset Service Providers with information with respect to the issuance, collection and, to the extent possible and practical, structure and other specifications of taxpayer identification numbers. The OECD will endeavour to facilitate its dissemination.

Place of birth

32. Paragraph C contains an exception with respect to place of birth information, which is not required to be reported, unless the Reporting Crypto-Asset Service Provider is otherwise required to obtain and report it under domestic law and it is available in the electronically searchable data maintained by the Reporting Crypto-Asset Service Provider. Thus, the place of birth is required to be reported if, with respect to the Reportable Person, both:

- the Reporting Crypto-Asset Service Provider is otherwise required to obtain the place of birth and report it under domestic law; and
- the place of birth is available in the electronically searchable information maintained by the Reporting Crypto-Asset Service Provider.

Paragraphs II (D), (E) and (F) – Valuation and currency

Valuation and currency translation rules for Crypto-Asset-to-Fiat Currency transactions

33. Paragraph D provides that, for the purposes of subparagraph A(3)(b) and A(3)(c), the amounts must be reported in the Fiat Currency in which they were paid. However, in case amounts were paid or received in multiple Fiat Currencies, they must be reported in a single Fiat Currency, converted at the time of each Relevant Transaction in a manner that is consistently applied by the Reporting Crypto-Asset Service Provider. For example, the Reporting Crypto-Asset Service Provider may apply the spot rate(s) as at the time of the transaction(s) to translate such amounts into a single Fiat Currency determined by the Reporting Crypto-Asset Service Provider. The information reported must also identify the Fiat Currency in which each amount is reported.

34. Further, for the purposes of reporting under subparagraphs A(3)(b) and A(3)(c), the Reporting Crypto-Asset Service Provider must aggregate, i.e. sum up, all transactions attributable to each reporting category for each type of Relevant Crypto-Asset, as converted pursuant to paragraph D.

Valuation and currency translation rules for Crypto-Asset-to-Crypto-Asset transactions

35. For the purposes of subparagraphs A(3)(d) and A(3)(e), the fair market value must be determined and reported in a single currency, valued at the time of each Relevant Transaction in a reasonable manner that is consistently applied by the Reporting Crypto-Asset Service Provider. In this respect, a Reporting Crypto-Asset Service Provider may rely on applicable Crypto-Asset-to-Fiat Currency trading pairs that it

maintains to determine the fair market value of both Relevant Crypto-Assets. For instance, in respect of a disposal of Relevant Crypto-Asset A against Relevant Crypto-Asset B, the Reporting Crypto-Asset Service Provider may, at the time the transaction is executed: (i) perform an implicit conversion of Relevant Crypto-Asset A to Fiat Currency to determine the fair market value of the disposed Relevant Crypto-Asset A for the purposes of reporting under subparagraph A(3)(e); and (ii) perform an implicit conversion of the acquired Relevant Crypto-Asset B to Fiat Currency to determine the fair market value of the acquired Relevant Crypto-Asset B for the purposes of reporting under subparagraph A(3)(d).

36. It may arise that a difficult-to-value Relevant Crypto-Asset is exchanged for a Relevant Crypto-Asset that can be readily valued. In such cases, the valuation in Fiat Currency of the Relevant Crypto-Asset against which the difficult-to-value Relevant Crypto-Asset is exchanged should be relied upon to establish a Fiat Currency value for the difficult-to-value Relevant Crypto-Asset, as illustrated by the below example:

- **Example**: a Crypto-Asset User makes use of a Reporting Crypto-Asset Service Provider to dispose of Relevant Crypto-Asset A against the acquisition of Relevant Crypto-Asset B. Relevant Crypto-Asset A has a readily obtainable Fiat Currency equivalent value and the Reporting Crypto-Asset Service Provider can perform an implicit conversion to determine the fair market value of the disposal of Relevant Crypto-Asset A. However, Relevant Crypto-Asset B is a recently launched Crypto-Asset and the Reporting Crypto-Asset Service Provider is not able to determine an equivalent fair market value as there is no available Fiat Currency conversion amount. In this case, to determine the acquisition value attributable to the Crypto-Asset User's acquisition of Crypto-Asset B, the Reporting Crypto-Asset Service Provider can perform an implicit conversion of Relevant Crypto-Asset B by attributing to it the same Fiat Currency amount attributed to Relevant Crypto-Asset A.

37. Further, for the purposes of reporting under subparagraphs A(3)(d) and A(3)(e), the Reporting Crypto-Asset Service Provider must aggregate, i.e. sum up, all transactions attributable to each reporting category, as converted pursuant to paragraph D.

Valuation and currency translation rules for Reportable Retail Payment Transactions and other Transfers

38. For the purposes of subparagraphs A(3)(f), A(3)(g), A(3)(h) and A(3)(i), the fair market value must be determined and reported in a single currency, using a reasonable valuation method that looks to contemporaneous evidence of value at the time of each Relevant Transaction in a manner that is consistently applied by the Reporting Crypto-Asset Service Provider. In performing such valuation, the Reporting Crypto-Asset Service Provider may use as a reference the values of Relevant Crypto-Asset and Fiat Currency trading pairs it maintains to determine the fair market value of the Relevant Crypto-Asset at the time it is transferred. The information reported must also identify the Fiat Currency in which each amount is reported. The following example illustrates this approach:

- **Example**: A Reporting Crypto-Asset Service Provider maintains a trading platform and also facilitates Transfers of Relevant Crypto-Assets. The Reporting Crypto-Asset Service Provider effectuates a Transfer of Relevant Crypto-Asset A for Crypto-Asset User A. Relevant Crypto-Asset A is also regularly traded for Fiat Currency on Reporting Crypto-Asset Service Provider's trading platform. The Reporting Crypto-Asset Service Provider A may rely on such trading data to determine the fair market value of Relevant Crypto-Asset A at the time of the Transfer.

39. Where the Reporting Crypto-Asset Service Provider effectuating the Transfer does not maintain an applicable reference value of the Relevant Crypto-Asset and Fiat Currency trading pairs, the following valuation methods must be relied upon:

- firstly, the internal accounting book values the Reporting Crypto-Asset Service Provider maintains with respect to the Relevant Crypto-Asset must be used;
- if a book value is not available, a value provided by third-party companies or websites that aggregate current prices of Relevant Crypto-Assets must be used, if the valuation method used by that third party is reasonably expected to provide a reliable indicator of value;
- if neither of the above is available, the most recent valuation of the Relevant Crypto-Asset by the Reporting Crypto-Asset Service Provider must be used; and
- if a value can still not be attributed, a reasonable estimate may be applied as a measure of last resort.

40. With respect to each Relevant Crypto-Asset for which the Reporting Crypto-Asset Service Provider has relied on an alternative valuation method outlined in paragraph 39, the method must be indicated via the appropriate element in the relevant XML Schema.

41. Further, for the purposes of reporting under subparagraphs A(3)(f), A(3)(g) A(3)(h) and A(3)(i), the Reporting Crypto-Asset Service Provider must aggregate, i.e. sum up, all transactions attributable to each reporting category for each type of Relevant Crypto-Asset, as converted pursuant to paragraph D.

Paragraph II (G) – Timing of reporting

42. Paragraph G provides the time by which the information pursuant to paragraph A needs to be reported. While the selection of the date by which information is to be reported by the Reporting Crypto-Asset Service Provider is a decision of the jurisdiction implementing the rules, it is expected that such date will allow the jurisdiction to exchange the information within the timelines specified in the competent authority agreement.

Commentary on Section III: Due diligence procedures

1. Section III contains the due diligence procedures for identifying Reportable Persons. These requirements are split into four paragraphs:

- paragraph A sets out the procedures for Individual Crypto-Asset Users;
- paragraph B sets out the procedures for Entity Crypto-Asset Users;
- paragraph C specifies the validity requirements for self-certifications of Individual Crypto-Asset Users, Controlling Persons and Entity Crypto-Asset Users; and
- paragraph D specifies the general due diligence requirements.

Paragraph A – Due diligence procedures for Individual Crypto-Asset Users

2. Paragraph A sets out that a Reporting Crypto-Asset Service Provider must collect a self-certification, and confirm its reasonableness, in respect of its Individual Crypto-Asset Users.

3. Subparagraph A(1) specifies that, upon the establishment of a relationship with the user, which may include a one-off transaction, a Reporting Crypto-Asset Service Provider must:

- obtain a self-certification that allows the Reporting Crypto-Asset Service Provider to determine the Individual Crypto-Asset User's residence(s) for tax purposes; and
- confirm the reasonableness of such self-certification based on the information obtained by the Reporting Crypto-Asset Service Provider in connection with the establishment of a relationship with the user. Such information includes information the Reporting Crypto-Asset Service Provider collected for AML/KYC Procedures.

4. With respect to Preexisting Individual Crypto-Asset Users, subparagraph A(1) clarifies that Reporting Crypto-Asset Service Providers must obtain a valid self-certification and confirm its reasonableness at the latest 12 months after the jurisdiction introduces the rules.

Obtaining a self-certification

5. The self-certification obtained under subparagraph A(1) must allow the determination of the Individual Crypto-Asset User's residence(s) for tax purposes. See Commentary on subparagraph C(1) of Section III for further details on the required contents of self-certifications for Individual Crypto-Asset Users. The domestic laws of the various jurisdictions lay down the conditions under which an individual is to be treated as fiscally "resident". They cover various forms of attachment to a jurisdiction which, in the domestic taxation laws, form the basis of a comprehensive taxation (full liability to tax). They also cover cases where an individual is deemed, according to the taxation laws of a jurisdiction, to be resident of that jurisdiction (e.g. diplomats or other persons in government service). Generally, an individual will only have one jurisdiction of residence. However, an individual may be resident for tax purposes in two or more jurisdictions. In those circumstances, the expectation is that all jurisdictions of residence are to be declared in a self-certification and that the Reporting Crypto-Asset Service Provider must treat the Individual Crypto-Asset User as a Reportable User in respect of each Reportable Jurisdiction.

6. Reportable Jurisdictions are expected to help taxpayers determine, and provide them with information with respect to, their residence(s) for tax purposes. That may be done, for example, through the various service channels used for providing information or guidance to taxpayers on the application of tax laws. The OECD will endeavour to facilitate the dissemination of such information.

Reasonableness of self-certifications

7. Subparagraph A(1) specifies that the Reporting Crypto-Asset Service Provider must confirm the reasonableness of the self-certification.

8. A Reporting Crypto-Asset Service Provider is considered to have confirmed the "reasonableness" of a self-certification if, in the course of establishing a relationship with an Individual Crypto-Asset User and upon review of the information obtained in connection with the establishment of the relationship (including any documentation collected pursuant to AML/KYC Procedures), it does not know or have reason to know that the self-certification is incorrect or unreliable. Reporting Crypto-Asset Service Providers are not expected to carry out an independent legal analysis of relevant tax laws to confirm the reasonableness of a self-certification.

9. The following examples illustrate the application of the "reasonableness" test:

- **Example 1**: A Reporting Crypto-Asset Service Provider obtains a self-certification from the Individual Crypto-Asset User upon the establishment of the relationship. The jurisdiction of the residence address contained in the self-certification conflicts with that contained in the documentation collected pursuant to AML/KYC Procedures. Because of the conflicting information, the self-certification is incorrect or unreliable and, as a consequence, it fails the reasonableness test.
- **Example 2**: A Reporting Crypto-Asset Service Provider obtains a self-certification from the Individual Crypto-Asset User upon the establishment of the relationship. The residence address contained in the self-certification is not in the jurisdiction in which the Individual Crypto-Asset User claims to be resident for tax purposes. Because of the conflicting information, the self-certification fails the reasonableness test.

10. In the case of a self-certification that fails the reasonableness test, it is expected that the Reporting Crypto-Asset Service Provider would obtain either (i) a valid self-certification, or (ii) a reasonable explanation and documentation (as appropriate) supporting the reasonableness of the self-certification

(and retain a copy or a notation of such explanation and documentation) before providing services effectuating Relevant Transactions to the Individual Crypto-Asset User. Examples of such "reasonable explanation" include a statement by the individual that he or she (1) is a student at an educational institution in the relevant jurisdiction and holds the appropriate visa (if applicable); (2) is a teacher, trainee, or intern at an educational institution in the relevant jurisdiction or a participant in an educational or cultural exchange visitor program, and holds the appropriate visa (if applicable); (3) is a foreign individual assigned to a diplomatic post or a position in a consulate or embassy in the relevant jurisdiction; or (4) is a frontier worker or employee working on a truck or train travelling between jurisdictions. The following example illustrates the application of this paragraph: A Reporting Crypto-Asset Service Provider obtains a self-certification for the Individual Crypto-Asset User upon the establishment of the relationship. The jurisdiction of residence for tax purposes contained in the self-certification conflicts with the residence address contained in the documentation collected pursuant to AML/KYC Procedures. The Individual Crypto-Asset User explains that she is a diplomat from a particular jurisdiction and that, as a consequence, she is resident in such jurisdiction; she also presents her diplomatic passport. Because the Reporting Crypto-Asset Service Provider obtained a reasonable explanation and documentation supporting the reasonableness of the self-certification, the self-certification passes the reasonableness test.

Reliance on self-certifications

11. Subparagraph A(2) specifies that if, at any point, there is a change of circumstances with respect to an Individual Crypto-Asset User that causes the Reporting Crypto-Asset Service Provider to know, or have reason to know, that the original self-certification is incorrect or unreliable, the Reporting Crypto-Asset Service Provider cannot rely on the original self-certification and must obtain a valid self-certification, or a reasonable explanation and documentation (as appropriate) supporting the validity of the original self-certification.

Standards of knowledge applicable to self-certifications

12. A Reporting Crypto-Asset Service Provider has reason to know that a self-certification is unreliable or incorrect if its knowledge of relevant facts or statements contained in the self-certification or other documentation is such that a reasonably prudent person in the position of the Reporting Crypto-Asset Service Provider would question the claim being made. A Reporting Crypto-Asset Service Provider also has reason to know that a self-certification or is unreliable or incorrect if there is information in the documentation or in the Reporting Crypto-Asset Service Provider's files that conflicts with the person's claim regarding its status.

13. A Reporting Crypto-Asset Service Provider has reason to know that a self-certification provided by a person is unreliable or incorrect if the self-certification is incomplete with respect to any item on the self-certification that is relevant to the claims made by the person, the self-certification contains any information that is inconsistent with the person's claim, or the Reporting Crypto-Asset Service Provider has other information that is inconsistent with the person's claim. A Reporting Crypto-Asset Service Provider that relies on a service provider to review and maintain a self-certification is considered to know or have reason to know the facts within the knowledge of the service provider.

14. A Reporting Crypto-Asset Service Provider may not rely on documentation provided by a person if the documentation does not reasonably establish the identity of the person presenting the documentation. For example, documentation is not reliable if it is provided in person by an individual and the photograph or signature on the documentation does not match the appearance or signature of the person presenting the document. A Reporting Crypto-Asset Service Provider may not rely on documentation if the documentation contains information that is inconsistent with the person's claim as to its status, the Reporting Crypto-Asset Service Provider has other information that is inconsistent with the person's status, or the documentation lacks information necessary to establish the person's status.

Change of circumstances

15. A "change of circumstances" includes any change that results in the addition of information relevant to an Individual Crypto-Asset User's status or otherwise conflicts with such user's status or any change or addition of information to any profile associated with such Individual Crypto-Asset User if such change or addition of information affects the status of the Individual Crypto-Asset User. For these purposes, the Reporting Crypto-Asset Service Provider should determine whether new information that is obtained with respect to the Individual Crypto-Asset User's profile in accordance with re-documentation undertaken in accordance with AML/KYC Procedures or other regulatory obligations includes new information that constitutes a change of circumstances. A change of circumstances affecting the self-certification provided to the Reporting Crypto-Asset Service Provider will terminate the validity of the self-certification with respect to the information that is no longer reliable, until the information is updated.

16. When a change of circumstances occurs, according to subparagraph A(2), the Reporting Crypto-Asset Service Provider cannot rely on the original self-certification and must obtain either (i) a valid self-certification that establishes the residence(s) for tax purposes of the Individual Crypto-Asset User, or (ii) a reasonable explanation and documentation (as appropriate) supporting the validity of the original self-certification (and retain a copy or a notation of such explanation and documentation). Therefore, a Reporting Crypto-Asset Service Provider is expected to institute procedures to ensure that any change that constitutes a change in circumstances is identified by the Reporting Crypto-Asset Service Provider. In addition, a Reporting Crypto-Asset Service Provider is expected to notify any person providing a self-certification of the person's obligation to notify the Reporting Crypto-Asset Service Provider of a change in circumstances.

17. A self-certification becomes invalid on the date that the Reporting Crypto-Asset Service Provider holding the self-certification knows or has reason to know that circumstances affecting the correctness of the self-certification have changed. However, a Reporting Crypto-Asset Service Provider may choose to treat a person as having the same status that it had prior to the change in circumstances until the earlier of 90 calendar days from the date that the self-certification became invalid due to the change in circumstances, the date that the validity of the self-certification is confirmed, or the date that a new self-certification is obtained. If the Reporting Crypto-Asset Service Provider cannot obtain a confirmation of the validity of the original self-certification or a valid self-certification during such 90-day period, the Reporting Crypto-Asset Service Provider must treat the Individual Crypto-Asset User as resident of the jurisdiction(s) in which the Individual Crypto-Asset User claimed to be resident in the original self-certification and the jurisdiction(s) in which the Individual Crypto-Asset User may be resident as a result of the change in circumstances. A Reporting Crypto-Asset Service Provider may rely on a self-certification without having to inquire into possible changes of circumstances that may affect the validity of the statement, unless it knows or has reason to know that circumstances have changed. For instance, where the Reporting Crypto-Asset Service Provider obtains information pursuant to its AML/KYC Procedures or other regulatory requirements that information contained in the self-certification is no longer accurate or reliable, the Reporting Crypto-Asset Service Provider must update the self-certification with respect to the information identified, before the self-certification can be relied on.

18. A Reporting Crypto-Asset Service Provider may retain an original, certified copy, or photocopy (including a microfiche, electronic scan, or similar means of electronic storage) or electronic copy of the self-certification. The self-certification (including the original) may also exist solely in electronic format.

Curing self-certification errors

19. A Reporting Crypto-Asset Service Provider may treat a self-certification as valid, notwithstanding that the self-certification contains an inconsequential error, if the Reporting Crypto-Asset Service Provider has sufficient documentation on file to supplement the information missing from the self-certification due to the error. In such case, the documentation relied upon to cure the inconsequential error must be

conclusive. For example, a self-certification in which the Individual Crypto-Asset User submitting the form abbreviated the jurisdiction of residence may be treated as valid, notwithstanding the abbreviation, if the Reporting Crypto-Asset Service Provider has government issued identification for the person from a jurisdiction that reasonably matches the abbreviation. On the other hand, an abbreviation for the jurisdiction of residence that does not reasonably match the jurisdiction of residence shown on the person's passport is not an inconsequential error. A failure to provide a jurisdiction of residence is not an inconsequential error. In addition, information on a self-certification that contradicts other information contained on the self-certification or in the files of the Reporting Crypto-Asset Service Provider is not an inconsequential error.

Paragraph B – Due diligence procedures for Entity Crypto-Asset Users

20. Paragraph B contains the due diligence procedures for Entity Crypto-Asset Users. Such procedures require Reporting Crypto-Asset Service Providers to determine:

- whether the Entity Crypto-Asset User is a Reportable User; and
- whether an Entity Crypto-Asset User has one or more Controlling Persons who are Reportable Persons, unless the Entity Crypto-Asset User is an Excluded Person or an Active Entity.

21. With respect to Preexisting Entity Crypto-Asset Users, subparagraph B(1)(a) clarifies that Reporting Crypto-Asset Service Providers must obtain a valid self-certification and confirm its reasonableness at the latest 12 months after the jurisdiction introduces these rules.

Review procedure for Entity Crypto-Asset Users

22. Subparagraph B(1) contains the review procedure to determine whether an Entity Crypto-Asset User is a Reportable User. In order to determine whether an Entity Crypto-Asset User is a Reportable User, subparagraph B(1)(a) requires that, when establishing a relationship with the Entity Crypto-Asset User, or with respect to Preexisting Entity Crypto-Assets Users by 12 months after the introduction of the rules, the Reporting Crypto-Asset Service Provider:

- obtains a self-certification that allows the Reporting Crypto-Asset Service Provider to determine the Entity Crypto-Asset User's residence(s) for tax purposes; and
- confirms the reasonableness of such self-certification based on the information obtained by the Reporting Crypto-Asset Service Provider in connection with the establishment of the relationship with the Entity Crypto-Asset User, including any documentation collected pursuant to AML/KYC Procedures. If the Entity Crypto-Asset User certifies that it has no residence for tax purposes, the Reporting Crypto-Asset Service Provider may rely on the place of effective management or the address of the principal office to determine the residence of the Entity Crypto-Asset User.

23. If the self-certification indicates that the Entity Crypto-Asset User is resident in a Reportable Jurisdiction, then, as provided in subparagraph B(1)(b), the Reporting Crypto-Asset Service Provider must treat the Entity Crypto-Asset User as a Reportable User unless it reasonably determines based on the self-certification or information in its possession or that is publicly available, that the Entity Crypto-Asset User is an Excluded Person. Such information includes information that was obtained for the purpose of completing the due diligence procedures pursuant to the Common Reporting Standard.

24. "Publicly available" information includes information published by an authorised government body (for example, a government or an agency thereof, or a municipality) of a jurisdiction, such as information in a list published by a tax administration; information in a publicly accessible register maintained or authorised by an authorised government body of a jurisdiction; or information disclosed on an established

securities market. In this respect, the Reporting Crypto-Asset Service Provider is expected to retain a notation of the type of information reviewed, and the date the information was reviewed.

25. In determining whether an Entity Crypto-Asset User is a Reportable User, the Reporting Crypto-Asset Service Provider may follow the guidance on subparagraphs B(1)(a) and (b) in the order most appropriate under the circumstances. That would allow a Reporting Crypto-Asset Service Provider, for example, to determine under subparagraph B(1)(b) that an Entity Crypto-Asset User is an Excluded Person and, thus, is not a Reportable User.

26. The self-certification must allow the determination of the Entity Crypto-Asset User's residence(s) for tax purposes. The domestic laws of the various jurisdictions lay down the conditions under which an Entity is to be treated as fiscally "resident". They cover various forms of attachment to a jurisdiction which, in the domestic taxation laws, form the basis of a comprehensive taxation (full tax liability). Generally, an Entity will be resident for tax purposes in a jurisdiction if, under the laws of that jurisdiction, it pays or should be paying tax therein by reason of its place of management or incorporation, or any other criterion of a similar nature, and not only from sources in that jurisdiction. If an Entity is subject to tax as a resident in more than one jurisdiction, all jurisdictions of residence are to be declared in a self-certification and the Reporting Crypto-Asset Service Provider must treat the Entity Crypto-Asset User as a Reportable User in respect of each Reportable Jurisdiction.

27. Reportable Jurisdictions are expected to help taxpayers determine, and provide them with information with respect to, their residence(s) for tax purposes. That may be done, for example, through the various service channels used for providing information or guidance to taxpayers on the application of tax laws. The OECD will endeavour to facilitate the dissemination of such information.

28. If an Entity Crypto-Asset User certifies that it has no residence for tax purposes, the Reporting Crypto-Asset Service Provider may rely on the place of effective management or, as a proxy, on the address of the principal office of the Entity Crypto-Asset User to determine its residence. Examples of cases where an Entity Crypto-Asset User has no residence for tax purposes includes Entities treated as fiscally transparent and Entities resident in a jurisdiction with no corporate income tax system.

Reasonableness of self-certifications

29. Once the Reporting Crypto-Asset Service Provider has obtained a self-certification that allows it to determine the Entity Crypto-Asset User's residence(s) for tax purposes, the Reporting Crypto-Asset Service Provider must confirm the reasonableness of such self-certification based on the information obtained in connection with the establishment of the relationship, including any documentation collected pursuant to AML/KYC Procedures.

30. A Reporting Crypto-Asset Service Provider is considered to have confirmed the "reasonableness" of a self-certification if, in the course of establishing a relationship with the Entity Crypto-Asset User and upon review of the information obtained in connection with the establishment of the relationship (including any documentation collected pursuant to AML/KYC Procedures), it does not know or have reason to know that the self-certification is incorrect or unreliable. Reporting Crypto-Asset Service Providers are not expected to carry out an independent legal analysis of relevant tax laws to confirm the reasonableness of a self-certification.

31. The following examples illustrate the application of the "reasonableness" test:

- **Example 1**: A Reporting Crypto-Asset Service Provider obtains a self-certification from the Entity Crypto-Asset User upon the establishment of the relationship. The address contained in the self-certification conflicts with that contained in the documentation collected pursuant to AML/KYC Procedures. Because of the conflicting information, the self-certification is incorrect or unreliable and, as a consequence, it fails the reasonableness test.

- **Example 2**: A Reporting Crypto-Asset Service Provider obtains a self-certification from the Entity Crypto-Asset User upon the establishment of the relationship. The documentation collected pursuant to AML/KYC Procedures only indicates the Entity Crypto-Asset User's place of incorporation. In the self-certification, the Entity Crypto-Asset User claims to be resident for tax purposes in a jurisdiction that is different from its jurisdiction of incorporation. The Entity Crypto-Asset User explains to the Reporting Crypto-Asset Service Provider that under relevant tax laws its residence for tax purposes is determined by reference to place of effective management, and that the jurisdiction where its effective management is situated differs from the jurisdiction in which it was incorporated. Thus, because there is a reasonable explanation of the conflicting information, the self-certification is not incorrect or unreliable and, as a consequence, passes the reasonableness test.

32. In the case of a self-certification that fails the reasonableness test, it is expected that the Reporting Crypto-Asset Service Provider would obtain either (i) a valid self-certification, or (ii) a reasonable explanation and documentation (as appropriate) supporting the reasonableness of the self-certification (and retain a copy or a notation of such explanation and documentation) before providing services effectuating Relevant Transactions to the Entity Crypto-Asset User. Further guidance in this respect can be found in the Commentary to paragraph A of Section III.

Review procedure for Controlling Persons

33. Subparagraph B(2) contains the review procedure to determine whether an Entity Crypto-Asset User, other than an Excluded Person, is held by one or more Controlling Persons that are Reportable Persons, unless it determines that the Entity Crypto-Asset User is an Active Entity. Such determination should be made based on a self-certification, the reasonableness of which should be confirmed based on any relevant information available to the Reporting Crypto-Asset Service Provider. When the Reporting Crypto-Asset Service Provider has not determined that the Entity Crypto-Asset User is an Active Entity, then the Reporting Crypto-Asset Service Provider must follow the guidance in subparagraphs B(2)(a) and (b) in the order most appropriate under the circumstances. Those subparagraphs are aimed at:

- determining the Controlling Persons of an Entity Crypto-Asset User; and
- determining whether any Controlling Persons of the Entity Crypto-Asset User are Reportable Persons.

34. For the purposes of determining the Controlling Persons of an Entity Crypto-Asset User, according to subparagraph B(2)(a), a Reporting Crypto-Asset Service Provider may rely on information collected and maintained pursuant to AML/KYC Procedures, provided that such procedures are consistent with the 2012 FATF Recommendations (as updated in June 2019 pertaining to virtual asset service providers). If the Reporting Crypto-Asset Service Provider is not legally required to apply AML/KYC Procedures that are consistent with the 2012 FATF Recommendations (as updated in June 2019 pertaining to virtual asset service providers), it must apply substantially similar procedures for the purpose of determining the Controlling Persons.

35. For the purposes of determining whether a Controlling Person of an Entity Crypto-Asset User is a Reportable Person, a Reporting Crypto-Asset Service Provider must, pursuant to subparagraph B(2)(b), rely on a self-certification from either the Entity Crypto-Asset User or the Controlling Person and confirm the reasonableness of such self-certification based on the information obtained by the Reporting Crypto-Asset Service Provider, including any documentation collected pursuant to AML/KYC Procedures.

Change of circumstances

36. Subparagraph B(3) specifies that if, at any point, there is a change of circumstances with respect to an Entity Crypto-Asset User or its Controlling Person(s) that causes the Reporting Crypto-Asset Service

Provider to know, or have reason to know, that the self-certification or other documentation associated with an Entity Crypto-Asset User or its Controlling Person(s) is incorrect or unreliable, the Reporting Crypto-Asset Service Provider cannot rely on the original self-certification and must re-determine their status. In doing so, the procedures set forth in paragraphs 15 through 18 of the Commentary on Section III should be applied.

Paragraph C – Requirements for validity of self-certifications

37. Paragraph C sets out the requirements for obtaining valid self-certifications with respect to Individual and Entity Crypto-Asset Users, as well as Controlling Persons.

Validity of self-certifications for Individual Crypto-Asset Users and Controlling Persons

38. A self-certification referred to in subparagraph C(1) is a certification by the Individual Crypto-Asset User or Controlling Person that provides the Individual Crypto-Asset User's or Controlling Person's status and any other information that may be reasonably requested by the Reporting Crypto-Asset Service Provider to fulfil its reporting and due diligence obligations, such as whether the Individual Crypto-Asset User or the Controlling Person is resident for tax purposes in a Reportable Jurisdiction. A self-certification is valid only if it is signed (or otherwise positively affirmed) by the Individual Crypto-Asset User or Controlling Person, it is dated at the latest at the date of receipt, and it contains the following information with respect to the Individual Crypto-Asset User or Controlling Person:

a) first and last name;

b) residence address;

c) jurisdiction(s) of residence for tax purposes;

d) with respect to each Reportable Person, the TIN with respect to each Reportable Jurisdiction; and

e) date of birth.

39. The self-certification may be pre-populated by the Reporting Crypto-Asset Service Provider to include the Individual Crypto-Asset User's or Controlling Person's information, except for the jurisdiction(s) of residence for tax purposes, to the extent already available in its records. Further, the Reporting Crypto-Asset Service Provider may rely on a self-certification collected in respect of the Individual Crypto-Asset User or Controlling Person under the Common Reporting Standard or a self-certification already collected for other tax purposes, such as for domestic reporting purposes, in the context of the Foreign Account Tax Compliance Act (FATCA), or for purposes of a FATCA Intergovernmental Agreement, to the extent it contains all of the information referred to in subparagraph C(1).

40. If the Individual Crypto-Asset User or Controlling Person is resident for tax purposes in a Reportable Jurisdiction, the self-certification must include the Individual Crypto-Asset User's or Controlling Person's TIN with respect to each Reportable Jurisdiction, subject to subparagraph C(3).

41. The self-certification may be provided in any manner and in any form. If the self-certification is provided electronically, the electronic system must ensure that the information received is the information sent, and must document all occasions of user access that result in the submission, renewal, or modification of a self-certification. In addition, the design and operation of the electronic system, including access procedures, must ensure that the person accessing the system and furnishing the self-certification is the person named in the self-certification, and must be capable of providing upon request a hard copy of all self-certifications provided electronically.

42. A self-certification may be signed (or otherwise positively affirmed) by any person authorised to sign on behalf of the Individual Crypto-Asset User or Controlling Person under domestic law.

43. Subparagraph C(3) specifies that, notwithstanding the requirements under subparagraphs C(1) and (2) to obtain a TIN in respect of Reportable Users and of Controlling Persons of Entity Crypto-Asset Users that are Reportable Persons, the TIN is not required to be collected if the jurisdiction of residence of the Reportable Person does not issue a TIN to the Reportable Person.

Validity of self-certifications for Entity Crypto-Asset Users

44. A self-certification is a certification by the Entity Crypto-Asset User that provides the Entity Crypto-Asset User's status and any other information that may be reasonably requested by the Reporting Crypto-Asset Service Provider to fulfil its reporting and due diligence obligations, such as whether the Entity Crypto-Asset User is resident for tax purposes in a Reportable Jurisdiction. A self-certification is valid only if it is dated at the latest at the date of receipt, and it contains the Entity Crypto-Asset User's:

a) legal name;
b) address;
c) jurisdiction(s) of residence for tax purposes; and
d) with respect to each Reportable Person, the TIN with respect to each Reportable Jurisdiction; and
e) in case of an Entity Crypto-Asset User other than an Active Entity or an Excluded Person, the information described in subparagraph C(1) with respect to each Controlling Person of the Entity Crypto-Asset User, unless such Controlling Person has provided a self-certification pursuant to subparagraph C(1), as well as the role(s) by virtue of which each Reportable Person is a Controlling Person of the Entity, if not already determined on the basis of AML/KYC Procedures; and
f) if applicable, information as to the criteria it meets to be treated as an Active Entity or Excluded Person.

45. The self-certification may be pre-populated by the Reporting Crypto-Asset Service Provider to include the Entity Crypto-Asset User's information, except for the jurisdiction(s) of residence for tax purposes, to the extent already available in its records. Further, the Reporting Crypto-Asset Service Provider may rely on a self-certification collected in respect of the Entity Crypto-Asset User under the Common Reporting Standard or a self-certification already collected for other tax purposes, such as for domestic reporting purposes, in the context of FATCA, or for purposes of a FATCA Intergovernmental Agreement, to the extent it contains all of the information referred to in subparagraph C(2).

46. A self-certification may be signed (or otherwise positively affirmed) by any person authorised to sign on behalf of the Entity Crypto-Asset User under domestic law. A person with authority to sign a self-certification of an Entity Crypto-Asset User generally includes an officer or director of a corporation, a partner of a partnership, a trustee of a trust, any equivalent of the former titles, and any other person that has been provided written authorisation by the Entity Crypto-Asset User to sign documentation on such person's behalf.

47. The requirements for the validity of self-certifications with respect to Individual Crypto-Asset Users or Controlling Persons in paragraphs 40 and 41 of this section are also applicable for the validity of self-certifications with respect to Entity Crypto-Asset Users.

Paragraph D – General due diligence requirements

48. Subparagraph D(1) seeks to ensure consistent application of the due diligence procedures when a Reporting Crypto-Asset Service Provider is also a Reporting Financial Institution pursuant to the Common Reporting Standard. In such instances, where a Reporting Crypto-Asset Service Provider, by virtue of also being a Reporting Financial Institution, has completed the due diligence procedures pursuant

to Sections IV and VI of the Common Reporting Standard, such Reporting Crypto-Asset Service Provider may rely on such procedures to fulfil its due diligence obligations under the Crypto-Asset Reporting Framework.

49. A Reporting Crypto-Asset Service Provider may also rely on a self-certification already collected for other tax purposes, such as for domestic reporting purposes, in the context of FATCA, or for purposes of a FATCA Intergovernmental Agreement, provided such self-certification meets the requirements of paragraph C of this Section. In such instances, a Reporting Crypto-Asset Service Provider is still subject to the other elements of the due diligence procedures of Section III.

50. A Reporting Crypto-Asset Service Provider may rely on a third party to fulfil the due diligence obligations. The following situations apply in which Reporting Crypto-Asset Service Provider will rely on documentation of a third party to fulfil its due diligence obligations: first, with respect to documentation collected by third party service providers, agents or where a Reporting Crypto-Asset Service Provider relies on documentation of an acquired business and, secondly, with respect to the situation where a Reporting Crypto-Asset Service Provider relies on other Reporting Crypto-Asset Service Providers that handle the same Relevant Transaction. These scenarios are described, in turn, below.

51. Pursuant to subparagraph D(2), [Jurisdiction] may allow Reporting Crypto-Asset Service Providers to use service providers to fulfil their due diligence obligations. In such cases, Reporting Crypto-Asset Service Providers may use the documentation (including a self-certification) collected by service providers, subject to the conditions described in domestic law. The due diligence obligations remain, however, the responsibility of the Reporting Crypto-Asset Service Providers.

52. A Reporting Crypto-Asset Service Provider may also rely on documentation (including a self-certification) collected by an agent of the Reporting Crypto-Asset Service Provider. The agent may retain the documentation as part of an information system maintained for a single Reporting Crypto-Asset Service Provider or multiple Reporting Crypto-Asset Service Providers provided that under the system, any Reporting Crypto-Asset Service Provider on behalf of which the agent retains documentation may easily access data regarding the nature of the documentation, the information contained in the documentation (including a copy of the documentation itself) and its validity, and must allow such Reporting Crypto-Asset Service Provider to easily transmit data, either directly into an electronic system or by providing such information to the agent, regarding any facts of which it becomes aware that may affect the reliability of the documentation. The Reporting Crypto-Asset Service Provider must be able to establish, to the extent applicable, how and when it has transmitted data regarding any facts of which it became aware that may affect the reliability of the documentation and must be able to establish that any data it has transmitted has been processed and appropriate due diligence has been exercised regarding the validity of the documentation. The agent must have a system in effect to ensure that any information it receives regarding facts that affect the reliability of the documentation or the status assigned to the Crypto-Asset User are provided to all Reporting Crypto-Asset Service Providers for which the agent retains the documentation.

53. A Reporting Crypto-Asset Service Provider that acquires the business of another Reporting Crypto-Asset Service Provider that has completed all the due diligence required under Section III with respect to the Individual Crypto-Asset Users transferred, would generally be permitted to also rely upon the predecessor's or transferor's determination of status of an Individual Crypto-Asset User until the acquirer knows, or has reason to know, that the status is inaccurate or a change in circumstances occurs.

54. Subparagraph D(2) also seeks to avoid duplicative or multiple application of the due diligence procedures by individuals or Entities that are all Reporting Crypto-Asset Service Providers effectuating the same Relevant Transaction with respect to the same Crypto-Asset User. This is particularly relevant in instances where another Reporting Crypto-Asset Service Provider may have better access to information to carry out the due diligence procedures, as it is recognised that not all functionalities or services associated with a given Relevant Transaction are necessarily provided by a single individual or Entity. In

certain instances, these functionalities may be split among different individuals or Entities that could each be a Reporting Crypto-Asset Service Provider in respect of the Relevant Transaction. For instance, a broker in Relevant Crypto-Assets may receive an order from a client to conduct a Relevant Transaction in Crypto-Assets. The broker could transmit the client's order to a trading platform, which effectuates the transaction on behalf of the client. In this case, the broker is a Reporting Crypto-Asset Service Provider where it acts on behalf of a client to complete orders to buy or sell interest in Relevant Crypto-Assets. Similarly, the trading platform is also a Reporting Crypto-Asset Service Provider as it conducts the actual Exchange Transaction. As a result there may be more than one Reporting Crypto-Asset Service Provider effectuating the same Relevant Transaction with respect to the same Crypto-Asset User.

55. Subparagraph D(2) allows Reporting Crypto-Asset Service Providers to designate a single Reporting Crypto-Asset Service Provider to comply with all due diligence requirements, in case multiple Reporting Crypto-Asset Service Providers provide services effectuating the same Relevant Transaction.

56. To that end, a Reporting Crypto-Asset Service Provider may rely on a third party to fulfil the due diligence obligations set out in Section III. In order for a Reporting Crypto-Asset Service Provider to be able to rely on a third party (including another Reporting Crypto-Asset Service Provider) for the performance of the due diligence obligations under Section III, appropriate contractual arrangements should be put in place. Such arrangements should include an obligation for the Reporting Crypto-Asset Service Provider to make the information necessary to comply with the due diligence procedures of the Crypto-Asset Reporting Framework available to the third party(ies) fulfilling such obligations. This would include information held by the Reporting Crypto-Asset Service Provider that is needed by a third party(ies) to complete the due diligence procedures. The arrangements should also ensure that the Reporting Crypto-Asset Service Provider can obtain any information collected and verified in respect of Crypto-Asset Users from the third party(ies) to allow the Reporting Crypto-Asset Service Provider to demonstrate compliance with the requirements of Section III, for instance in the framework of an audit.

57. It is important to note that the fact that a Reporting Crypto-Asset Service Provider relies on a third party (including another Reporting Crypto-Asset Service Provider) to complete the due diligence procedures does not mean that the Reporting Crypto-Asset Service Provider is discharged from its obligations under Section III. Rather, subparagraph D(2) stipulates that the Reporting Crypto-Asset Service Provider remains responsible for the completion of the due diligence procedures.

58. Subparagraph D(3) specifies relevant information retention obligations, whereby a Reporting Crypto-Asset Service Provider is required to ensure that all documentation and data remain available for a period of not less than five years (in order to correspond to the requirements for record-keeping pursuant to the Global Forum Standard for the Exchange of Information upon Request) after the end of the period within which the Reporting Crypto-Asset Service Provider must report the information required to be reported pursuant to Section II, including in instances where the Reporting Crypto-Asset Service Provider is liquidated or otherwise terminates its business. Such information includes any information used to identify the Crypto-Asset User, as well as any external wallet addresses (or other equivalent identifiers) associated with Transfers of Relevant Crypto-Assets that are subject to reporting under subparagraph A(3)(i).

Commentary on Section IV: Defined terms

Paragraph IV (A) – Relevant Crypto-Asset

Subparagraph A(1) – Crypto-Asset

1. The term "Crypto-Asset", as defined in subparagraph A(1), refers to a digital representation of value that relies on a cryptographically secured distributed ledger or a similar technology to validate and secure transactions.

2. In this context, a "digital representation of value" means that a Crypto-Asset must represent a right to value, and that the ownership of, or right to, such value can be traded or transferred to other individuals or Entities in a digital manner. For instance, a token based on cryptography that allows individuals to store value, engage in payments and that does not represent any claims or rights of memberships against a person, rights to property or other absolute or relative rights is a Crypto-Asset.

3. Furthermore, a cryptographic token that represents claims or rights of membership against an individual or Entity, rights to property or other absolute or relative rights (e.g. a security token or a derivative contract or right to purchase or sell an asset, including a Financial Asset and a Crypto-Asset, at a set date, price or other pre-determined factor), and that can be digitally exchanged for Fiat Currencies or other Crypto-Assets, is a Crypto-Asset. For instance, the following examples illustrate the reporting requirements in respect of derivatives:

- **Example 1**: (Crypto-Derivative A, a cryptographic token, purchased with Relevant Crypto-Assets (i.e. stablecoins that are not Specified Electronic Money Products)): Crypto-Derivative A, represents a leveraged interest in an underlying Relevant Crypto-Asset, such that, the value of Crypto-Derivative A will mirror changes in the price of the underlying Relevant Crypto-Asset (either upwards or downwards) at three times the change in market price.

  User 1 purchases one unit of Crypto-Derivative A through consideration in the form of stablecoins. As Crypto-Derivative A is a Relevant Crypto-Asset, it is reportable under the Crypto-Asset Reporting Framework, provided the trade is carried out through a Reporting Crypto-Asset Service Provider. The trade entails the following Relevant Transactions:

  1. Disposal of the stablecoin by User 1, reported in Fiat Currency at the fair market value, along with the number of units; and
  2. Acquisition of Crypto-Derivative A by User 1, reported in Fiat Currency at the fair market value, along with the number of units.

- **Example 2**: (Redeeming Crypto-Derivative A, with settlement in stablecoins): Further to the trade in Example 1, User 1 redeems Crypto-Derivative A with the issuer. When User 1 redeems Crypto-Derivative A, the market price of the underlying Relevant Crypto-Asset has gained 10% since User 1 purchased Crypto-Derivative A. User 1's gains are magnified by the leverage of the token, and User 1 redeems Crypto-Derivative A with the issuer for a value 30% greater than the initial purchase price. The Reporting Crypto-Asset Service Provider pays this redemption amount to User 1's wallet in stablecoins. The trade entails the following Relevant Transactions:

  1. Disposal of Crypto-Derivative A, valued in Fiat Currency at its fair market value, along with the number of units; and
  2. Acquisition of stablecoin, valued in Fiat Currency at their fair market value, along with the number of units.

- **Example 3**: (Traditional derivative contract settled by physical delivery of a Relevant Crypto-Asset): Two counterparties, Buyer and Seller, enter into opposing positions of a futures contract to, respectively, purchase and sell Relevant Crypto-Asset B on a specified date. The settlement of the derivative requires Buyer to purchase Relevant Crypto-Asset B from Seller on a specified date and at a pre-determined price, paid in Fiat Currency. Seller is then obliged to physically deliver Relevant Crypto-Asset B to Buyer's wallet address. On the specified date, Buyer and Seller conduct the transaction, by using a Reporting Crypto-Asset Service Provider to facilitate the following Relevant Transactions in respect of Relevant Crypto-Asset B:

1. Disposal of Relevant Crypto-Asset B by Seller, reported at the Fiat Currency received, along with the number of units; and
2. Acquisition of Relevant Crypto-Asset B by Buyer, reported at the Fiat Currency paid, along with the number of units.

4. The term "Crypto-Asset" is intended to cover any digital representation of value that relies on a cryptographically secured distributed ledger or a similar technology to validate and secure transactions, where the ownership of, or right to, such value can be traded or transferred to other individuals or Entities in a digital manner. As such, the term "Crypto-Asset" encompasses both fungible and non-fungible tokens and therefore includes non-fungible tokens (NFTs) representing rights to collectibles, games, works of art, physical property or financial documents that can be traded or transferred to other individuals or Entities in a digital manner.

5. Other uses of cryptographic technology that are not digital representations of value, are not Crypto-Assets. Examples include the use of cryptography to:

- create a decentralized immutable record of activities or materials involved in making, storing, shipping or delivering a product, where the record does not convey any ownership rights in such product; or
- a declarative record of ownership of assets (such as a real estate ledger or similar agreement) where the record does not convey any ownership rights in the assets represented by such record.

6. In addition to having inherent value that is digitally tradable or transferable, a Crypto-Asset must rely on a cryptographically secured distributed ledger or similar technology to validate and secure transactions whether or not the transaction is actually recorded on such distributed ledger or similar technology. A distributed ledger is a decentralised manner for recording transactions in Crypto-Assets in multiple places and at the same time. Cryptography refers to a mathematical and computational practice of encoding and decoding data that is used to validate and secure transactions in a decentralised or non-intermediated manner. The cryptographic process is used to ensure, in a decentralised manner, the integrity of Crypto-Assets, the clear assignment of Crypto-Assets to users, and the disposal of Crypto-Assets.

7. This cryptographic process allows multiple parties to engage in disintermediated validations of transactions in the Crypto-Asset, often by verifying public and private cryptographic keys to a transaction. This validation ensures that users in possession of a Crypto-Asset have not already exchanged the same Crypto-Asset in another transaction. The cryptographic process also secures transactions made in Crypto-Assets by compiling each transaction within a block of other transactions. The block of transactions is then added to the official, publicly accessible, transaction ledger (such as a blockchain) once the user completes a cryptographic hash.

8. Crypto-Assets may also rely on similar technology that allows for the disintermediated holding or validating of Crypto-Assets. Regardless of the type of software used, if the technology underpinning the Crypto-Asset allows for validating and securing digital transactions in a decentralised or disintermediated manner, it is considered a similar technology to a cryptographically secured distributed ledger.

Subparagraph A(2) – Relevant Crypto-Assets

9. Relevant Crypto-Assets are Crypto-Assets in respect of which Reporting Crypto-Asset Service Providers must fulfil reporting and due diligence requirements. The term Relevant Crypto-Assets applies to all Crypto-Assets except Central Bank Digital Currencies, Specified Electronic Money Products and Crypto-Assets for which the Reporting Crypto-Asset Service Provider has adequately determined that they cannot be used for payment or investment purposes. If an individual or Entity is a Reporting Crypto-Asset Service Provider (e.g. because it otherwise carries out exchanges in Relevant Crypto-Assets), it would nevertheless not be required to report information with respect to exchanges carried out in Crypto-Assets that are not Relevant Crypto-Assets.

10. For the purpose of adequately determining whether a Crypto-Asset cannot be used for payment or investment purposes, Reporting Crypto-Asset Service Providers may, in a first step, rely on the classification of the Crypto-Asset that was made for the purpose of determining whether the Crypto-Asset is a virtual asset for AML/KYC purposes pursuant to the FATF Recommendations. In case a Crypto-Asset is considered a virtual asset pursuant to FATF Recommendations by virtue of being able to be used for payment or investment purposes, it is to be considered a Relevant Crypto-Asset for purposes of the Crypto-Asset Reporting Framework.

11. Where an asset is not a virtual asset pursuant to FATF Recommendations or the Reporting Crypto-Asset Service Provider has not made a determination to that effect, the Reporting Crypto-Asset Service Provider must determine, for each Crypto-Asset, whether it cannot be used for payment or investment purposes. Only when this test can be positively affirmed, the Crypto-Asset is not to be considered a Relevant Crypto-Asset. In case of doubts as to whether the Crypto-Asset can be used for payment or investment purposes, the Crypto-Asset is to be considered a Relevant Crypto-Asset.

12. In assessing whether a Crypto-Asset cannot be used for payment or investment purposes, the following aspects may be taken into account:

- Crypto-Assets that represent Financial Assets or are subject to financial regulation can be used for payment or investment purposes and are therefore to be considered Relevant Crypto-Assets.
- NFTs are in many instances marketed as collectibles. This function does, however, by itself not prevent an NFT from being able to be used for payment or investment purposes. It is important to consider the nature of the NFT and its function in practice and not what terminology or marketing terms are used. NFTs that can be used for payment or investment purposes in practice are Relevant Crypto-Assets. Reporting Crypto-Asset Service Providers should therefore consider on a case-by-case basis whether an NFT cannot be used for payment or investment purposes, taking into account the commonly accepted usage of the Crypto-Asset. NFTs that are traded on a marketplace can be used for payment or investment purposes and are therefore to be considered Relevant Crypto-Assets.
- Certain Crypto-Assets can only be exchanged or redeemed within a limited fixed network or environment for specified goods and services, such as food, book, and restaurant vouchers, as well airline miles or other loyalty program rewards. In this context, the term “goods and services” may also include digital goods and services, such as digital music, games, books or other media, as well as tickets, software applications and online subscriptions. Provided these Crypto-Assets are characterised by operating in a limited fixed network or environment beyond which the Crypto-Assets cannot be transferred or exchanged in a secondary market outside of the closed-loop system, and cannot be sold or exchanged at a market rate inside or outside of the closed-loop, such Crypto-Assets would generally not be able to be used for payment or investment purposes.

Subparagraph A(3) – Central Bank Digital Currency

13. The term "Central Bank Digital Currencies" means any digital Fiat Currency issued by a Central Bank. Central Bank Digital Currencies are not considered Relevant Crypto-Assets, given that they are a digital form of Fiat Currency.

Subparagraph A(4) – Specified Electronic Money Product

14. Subparagraph A(4) defines the term "Specified Electronic Money Product" as any Crypto-Asset that is:

a) a digital representation of a single Fiat Currency;

b) issued on receipt of funds for the purpose of making payment transactions;

c) represented by a claim on the issuer denominated in the same Fiat Currency;

d) accepted in payment by a natural or legal person other than the issuer; and

e) by virtue of regulatory requirements to which the issuer is subject, redeemable at any time and at par value for the same Fiat Currency upon request of the holder of the product.

The term "Specified Electronic Money Product" does not include a product created for the sole purpose of facilitating the transfer of funds from a customer to another person pursuant to instructions of the customer. A product is not created for the sole purpose of facilitating the transfer of funds if, in the ordinary course of business of the transferring Entity, either the funds connected with such product are held longer than 60 days after receipt of instructions to facilitate the transfer, or, if no instructions are received, the funds connected with such product are held longer than 60 days after receipt of the funds.

15. Subparagraph A(4)(a) requires that a Crypto-Asset must be a digital representation of a single Fiat Currency, in order to be a Specified Electronic Money Product. A Crypto-Asset will be considered to digitally represent and reflect the value of the Fiat Currency that it is denominated in. Consequently, a Crypto-Asset that reflects the value of multiple currencies or assets is not a Specified Electronic Money Product.

16. Subparagraph A(4)(b) provides that the Crypto-Asset must be issued on receipt of funds. This part of the definition means that a Specified Electronic Money Products is a prepaid product. The act of "issuing" is interpreted broadly to include the activity of making available pre-paid stored value and means of payment in exchange for funds. In addition, this subparagraph provides that the Crypto-Asset must be issued for the purpose of making payment transactions.

17. Subparagraph A(4)(c) requires that, in order to be a Specified Electronic Money Product, a Crypto-Asset must be represented by a claim on the issuer denominated in the same Fiat Currency. In this respect, a "claim" includes any monetary claim against the issuer, reflecting the value of the Fiat Currency represented by the Crypto-Asset issued to the customer.

18. Under subparagraph A(4)(d), a Crypto-Asset must be accepted by a natural or legal person other than the issuer in order to be a Specified Electronic Money Product, whereby such third parties must accept the Crypto-Asset as a means of payment. Consequently, monetary value stored on specific pre-paid instruments, designed to address precise needs that can be used only in a limited way, because they allow the electronic money holder to purchase goods or services only in the premises of the electronic money issuer or within a limited network of service providers under direct commercial agreement with a professional issuer, or because they can be used only to acquire a limited range of goods or services, are not considered Specified Electronic Money Products.

19. Subparagraph A(4)(e) provides that the issuer of the Crypto-Assets must be subject to supervision to ensure the product is redeemable at any time and at par value for the same Fiat Currency upon request

of the holder of the Crypto-Asset, in order to be a Specified Electronic Money Product. In this respect, the "same" Fiat Currency refers to the Fiat Currency that the Crypto-Asset is a digital representation of. When proceeding to a redemption, it is acknowledged that the issuer can deduct from the redemption amount any fees or transaction costs.

20. The definition excludes those products that are created solely to facilitate a funds transfer pursuant to instructions of a customer and that cannot be used to store value. For example, such products may be used to enable an employer to transfer the monthly wages to its employees or to enable a migrant worker to transfer funds to relatives living in another country. A product is not created for the sole purpose of facilitating the transfer of funds if, in the ordinary course of business of the transferring Entity, either the funds connected with such product are held longer than 60 days after receipt of instructions to facilitate the transfer, or, if no instructions are received, the funds connected with such product are held longer than 60 days after receipt of the funds.

Paragraph IV (B) – Reporting Crypto-Asset Service Provider

Subparagraph B(1) – Reporting Crypto-Asset Service Provider

21. The term "Reporting Crypto-Asset Service Provider" refers to any individual or Entity that, as a business, provides a service effectuating Exchange Transactions for or on behalf of customers (which for the purposes of this definition includes users of services of Reporting Crypto-Asset Service Providers), including by acting as a counterparty, or as an intermediary, to Exchange Transactions, or by making available a trading platform.

22. The phrase "as a business" excludes individuals or Entities who carry out a service on a very infrequent basis for non-commercial reasons. In determining what is meant by "as a business", reference can be made to each jurisdiction's relevant rules.

23. A service effectuating Exchange Transactions includes any service through which the customer can receive Relevant Crypto-Assets for Fiat Currencies, or vice versa, or exchange Relevant Crypto-Assets for other Relevant Crypto-Assets. The activities of an investment fund investing in Relevant Crypto-Assets do not constitute a service effectuating Exchange Transactions since such activities do not permit the investors in the fund to effectuate Exchange Transactions.

24. An individual or Entity effectuating Exchange Transactions will only be a Reporting Crypto-Asset Service Provider if it carries out such activities for or on behalf of customers. This means, for example, that an individual or Entity that is solely engaged in validating distributed ledger transactions in Relevant Crypto-Assets is not a Reporting Crypto-Asset Service Provider, even where such validation is remunerated.

25. An individual or Entity may effectuate Exchange Transactions for or on behalf of customers by acting as a counterparty or intermediary to the Exchange Transactions. Examples of individuals or Entities that may provide services effectuating Exchange Transactions as a counterparty, or as an intermediary, include:

- dealers acting for their own account to buy and sell Relevant Crypto-Assets to customers;
- operators of Crypto-Asset ATMs, permitting the exchange of Relevant Crypto-Assets for Fiat Currencies or other Relevant Crypto-Assets through such ATMs;
- Crypto-Asset exchanges that act as a market makers and take a bid-ask spread as a transaction commission for their services;
- brokers in Relevant Crypto-Assets where they act on behalf of clients to complete orders to buy or sell an interest in Relevant Crypto-Assets; and

- individuals or Entities subscribing one or more Relevant Crypto-Assets. While the sole creation and issuance of a Relevant Crypto-Asset would not be considered a service effectuating Exchange Transactions as a counterparty or intermediary, the direct purchase of Relevant Crypto-Assets from an issuer, to resell and distribute such Relevant Crypto-Assets to customers would be considered effectuating an Exchange Transaction.

26. An individual or Entity may also effectuate Exchange Transactions for or on behalf of customers by making available a trading platform that provides the ability for such customers to effectuate Exchange Transactions on such platform. A "trading platform" includes any software program or application that allows users to effectuate (either partially or in their entirety) Exchange Transactions. An individual or Entity that is making available a platform that solely includes a bulletin board functionality for posting buy, sell or conversion prices of Relevant Crypto-Assets would not be a Reporting Crypto-Asset Service Provider as it would not provide a service allowing users to effectuate Exchange Transactions. For the same reason, an individual or Entity that solely creates or sells software or an application is not a Reporting Crypto-Asset Service Provider, as long as it is not using such software or application for the provision of a service effectuating Exchange Transactions for or on behalf of customers.

27. An individual or Entity will be considered to make available a trading platform to the extent it exercises control or sufficient influence over the platform, allowing it to comply with the due diligence and reporting obligations with respect to Exchange Transactions concluded on the platform. Whether an individual or Entity exercises such control or sufficient influence should be assessed in a manner consistent with the 2012 FATF Recommendations (as amended in June 2019 with respect to virtual assets and virtual asset service providers) and related FATF guidance.

28. An individual or Entity may be a Reporting Crypto-Asset Service Provider by carrying out activities other than acting as a counterparty, or intermediary, to an Exchange Transaction, or making available a trading platform, as long as it functionally provides a service, as a business, effectuating Exchange Transactions for or on behalf of customers. The technology involved in providing such service is irrelevant to determine whether an individual or Entity is a Reporting Crypto-Asset Service Provider.

Paragraph IV (C) – Relevant Transaction

Subparagraph C(1) – Relevant Transaction

29. The term "Relevant Transaction" refers to any exchange of Relevant Crypto-Assets and Fiat Currencies, any exchange between one or more forms of Relevant Crypto-Assets and Transfers of Relevant Crypto-Assets, including Reportable Retail Payment Transactions. This definition targets those transactions likely to give rise to taxation events (i.e. capital gains and income taxation).

Subparagraph C(2) – Exchange Transaction

30. An Exchange Transaction, as defined in subparagraph C(2), refers to any exchange between Relevant Crypto-Assets and Fiat Currencies as well as any exchange between one or more forms of Relevant Crypto-Assets. For this purpose, an exchange includes the movement of a Relevant Crypto-Asset from one wallet address to another, in consideration of another Relevant Crypto-Asset or Fiat Currency.

Subparagraph C(3) – Reportable Retail Payment Transaction

31. Subparagraph C(3) defines the term "Reportable Retail Payment Transaction" as a Transfer of Relevant Crypto-Assets in consideration of goods or services for a value exceeding USD 50,000. This term covers situations where a Reporting Crypto-Asset Service Provider transfers Relevant Crypto-Assets used by a customer to purchase goods or services from a merchant who receives the Relevant Crypto-Assets

as consideration. For example, a Reporting Crypto-Asset Service Provider may carry out Relevant Transactions between a merchant and its customers to allow payment for goods or services with Relevant Crypto-Assets. Where a Reporting Crypto-Asset Service Provider transfers payment made in Relevant Crypto-Assets from a customer to the merchant for a value above the specified threshold, the Reporting Crypto-Asset Service Provider should report such Transfer as a Reportable Retail Payment Transaction. With respect to such Transfers, the Reporting Crypto-Asset Service Provider is required to also treat the customer of the merchant as the Crypto-Asset User, provided that the Reporting Crypto-Asset Service Provider is required to verify the identity of such customer pursuant to domestic anti-money laundering rules, by virtue of the Reportable Retail Payment Transaction.

Subparagraph C(4) –Transfers

32. The term "Transfer" means a transaction that moves a Relevant Crypto-Asset from or to the Crypto-Asset address or account of one Crypto-Asset User, other than one maintained by the Reporting Crypto-Asset Service Provider on behalf of same Crypto-Asset User. A Reporting Crypto-Asset Service Provider can only classify a Relevant Transaction as a Transfer if, based on the knowledge of the Reporting Crypto-Asset Service Provider at the time of transaction, the Reporting Crypto-Asset Service Provider cannot determine that the transaction is an Exchange Transaction. Such knowledge should be determined by reference to the Reporting Crypto-Asset Service Provider's actual knowledge based on readily available information and the degree of expertise and understanding required to conduct the Relevant Transaction. For example, there may be instances where a Crypto-Asset User acquires or disposes of a Relevant Crypto-Asset against Fiat Currency, although the Reporting Crypto-Asset Service Provider does not have actual knowledge of the underlying consideration. This would, for example, be the case if the Reporting Crypto-Asset Service Provider only conducted the Transfer of the Relevant Crypto-Assets to and from the Crypto-Asset User's account, without visibility over the Fiat Currency leg of the transaction. Such transactions would still be considered Relevant Transactions, but the Reporting Crypto-Asset Service Provider would need to report such Relevant Transactions as Transfers.

33. A "Transfer" would also include the instance where a Reporting Crypto-Asset Service Provider facilitates an individual or Entity receiving a Relevant Crypto-Asset by means of an airdrop when the Crypto-Asset is newly issued. For instance, in the context of a "hard-fork" a new Relevant Crypto-Asset diverges from a legacy Relevant Crypto-Asset. As a result, developers of the hard fork typically send an airdrop of new Relevant Crypto-Assets to all holders of the legacy Relevant Crypto-Asset and such Crypto-Asset Users will hold the new Relevant Crypto-Assets in addition to the legacy Relevant Crypto-Assets. For example, the receipt of an airdrop of a new Relevant Crypto-Asset is considered an inbound Transfer to the receiving Crypto-Asset User.

Subparagraph C(5) – Fiat Currency

34. The term Fiat Currency refers to the official currency of a jurisdiction, issued by a jurisdiction or by a jurisdiction's designated Central Bank or monetary authority, as represented by physical banknotes or coins or by money in different digital forms, including bank reserves, and Central Bank Digital Currencies. The term also includes commercial bank money and electronic money products (including Specified Electronic Money Products). Accordingly, a stablecoin that qualifies as a Specified Electronic Money Product is treated as Fiat Currency.

Paragraph IV (D) – Reportable User

Subparagraph D(1) – Reportable User

35. The term "Reportable User", as defined in subparagraph D(1), means a Crypto-Asset User that is a Reportable Person.

Subparagraph D(2) – Crypto-Asset User

36. Subparagraph D(2) defines the term "Crypto-Asset User" as a customer of a Reporting Crypto-Asset Service Provider for purposes of carrying out Relevant Transactions. Any individual or Entity identified by the Reporting Crypto Asset Service Provider for purposes of carrying out Relevant Transactions is treated as a Crypto Asset User, irrespective of whether the Reporting Crypto-Asset Service Provider is safekeeping the Relevant Crypto-Assets on behalf of the Crypto-Asset User or the legal characterisation of the relationship between the Reporting Crypto-Asset Service Provider and such individual or Entity.

37. An individual or Entity, other than a Financial Institution or Reporting Crypto-Asset Service Provider, acting as a Crypto-Asset User for the benefit or account of another individual or Entity as agent, custodian, nominee, signatory, investment advisor, or intermediary, is not treated as a Crypto-Asset User, and such other individual or Entity is treated as the Crypto-Asset User. For these purposes a Reporting Crypto-Asset Service Provider may rely on information in its possession (including information collected pursuant to AML/KYC Procedures), based on which it can reasonably determine whether the individual or Entity is acting for the benefit or account of another individual or Entity. In confirming whether a Crypto-Asset User may be a Reporting Crypto-Asset Service Provider or a Financial Institution, a Reporting Crypto-Asset Service provider may, for instance, rely on cross-checking the information provided by its Crypto-Asset User with regulated institutions lists that indicate other Reporting Crypto-Asset Service Providers or Financial Institutions, where available.

38. The following examples illustrate the application of this definition:

- F holds a power of attorney from U that authorises F to establish a relationship as a Crypto-Asset User at Reporting Crypto-Asset Service Provider X for carrying out Relevant Transactions on behalf of U. F has established a relationship at Reporting Crypto-Asset Service Provider X as the person who can carry out Relevant Transactions. However, because F is not a Financial Institution or Reporting Crypto-Asset Service Provider and the Reporting Crypto-Asset Service Provider has information in its AML/KYC files indicating that F acts as an agent for the benefit of U, the Reporting Crypto-Asset Service Provider must treat U as the Crypto-Asset User;
- Reporting Crypto-Asset Service Provider A uses the services of Reporting Crypto-Asset Service Provider B to effectuate Relevant Transactions on the exchange platform maintained by B. Therefore, A is a Crypto-Asset User for B, and B will report the Relevant Transactions effectuated by A. Because A is a Reporting Crypto-Asset Service Provider, it is immaterial whether A effectuates such Relevant Transactions in its own name or as an agent, custodian, nominee, signatory, investment advisor or intermediary.

39. A Reporting Crypto-Asset Service Provider may conduct Relevant Transactions that allow a merchant to offer its customers payment in the form of Relevant Crypto-Assets, in consideration of a purchase of goods or services. In those instances, and provided that the value of the transaction exceeds USD 50 000, the transaction is considered a Relevant Transaction by virtue of being a Reportable Retail Payment Transaction. See Commentary to subparagraph C(3). For Reportable Retail Payment Transactions, the Reporting Crypto-Asset Service Provider must treat the customer of the merchant as the Crypto-Asset User and the transaction should be reported as a Reportable Retail Payment Transaction pursuant to subparagraph A(3)(f) of Section II, provided that the Reporting Crypto-Asset Service Provider is required to verify the identity of such customer pursuant to domestic anti-money laundering rules, by virtue of the Reportable Retail Payment Transaction. The requirement to verify the identity of the customer means a requirement pursuant to domestic anti-money laundering rules that requires the Reporting Crypto-Asset Service Provider to verify the identity using reliable, independent source documents, data or information.

Subparagraphs D(3) through (6) – Preexisting, Individual and Entity Crypto-Asset Users

40. Subparagraphs D(3) through (6) contain the various categories of Crypto-Asset Users classified by reference to date of the establishment of the relationship or type of Crypto-Asset User: "Individual Crypto-Asset User", "Preexisting Individual Crypto-Asset User", "Entity Crypto-Asset User", "Preexisting Entity Crypto-Asset User".

41. A Crypto-Asset User is classified, firstly, depending on whether it is an individual or an Entity and, secondly, depending on the date it established a relationship as such with a Reporting Crypto-Asset Service Provider. Thus, a Crypto-Asset User can be either a "Preexisting Individual Crypto-Asset User", a "Preexisting Entity Crypto-Asset User", an "Individual Crypto-Asset User" and/or an "Entity Crypto-Asset User".

42. As such, Preexisting Individual Crypto-Asset Users and Preexisting Entity Crypto-Asset Users are Crypto-Asset Users that have established a relationship as a customer of the Reporting Crypto-Asset Service Provider as of [xx/xx/xxxx] and are therefore a subset of Individual Crypto-Asset Users and Entity Crypto-Asset Users, respectively.

Subparagraph D(7) – Reportable Person

43. Subparagraph D(7) defines the term "Reportable Person" as a Reportable Jurisdiction Person other than an Excluded Person.

Subparagraph D(8) – Reportable Jurisdiction Person

44. As a general rule, an individual or Entity is a "Reportable Jurisdiction Person" if it is resident in a Reportable Jurisdiction under the tax laws of such jurisdiction.

45. Domestic laws differ in the treatment of partnerships (including limited liability partnerships). Some jurisdictions treat partnerships as taxable units (sometimes even as companies) whereas other jurisdictions adopt what may be referred to as the fiscally transparent approach, under which the partnership is disregarded for tax purposes. Where a partnership is treated as a company or taxed in the same way, it would generally be considered to be a resident of the Reportable Jurisdiction that taxes the partnership. Where, however, a partnership is treated as fiscally transparent in a Reportable Jurisdiction, the partnership is not "liable to tax" in that jurisdiction, and so cannot be a resident thereof.

46. An Entity such as a partnership, limited liability partnership or similar legal arrangement that has no residence for tax purposes shall be treated as resident in the jurisdiction in which its place of effective management is situated. For these purposes, a legal person or a legal arrangement is considered "similar" to a partnership and a limited liability partnership where it is not treated as a taxable unit in a Reportable Jurisdiction under the tax laws of such jurisdiction.

47. The "place of effective management" is the place where key management and commercial decisions that are necessary for the conduct of the Entity's business as a whole are in substance made. All relevant facts and circumstances must be examined to determine the place of effective management.

48. The term "Reportable Jurisdiction Person" also includes an estate of a decedent that was a resident of a Reportable Jurisdiction. In determining what is meant by "estate", reference must be made to each jurisdiction's particular rules on the transfer or inheritance of rights and obligations in the event of death (e.g. the rules on universal succession).

Subparagraph D(9) – Reportable Jurisdiction

49. Subparagraph D(9) defines "Reportable Jurisdiction" as any jurisdiction (a) with which an agreement or arrangement is in effect pursuant to which [Jurisdiction] is obligated to provide the information

specified in Section II with respect to Reportable Persons resident in such jurisdiction, and (b) which is identified as such in a list published by [Jurisdiction]. Subparagraph D(9) therefore requires that the jurisdiction is identified in a published list as a Reportable Jurisdiction. Each jurisdiction must make such a list publicly available, and update it as appropriate (e.g. every time the jurisdiction signs an agreement with respect to exchanging information under these rules, or such an agreement enters into force).

Subparagraph D(10) – Controlling Persons

50. Subparagraph D(10) sets forth the definition of the term "Controlling Persons". This term corresponds to the term "beneficial owner" as described in Recommendation 10 and the Interpretative Note on Recommendation 10 of the FATF Recommendations (as adopted in February 2012), and must be interpreted in a manner consistent with such Recommendations, with the aim of protecting the international financial system from misuse including with respect to tax crimes.

51. For an Entity that is a legal person, the term "Controlling Persons" means the natural person(s) who exercises control over the Entity. "Control" over an Entity is generally exercised by the natural person(s) who ultimately has a controlling ownership interest in the Entity. A "controlling ownership interest" depends on the ownership structure of the legal person and is usually identified on the basis of a threshold applying a risk-based approach (e.g. any person(s) owning more than a certain percentage of the legal person, such as 25%). Where no natural person(s) exercises control through ownership interests, the Controlling Person(s) of the Entity will be the natural person(s) who exercises control of the Entity through other means. Where no natural person(s) is identified as exercising control of the Entity, the Controlling Person(s) of the Entity will be the natural person(s) who holds the position of senior managing official.

52. In the case of a trust, the term "Controlling Persons" means the settlor(s), the trustee(s), the protector(s) (if any), the beneficiary(ies) or class(es) of beneficiaries, and any other natural person(s) exercising ultimate effective control over the trust. The settlor(s), the trustee(s), the protector(s) (if any), and the beneficiary(ies) or class(es) of beneficiaries, must always be treated as Controlling Persons of a trust, regardless of whether or not any of them exercises control over the trust. It is for this reason that the second sentence of subparagraph D(10) supplements the first sentence of such subparagraph. In addition, any other natural person(s) exercising ultimate effective control over the trust (including through a chain of control or ownership) must also be treated as a Controlling Person of the trust. With a view to establishing the source of funds in the account(s) held by the trust, where the settlor(s) of a trust is an Entity, Reporting Crypto-Asset Service Providers must also identify the Controlling Person(s) of the settlor(s) and report them as Controlling Person(s) of the trust. For beneficiary(ies) of trusts that are designated by characteristics or by class, Reporting Crypto-Asset Service Providers should obtain sufficient information concerning the beneficiary(ies) to satisfy the Reporting Crypto-Asset Service Provider that it will be able to establish the identity of the beneficiary(ies) at the time of the pay-out or when the beneficiary(ies) intends to exercise vested rights. Therefore, that occasion will constitute a change in circumstances and will trigger the relevant procedures.

53. In the case of a legal arrangement other than a trust, the term "Controlling Persons" means persons in equivalent or similar positions as those that are Controlling Persons of a trust. Thus, taking into account the different forms and structures of legal arrangements, Reporting Crypto-Asset Service Providers should identify and report persons in equivalent or similar positions, as those required to be identified and reported for trusts.

54. In relation to legal persons that are functionally similar to trusts (e.g. foundations), Reporting Crypto-Asset Service Providers should identify Controlling Persons through similar customer due diligence procedures as those required for trusts, with a view to achieving appropriate levels of reporting.

Subparagraph D(11) – Active Entity

55. An Entity is an Active Entity, provided that it meets any of the criteria listed in subparagraph D(11).

56. Subparagraph D(11)(a) describes the criterion to qualify for the Active Entity status by reason of income and assets as follows: less than 50% of the Entity's gross income for the preceding calendar year or other appropriate reporting period is passive income and less than 50% of the assets held by the Entity during the preceding calendar year or other appropriate reporting period are assets that produce or are held for the production of passive income.

57. In determining what is meant by "passive income", reference must be made to each jurisdiction's particular rules. Passive income would generally be considered to include the portion of gross income that consists of:

a) dividends;
b) interest;
c) income equivalent to interest or dividends;
d) rents and royalties, other than rents and royalties derived in the active conduct of a business conducted, at least in part, by employees of the Entity;
e) annuities;
f) income derived from Relevant Crypto-Assets;
g) the excess of gains over losses from the sale or exchange of Relevant Crypto-Assets or Financial Assets;
h) the excess of gains over losses from transactions (including futures, forwards, options, and similar transactions) in any Relevant Crypto-Assets or Financial Assets;
i) the excess of foreign currency gains over foreign currency losses;
j) net income from swaps; or
k) amounts received under cash value insurance contracts.

Notwithstanding the foregoing, passive income will not include, in the case of an Entity that regularly acts as a dealer in Relevant Crypto-Assets or Financial Assets, any income from any transaction entered into in the ordinary course of such dealer's business as such a dealer. Further, income received on assets to invest the capital of an insurance business can be treated as active income.

58. Subparagraph D(11)(b) describes the criterion to qualify for the Active Entity status for "holding Entities that are members of a nonfinancial group" as follows: substantially all of the activities of the Entity consist of holding (in whole or in part) the outstanding stock of, or providing financing and services to, one or more subsidiaries that engage in trades or businesses other than the business of a Financial Institution, except that an Entity does not qualify for this status if the Entity functions (or holds itself out) as an investment fund, such as a private equity fund, venture capital fund, leveraged buyout fund, or any investment vehicle whose purpose is to acquire or fund companies and then hold interests in those companies as capital assets for investment purposes.

59. With respect to the activities mentioned in subparagraph D(11)(b), "substantially all" means 80% or more. If, however, the Entity's holding or group finance activities constitute less than 80% of its activities but the Entity receives also active income (i.e. income that is not passive income) otherwise, it qualifies for the Active Entity status, provided that the total sum of activities meets the "substantially all test". For purposes of determining whether the activities other than holding and group finance activities of the Entity qualify it as an Active Entity, the test of subparagraph D(11)(a) can be applied to such other activities. For example, if a holding company has holding or finance and service activities to one or more subsidiaries for 60% and also functions for 40% as a distribution centre for the goods produced by the group it belongs to and the income of its distribution centre activities is active according to subparagraph D(11)(a), it is an

Active Entity, irrespective of the fact that less than 80% of its activities consist of holding the outstanding stock of, or providing finance and services to, one or more subsidiaries. The term "substantially all" covers also a combination of holding stock of and providing finance and services to one or more subsidiaries. The term "subsidiary" means any entity whose outstanding stock is either directly or indirectly held (in whole or in part) by the Entity.

60. One of the requirements listed in subparagraph D(11)(f) for "non-profit Entities" to qualify for the Active Entity status is that the applicable laws of the Entity's jurisdiction of residence or the Entity's formation documents do not permit any income or assets of the Entity to be distributed to, or applied for the benefit of, a private person or non-charitable Entity other than pursuant to the conduct of the Entity's charitable activities, or as payment of reasonable compensation for services rendered, or as payment representing the fair market value of property which the Entity has purchased. In addition, the income or assets of the Entity could be distributed to, or applied for the benefit of, a private person or noncharitable Entity as payment of reasonable compensation for the use of property.

Paragraph IV (E) – Excluded Person

Subparagraph E(1) – Excluded Person

61. Subparagraph E(1) defines the term "Excluded Person" as (a) an Entity the stock of which is regularly traded on one or more established securities markets; (b) any Entity that is a Related Entity of an Entity described in clause (a); (c) a Governmental Entity; (d) an International Organisation; (e) a Central Bank; or (f) a Financial Institution other than an Investment Entity described in Section IV E(5)(b). Those Entities that are covered by the term "Excluded Person" are not subject to reporting under the Crypto-Asset Reporting Framework, in light of the limited tax compliance risks these Entities represent and/or the other tax reporting obligations certain of these Entities are subject to, including pursuant to the Common Reporting Standard. As such, the scope of Excluded Persons is, wherever adequate, aligned to the exclusions from reporting foreseen in the Common Reporting Standard.

Subparagraphs E(2)-(4) – Financial Institution, Custodial Institution, and Depository Institution

62. The terms "Financial Institution", "Custodial Institution" and "Depository Institution" in subparagraphs E(2), (3) and (4), respectively, should be interpreted consistently with the Commentary of the Common Reporting Standard, as amended.

Subparagraph E(5) – Investment Entity

63. The term "Investment Entity" includes two types of Entities: Entities that primarily conduct, as a business, investment activities or operations on behalf of other persons, and Entities that are managed by those Entities or other Financial Institutions.

64. Subparagraph E(5)(a) defines the first type of "Investment Entity" as any Entity that primarily conducts as a business one or more of the following activities or operations for or on behalf of a customer:

a) trading in money market instruments (cheques, bills, certificates of deposit, derivatives, etc.); foreign exchange; exchange, interest rate and index instruments; transferable securities; or commodity futures trading;

b) individual and collective portfolio management; or

c) otherwise investing, administering, or managing Financial Assets, or money (including Central Bank Digital Currencies), or Relevant Crypto-Assets on behalf of other persons.

65. Such activities or operations do not include rendering non-binding investment advice to a customer. For purposes of subparagraph E(5)(a), the term “customer” includes the Equity Interest holder of a collective investment vehicle, whereby the collective investment vehicle is considered to conduct its activities or operations as a business. For purposes of subparagraph E(5)(a)(iii), the term "investing, administering, or trading" does not comprise the provision of services effectuating Exchange Transactions for or on behalf of customers.

66. Subparagraph E(5)(b) defines the second type of “Investment Entity” as any Entity the gross income of which is primarily attributable to investing, reinvesting, or trading in Financial Assets or Relevant Crypto-Assets, if the Entity is managed by another Entity that is a Depository Institution, a Custodial Institution, a Specified Insurance Company, or an Investment Entity described in subparagraph E(5)(a). An Entity is ‘managed by’ another Entity if the managing Entity performs, either directly or through another service provider, any of the activities or operations described in subparagraph E(5)(a) on behalf of the managed Entity. However, an Entity does not manage another Entity if it does not have discretionary authority to manage the Entity’s assets (in whole or part). Where an Entity is managed by a mix of Financial Institutions and individuals or Entities other than Financial Institutions, the Entity is considered to be managed by another Entity that is a Depository Institution, a Custodial Institution, a Specified Insurance Company, or an Investment Entity described in subparagraph E(5)(a), if any of the managing Entities is such another Entity. For example, a private trust company that acts as a registered office or registered agent of a trust or performs administrative services unrelated to the Financial Assets, Relevant Crypto-Assets or money of the trust, does not conduct the activities and operations described in subparagraph E(5)(a) on behalf of the trust and thus the trust is not “managed by” the private trust company within the meaning of subparagraph E(5)(b). Also, an Entity that invests all or a portion of its assets in a mutual fund, exchange traded fund, or similar vehicle will not be considered “managed by” the mutual fund, exchange traded fund, or similar vehicle. In both of these examples, a further determination needs to be made as to whether the Entity is managed by another Entity for the purpose of ascertaining whether the first-mentioned Entity falls within the definition of Investment Entity, as set out in subparagraph E(5)(b).

67. An Entity is treated as primarily conducting as a business one or more of the activities described in subparagraph E(5)(a), or an Entity’s gross income is primarily attributable to investing, reinvesting, or trading in Financial Assets or Relevant Crypto-Assets for purposes of subparagraph E(5)(b), if the Entity’s gross income attributable to the relevant activities equals or exceeds 50% of the Entity’s gross income during the shorter of:

- the three-year period ending on 31 December of the year preceding the year in which the determination is made; or
- the period during which the Entity has been in existence.

68. For the purposes of the gross income test, all remuneration for the relevant activities of an Entity is to be taken into account, independent of whether that remuneration is paid directly to the Entity to which the test is applied or to another Entity.

69. The term “Investment Entity”, as defined in subparagraph E(5), does not include an Entity that is an Active Entity because it meets any of the criteria in subparagraphs D(11)(b) through (e).

70. An Entity would generally be considered an Investment Entity if it functions or holds itself out as a collective investment vehicle, mutual fund, exchange traded fund, private equity fund, hedge fund, venture capital fund, leveraged buy-out fund or any similar investment vehicle established with an investment strategy of investing, reinvesting, or trading in Financial Assets or Relevant Crypto-Assets. An Entity that primarily conducts as a business investing, administering, or managing non-debt, direct interests in real property on behalf of other persons, such as a type of real estate investment trust, will not be an Investment Entity.

71. Subparagraph E(5) also states that the definition of the term "Investment Entity" shall be interpreted in a manner consistent with similar language set forth in the definition of "financial institution" in the Financial Action Task Force Recommendations.

Subparagraphs E(6)-(15) – "Specified Insurance Company", "Governmental Entity", "International Organisation", "Central Bank", "Financial Asset", "Equity Interest", "Insurance Contract", "Annuity Contract", "Cash Value Insurance Contract" and "Cash Value"

72. The terms "Specified Insurance Company", "Governmental Entity", "International Organisation", "Central Bank", "Financial Asset", "Equity Interest", "Insurance Contract", "Annuity Contract", "Cash Value Insurance Contract", and "Cash Value" in subparagraphs E(6) through (15) should be interpreted consistently with the Commentary of the Common Reporting Standard, as amended.

Paragraph IV (F) – Miscellaneous

Subparagraph F(1) – Partner Jurisdiction

73. The term "Partner Jurisdiction" means any jurisdiction that has put in place equivalent legal requirements and that is included in a public list issued by [Jurisdiction].

Subparagraph F(2) – AML/KYC Procedures

74. The term "AML/KYC Procedures", as defined in subparagraph F(2), means the customer due diligence procedures of a Reporting Crypto-Asset Service Provider pursuant to the anti-money laundering or similar requirements to which such Reporting Crypto-Asset Service Provider is subject (e.g. know your customer provisions). These procedures include identifying and verifying the identity of the customer (including the beneficial owners of the customer), understanding the nature and purpose of the transactions, and on-going monitoring.

Subparagraph F(3) and (4) – Entity and Related Entity

75. Subparagraph F(3) defines the term "Entity" as a legal person or a legal arrangement. This term is intended to cover any person other than an individual (i.e. a natural person), in addition to any legal arrangement. Thus, e.g. a corporation, partnership, trust, *fideicomiso*, foundation (*fondation*, *Stiftung*), company, co-operative, association, or *asociación en participación*, falls within the meaning of the term "Entity".

76. An Entity is a "Related Entity" of another Entity, as defined in subparagraph F(4), if either Entity controls the other Entity, or the two Entities are under common control. For this purpose control includes direct or indirect ownership of more than 50% of the vote and value in an Entity. In this respect, Entities are considered Related Entities if these Entities are connected through one or more chains of ownership by a common parent Entity and if the common parent Entity directly owns more than 50% of the stock or other equity interest in at least one of the other Entities. A chain of ownership is to be understood as the ownership by one or more Entities of more than 50% of the total voting power of the stock of an Entity and more than 50% of the total value of the stock of an Entity, as illustrated by the following example:

Entity A owns 51% of the total voting power and 51% of the total value of the stock of Entity B. Entity B in its turn owns 51% of the total voting power and 51% of the total value of the stock of Entity C. Entities A and C are considered "Related Entities" pursuant to subparagraph F(4) of Section IV because Entity A has a direct ownership of more than 50% of the total voting power of the stock and more than 50%of total value of the stock of Entity B, and because Entity B has a direct ownership of more than 50% of the total voting power of the stock and more than 50% of total value of the stock of Entity C. Entities A and C are, hence, connected through chains of ownership. Notwithstanding the fact that Entity A proportionally only owns 26% of the total value of the stock and voting rights of Entity C, Entity A and Entity C are Related Entities.

Subparagraph F(5) – Taxpayer Identification Number

77. According to subparagraph F(5), the term "TIN" means Taxpayer Identification Number (or functional equivalent in the absence of a Taxpayer Identification Number). A Taxpayer Identification Number is a unique combination of letters or numbers, however described, assigned by a jurisdiction to an individual or an Entity and used to identify the individual or Entity for purposes of administering the tax laws of such jurisdiction.

78. TINs are also useful for identifying taxpayers who invest in other jurisdictions. TIN specifications (i.e. structure, syntax, etc.) are set by each jurisdiction's tax administrations. Some jurisdictions even have a different TIN structure for different taxes or different categories of taxpayers (e.g. residents and non-residents).

79. While many jurisdictions utilise a TIN for personal or corporate taxation purposes, some jurisdictions do not issue a TIN. However, these jurisdictions often utilise some other high integrity number with an equivalent level of identification (a "functional equivalent"). Examples of that type of number include, for individuals, a social security/insurance number, citizen/personal identification/service code/number, and resident registration number; and for Entities, a business/company registration code/number.

80. In addition, some jurisdictions may also offer government verification services for the purpose of ascertaining the identity and tax residence of their taxpayers. Such government verification services are electronic processes made available by the jurisdiction to entities or individuals with third party reporting obligations (such as Reporting Crypto-Asset Service Providers) for the purposes of ascertaining the identity and tax residence of reportable persons (such as Crypto-Asset Users or their Controlling Persons). Where a tax administration opts for identification of Crypto-Asset Users or Controlling Persons based on an Application Programming Interface (API) solution, it would normally make an API portal accessible to Reporting Crypto-Asset Service Providers. Subsequently, if the Crypto-Asset User's or Controlling Person's self-certification indicates residence in that jurisdiction, the Reporting Crypto-Asset Service Provider can direct the Crypto-Asset User or Controlling Person to the API portal which would allow the jurisdiction to identify the Crypto-Asset User or Controlling Person based on its domestic taxpayer identification requirements (for example a government ID or username). Upon successful identification of the Crypto-Asset User or Controlling Person as a taxpayer of that jurisdiction, the jurisdiction, via the API portal, would provide the Reporting Crypto-Asset Service Provider with a unique reference number or code allowing the jurisdiction to match the Crypto-Asset User or Controlling Person to a taxpayer within its database. Where the Reporting Crypto-Asset Service Provider subsequently reports information concerning that Crypto-Asset User or Controlling Person, it would include the unique reference number or code to allow the jurisdiction receiving the information to enable matching of the Crypto-Asset User or Controlling Person. In this respect, a unique reference number, code or other confirmation received by a Reporting Crypto-Asset Service Provider in respect of a Crypto-Asset User or a Controlling Person via a government verification service is also a functional equivalent to a TIN.

81. Jurisdictions are expected to provide Reporting Crypto-Asset Service Providers with information with respect to the issuance, collection and, to the extent possible and practical, the structure and other specifications of taxpayer identification numbers and their functional equivalents. The OECD will endeavour to facilitate its dissemination. Such information will facilitate the collection of accurate TINs by Reporting Crypto-Asset Service Providers.

Subparagraph F(6) – Branch

82. The term "Branch" means a unit, business or office of a Reporting Crypto-Asset Service Provider that is treated as a branch under the regulatory regime of a jurisdiction or that is otherwise regulated under the laws of a jurisdiction as separate from other offices, units, or branches of the Reporting Crypto-Asset Service Provider. All units, businesses, or offices of a Reporting Crypto-Asset Service Provider in a single jurisdiction shall be treated as a single branch.

Commentary on Section V: Effective implementation

1. The CARF is built around the following key building blocks, designed to ensure the collection and automatic exchange of information on transactions in Relevant Crypto-Assets: (i) the scope of Crypto-Assets to be covered; (ii) the Entities and individuals subject to data collection and reporting requirements; (iii) the transactions subject to reporting as well as the information to be reported in respect of such transactions; and (iv) the due diligence procedures to identify Crypto-Asset Users and the relevant tax jurisdictions for reporting and exchange purposes.

2. For the CARF to deliver on its objectives, jurisdictions must ensure the correct implementation of each of these building blocks, such that they are complied with and that they are not circumvented. The aim of the Commentary on Section V is to describe these implementation requirements.

3. A jurisdiction should have in place a proportionate and risk-based comprehensive compliance strategy to ensure the effective implementation of the due diligence and reporting obligations in such jurisdiction, taking into account the jurisdiction's particular domestic context. This compliance strategy should address the following three main areas of focus. Firstly, a jurisdiction implementing the CARF should ensure the identification of all Entities and individuals that, by virtue of their activities, are Reporting Crypto-Asset Service Providers and have a nexus with such jurisdiction. Secondly, a jurisdiction should ensure that Reporting Crypto-Asset Service Providers accurately follow the reporting and due diligence procedures of the CARF. Finally, a jurisdiction should raise awareness of, and promote and enforce compliance with, the CARF. This should include a penalty framework to address instances of non-compliance, efforts to proactively promote and encourage compliance, as well as a compliance verification strategy to identify new practices that potentially pose high risks to the functioning of the CARF.

Ensuring the identification of all Reporting Crypto-Asset Service Providers

Potential challenges in identifying Reporting Crypto-Asset Service Providers

4. The nexus criteria of Section I will likely result in a broad range of Entities and individuals being considered Reporting Crypto-Asset Service Providers in a given jurisdiction. Among these, some Reporting Crypto-Asset Service Providers (e.g. Financial Institutions) are likely to be well-established actors in the traditional financial sector and are therefore likely aware of relevant regulatory and reporting requirements. However, many other Reporting Crypto-Asset Service Providers may be emerging actors less aware of such requirements. Depending on the jurisdiction, some of these emerging actors may currently be subject only to light or no regulation and therefore may not be identified by regulatory authorities. In addition, Reporting Crypto-Asset Service Providers with due diligence and reporting obligations as a result of having a place of business in, or being managed from, a jurisdiction may not regularly engage in activities that lend themselves to being easily identifiable to the jurisdiction.

5. Hence, a jurisdiction's compliance framework should consider the likelihood that some Reporting Crypto-Asset Service Providers with a nexus to the jurisdiction are not readily identifiable by such jurisdiction and may potentially not be aware of their due diligence and reporting obligations.

Potential approaches to ensure identification of Reporting Crypto-Asset Service Providers

6. To ensure identification of Reporting Crypto-Asset Service Providers in accordance with the requirements of Section I, jurisdictions should have mechanisms in place to identify Reporting Crypto-Asset Service Providers that have a nexus to their jurisdiction. As outlined below, these mechanisms may be included in an existing domestic regulatory framework, or a jurisdiction may need to design a new framework for this purpose.

7. In certain circumstances, a jurisdiction may rely on mechanisms already in place to identify Reporting Crypto-Asset Service Providers operating in its jurisdiction. For example, some jurisdictions may be able to rely on domestic regulatory frameworks already in place for other purposes (e.g. AML or financial markets registration requirements) to identify Reporting Crypto-Asset Service Providers. A jurisdiction that relies on an existing regulatory framework should first determine that such framework generally corresponds with the scope of the CARF, with respect to the different aspects of the Reporting Crypto-Asset Service Provider definition and the nexus rules, such that the domestic regulatory framework would ensure all individuals and Entities meeting the definition of Reporting Crypto-Asset Service Provider are identified.

8. If a jurisdiction determines that its domestic regulatory framework would not ensure the identification of certain or all Reporting Crypto-Asset Service Providers with a nexus to its jurisdiction, it should put in place additional mechanisms to ensure Reporting Crypto-Asset Service Providers with a nexus to its jurisdiction are identified. With respect to Reporting Crypto-Asset Service Providers whose only nexus with the jurisdiction is via its place of management or business, jurisdictions should take reasonable measures to ensure their identification.

9. There exist a number of examples of additional mechanisms, such as those described in this paragraph, that jurisdictions could adopt to identify Reporting Crypto-Asset Service Providers. For example, additional mechanisms for identifying all Reporting Crypto-Asset Service Providers, in particular those not already subject to registration or regulation, could include a requirement for Reporting Crypto-Asset Service Providers to proactively register with a domestic centralised registry. Jurisdictions could further consider imposing a nil reporting requirement on Reporting Crypto-Asset Service Providers. It could also be considered to establish a mechanism (e.g. an anonymous tip line or inbox) whereby information about non-compliant Reporting Crypto-Asset Service Providers could be reported to authorities. Furthermore, jurisdictions could consider introducing a requirement on their domestic Crypto-Asset Users to report, for instance in their tax returns, the name and address of the Reporting Crypto-Asset Service Providers they have used. This would allow tax authorities to identify Reporting Crypto-Asset Service Providers in either their own or a partner jurisdiction. Further coordination among partner jurisdictions may be necessary to ensure Reporting Crypto-Asset Service Providers operating in a cross-border context are identified. To that end, when a jurisdiction has reason to believe that a Reporting Crypto-Asset Service Provider with a nexus to another jurisdiction is not identified as such, it could rely on mechanisms foreseen in the competent authority agreements for the exchange of information pursuant to the CARF. Finally, jurisdictions could consider relying on publicly available resources, such as market research portals, to determine Reporting Crypto-Asset Service Providers with a nexus to their jurisdiction. The sufficiency of any additional mechanisms, combined with the domestic regulatory framework, would need to be evaluated in their totality. Jurisdictions that need additional mechanisms should ensure that the mechanism or mechanisms chosen are sufficiently robust as to achieve the objective of identifying Reporting Crypto-Asset Service Providers with a nexus to such jurisdiction.

Ensuring compliance of Reporting Crypto-Asset Service Providers with their due diligence and reporting requirements

10. Once a jurisdiction has identified Reporting Crypto-Asset Service Providers with due diligence and reporting obligations in such jurisdiction, the jurisdiction should ensure that such Reporting Crypto-Asset Service Providers continue to comply with the reporting and due diligence procedures in Sections II and III for as long as such obligations exist. To this end, a jurisdiction should designate one or more administrative bodies as responsible for ensuring, on the basis of a proportionate and risk-based compliance strategy, compliance of Reporting Crypto-Asset Service Providers with their due diligence and reporting obligations under Sections II and III.

Designated administrative bodies with powers to verify compliance of Reporting Crypto-Asset Service Providers

11. As an initial step, jurisdictions should designate one or more administrative bodies (e.g. a tax authority or financial supervisor), with the power to verify the compliance of Reporting Crypto-Asset Service Providers with the due diligence and reporting obligations in such jurisdiction. Jurisdictions should also ensure that any such designated bodies are adequately resourced to properly verify compliance of Reporting Crypto-Asset Service Providers with their due diligence and reporting requirements. A jurisdiction could also consider making use of alternative mechanisms that reduce burdens on domestic authorities' resources, to the extent such mechanisms are reliable for verifying the compliance of Reporting Crypto-Asset Service Providers (e.g. relying on other government departments or agencies or third-party service providers to verify that Reporting Crypto-Asset Service Providers comply with their due diligence and reporting requirements), provided the domestic authorities remain accountable.

12. To ensure that the domestic authorities can verify Reporting Crypto-Asset Service Providers' compliance, a jurisdiction should have rules in place requiring Reporting Crypto-Asset Service Providers with due diligence and reporting obligations in such jurisdiction to keep records of the steps undertaken and any evidence relied upon for the performance of the due diligence procedures set out in Section III, as well as for the classification of Relevant Transactions, Crypto-Assets and Relevant Crypto-Assets set out in Section IV.

13. Jurisdictions should have rules in place to compel the taxpayer or a third party to provide documents that are necessary to apply their domestic tax legislation. These rules should also apply to obtain information to respond to a request for information from an exchange partner under an exchange of information instrument. A jurisdiction should also have in place adequate measures to ensure the records of Reporting Crypto-Asset Service Providers with respect to the due diligence and reporting obligations in such jurisdiction are made available, upon request, to its domestic authorities in order for these authorities to carry out compliance reviews.

Verification issues related to reporting requirements under the CARF

14. A jurisdiction should verify whether Reporting Crypto-Asset Service Providers with due diligence and reporting obligations in such jurisdiction have complied with the requirements of Section II. This includes ensuring the Reporting Crypto-Asset Service Provider has correctly reported the information to the tax authority (or other appropriate authority) of the jurisdiction in a timely manner.

15. As a general matter, the reporting requirements of Section II are conditioned on a Reporting Crypto-Asset Service Provider's classification of Crypto-Assets. Notably, the CARF contains a number of exemptions relieving Reporting Crypto-Asset Service Providers from reporting obligations with respect to Crypto-Assets that cannot be used for payment or investment purposes, Specified Electronic Money Products and Crypto-Assets that are Central Bank Digital Currencies. Jurisdictions should therefore verify

that Reporting Crypto-Asset Service Providers correctly apply the definitions contained in Section IV with respect to Relevant Crypto-Assets.

16. Certain Transfers effectuated by Reporting Crypto-Asset Service Providers may also require additional scrutiny. For example, a jurisdiction may identify that Reporting Crypto-Asset Service Providers, individuals, Entities or merchants seek to fragment transaction amounts, such as retail sales amounts, to avoid reporting obligations with respect to transactions that otherwise meet the definition of Reportable Retail Payment Transactions. In such case, the jurisdiction should ensure that such transactions are treated as Reportable Retail Payment Transactions and reported as such.

Verification issues related to due diligence requirements under the CARF

17. In addition to the verification of compliance with reporting requirements, a jurisdiction should also verify whether Reporting Crypto-Asset Service Providers with due diligence and reporting obligations in such jurisdiction have complied with the due diligence requirements set out in Section III. Such verification should, in particular, ensure that Reporting Crypto-Asset Service Providers complete the collection and validation of self-certifications for Crypto-Asset Users and Controlling Persons in an accurate and timely manner. It is recognised that, depending on the status of a jurisdiction's domestic implementation of the FATF Recommendations pertaining to virtual asset service providers, it may arise that a Reporting Crypto-Asset Service Provider is not considered an AML-obliged person in the jurisdiction where it is subject to the reporting and due diligence obligations of Sections II and III. Section III.B(2)(a) clarifies that if a Reporting Crypto-Asset Service Provider is not legally required to apply AML/KYC Procedures that are consistent with the 2012 FATF Recommendations (as updated in June 2019 pertaining to virtual asset service providers), it should apply substantially similar procedures for the purpose of determining the Controlling Persons. Where a Reporting Crypto-Asset Service Provider is required to apply such substantially similar procedures, the jurisdiction should verify and ensure that such procedures are consistent with the requirements for purposes of identifying Controlling Persons.

Raising awareness of, and promoting and enforcing compliance with, the CARF

18. Jurisdictions should have in place effective measures to raise awareness of, and promote compliance with the due diligence and reporting obligations in such jurisdiction. Accordingly, jurisdictions should take appropriate measures aimed at ensuring that Reporting Crypto-Asset Service Providers in their jurisdiction are made aware of the nexus, due diligence and reporting requirements in the jurisdiction's laws. Jurisdictions should also make available to Reporting Crypto-Asset Service Providers in their jurisdiction the necessary information.

19. Jurisdictions should also have in place enforcement provisions to address instances of non-compliance and should have the ability to impose adequate administrative and/or criminal penalties on Reporting Crypto-Asset Service Providers for failure to comply with the reporting and due diligence procedures in Sections II and III, as well as for failure to respond to requests from authorities.

20. Jurisdictions should also have in place strong measures to ensure valid self-certifications are always collected for Crypto-Asset Users and Controlling Persons. What will constitute a "strong measure" in this context may vary from jurisdiction to jurisdiction and should be evaluated in light of the actual results of the measure. The crucial test for determining what measures can qualify as "strong measures" is whether the measures have a strong enough impact on Crypto-Asset Users, Controlling Persons and/or Reporting Crypto-Asset Service Providers to effectively ensure that self-certifications are obtained and validated in accordance with the rules set out in the CARF. An effective way to achieve this outcome would be to introduce legislation making the effectuating of transactions conditional upon the receipt of a valid self-certification. Other jurisdictions may choose different methods, taking into account their domestic law. This could include, for example, imposing significant penalties on Crypto-Asset Users and Controlling Persons that fail to provide a self-certification, or on Reporting Crypto-Asset Service Providers that do not

take appropriate measures to obtain a self-certification. Beyond administrative measures and penalties, strong measures could also include a requirement to apply a withholding tax on transactions conducted in the absence of a valid self-certification. Furthermore, to increase the reliability of self-certifications, jurisdictions should have a specific provision in their domestic legislation imposing sanctions for signing (or otherwise positively affirming) a false or materially incorrect self-certification.

21. In addition to enforcement provisions for dealing with instances of non-compliance, jurisdictions should seek to identify any practices which, based on the domestic context, potentially threaten the effectiveness of the due diligence and reporting obligations in such jurisdiction and take appropriate compliance measures in response. In particular, a jurisdiction should have rules to prevent any Reporting Crypto-Asset Service Providers, persons or intermediaries from adopting practices intended to circumvent the due diligence and reporting obligations in such jurisdiction. Examples of other actions a jurisdiction could take include considering whether risks resulting from the highly mobile nature of the Crypto-Asset market justify additional measures if it identifies that Reporting Crypto-Asset Service Providers in its jurisdiction are carrying out cross-border Crypto-Asset transactions in jurisdictions that are not Partner Jurisdictions, with the intention of avoiding reporting requirements under its legislation. Similarly, a jurisdiction could consider whether those parts of the Crypto-Asset market that have a decentralised nature (e.g. decentralised finance platforms) pose particular risks in its domestic context if it identifies that Entities or individuals falsely claim not to be a Reporting Crypto-Asset Service Provider even though they in fact exercise control or sufficient influence over a trading platform effectuating Exchange Transactions.

4 Multilateral Competent Authority Agreement

Multilateral Competent Authority Agreement on Automatic Exchange of Information pursuant to the Crypto-Asset Reporting Framework

DECLARATION

I, [NAME and TITLE], [on behalf of] the Competent Authority of [JURISDICTION], declare that it hereby agrees to comply with the provisions of the

Multilateral Competent Authority Agreement on Automatic Exchange of Information pursuant to the Crypto-Asset Reporting Framework

hereafter referred to as the "Agreement" and attached to this Declaration.

By means of the present Declaration, the Competent Authority of [JURISDICTION] is to be considered a signatory of the Agreement as from [DATE]. The Agreement will come into effect in respect of the Competent Authority of [JURISDICTION] in accordance with Section 7 thereof.

Signed in [PLACE] on [DATE]

MULTILATERAL COMPETENT AUTHORITY AGREEMENT ON AUTOMATIC EXCHANGE OF INFORMATION PURSUANT TO THE CRYPTO-ASSET REPORTING FRAMEWORK

Whereas, the Jurisdictions of the signatories to this Multilateral Competent Authority Agreement on the Automatic Exchange of Information pursuant to the Crypto-Asset Reporting Framework (the "Agreement") are Parties to, or territories covered by, the Convention on Mutual Administrative Assistance in Tax Matters or the Convention on Mutual Administrative Assistance in Tax Matters, as amended by the Protocol amending the Convention on Mutual Administrative Assistance in Tax Matters (the "Convention"); collectively the "Convention", individually the "original Convention" or the "amended Convention" respectively);

Whereas, the Jurisdictions intend to improve international tax compliance by further building on their relationship with respect to mutual assistance in tax matters;

Whereas, the Crypto-Asset Reporting Framework was developed by the OECD, with G20 countries, to tackle tax avoidance and evasion and improve tax compliance;

Whereas, the laws of the respective Jurisdictions require or are expected to require Reporting Crypto-Asset Service Providers to report information with respect to certain Crypto-Assets and follow related due diligence procedures, consistent with the scope of exchange contemplated by Section 2 of this Agreement and the reporting and due diligence procedures set out in the Crypto-Asset Reporting Framework;

Whereas, it is expected that the laws of the Jurisdictions would be amended from time to time to reflect updates to the Crypto-Asset Reporting Framework and once such amendments are enacted by a Jurisdiction the term Crypto-Asset Reporting Framework would be deemed to refer to the updated version in respect of that Jurisdiction;

Whereas, Chapter III of the Convention authorises the exchange of information for tax purposes, including the exchange of information on an automatic basis, and allows the competent authorities of the Jurisdictions to agree to the procedures to be applied to such automatic exchanges;

Whereas, Article 6 of the Convention provides that two or more Parties can mutually agree to exchange specified information automatically, the actual exchange of the information will be on a bilateral basis;

Whereas, the Jurisdictions have in place (i) appropriate safeguards to ensure that the information received pursuant to this Agreement remains confidential and is used solely for the purposes set out in the Convention, and (ii) the infrastructure for an effective exchange relationship (including established processes for ensuring timely, accurate, and confidential information exchanges, effective and reliable communications, and capabilities to promptly resolve questions and concerns about exchanges or requests for exchanges and to administer the provisions of Section 4 of this Agreement);

Whereas, the Competent Authorities of the Jurisdictions desire to conclude this Agreement to improve international tax compliance with respect to Crypto-Assets based on automatic exchange pursuant to the Convention, without prejudice to national legislative procedures (if any), and subject to the confidentiality, data safeguards and other protections provided for therein, including the provisions limiting the use of the information exchanged under the Convention;

Now, therefore, the Competent Authorities have agreed as follows:

SECTION 1

Definitions

1. For the purposes of the Agreement, the following terms have the following meanings:

a) the term "**Jurisdiction**" means a country or a territory in respect of which the Convention is in force or in effect under the original or amended Convention, respectively, either through signature and ratification in accordance with Article 28, or through territorial extension in accordance with Article 29, and which is a signatory to this Agreement.

b) the term "**Competent Authority**" means, for each respective Jurisdiction, the persons and authorities listed in Annex B of the Convention.

c) the term "**Crypto-Asset Reporting Framework**" means the international framework for the automatic exchange of information with respect to Crypto-Assets (which includes the Commentaries) developed by the OECD, with G20 countries.

d) the term "**Co-ordinating Body Secretariat**" means the OECD Secretariat that, pursuant to paragraph 3 of Article 24 of the Convention, provides support to the co-ordinating body that is composed of representatives of the competent authorities of the Parties to the Convention.

e) the term **"Agreement in effect"** means, in respect of any two Competent Authorities, that both Competent Authorities have provided notification to the Co-ordinating Body Secretariat under paragraph 1 of Section 7, including listing the other Competent Authority's Jurisdiction pursuant to subparagraph 1g) of Section 7. A list of Competent Authorities between which this Agreement is in effect is to be published on the OECD Website.

2. Any capitalised term not otherwise defined in this Agreement will have the meaning that it has at that time under the law of the Jurisdiction applying the Agreement, such meaning being consistent with the meaning set forth in the Crypto-Asset Reporting Framework. Any term not otherwise defined in this Agreement or in the Crypto-Asset Reporting Framework will, unless the context otherwise requires or the Competent Authorities agree to a common meaning (as permitted by domestic law), have the meaning that it has at that time under the law of the Jurisdiction applying this Agreement, any meaning under the applicable tax laws of that Jurisdiction prevailing over a meaning given to the term under other laws of that Jurisdiction.

SECTION 2

Exchange of Information with Respect to Reportable Persons

1. Pursuant to the provisions of Article 6 and 22 of the amended or original Convention, as applicable, and subject to the applicable reporting and due diligence rules consistent with the Crypto-Asset Reporting Framework, each Competent Authority will annually exchange with the other Competent Authorities on an automatic basis the information obtained pursuant to such rules and specified in paragraph 3.

2. Notwithstanding paragraph 1, the Competent Authorities of the Jurisdictions that have indicated that they are to be listed as non-reciprocal jurisdictions on the basis of their notification pursuant to subparagraph 1b) of Section 7 will send, but not receive, the information specified in paragraph 3. Jurisdictions that are not listed as non-reciprocal Jurisdictions will receive the information specified in paragraph 3, but will not send such information to the Jurisdictions included in the aforementioned list of non-reciprocal Jurisdictions.

3. The information to be exchanged is, with respect to each Reportable Person of another Jurisdiction:

a) the name, address, jurisdiction(s) of residence, TIN(s) and date and place of birth (in the case of an individual) of each Reportable User and, in the case of any Entity that, after application of the due diligence procedures, is identified as having one or more Controlling Persons that is a Reportable Person, the name, address, jurisdiction(s) of residence and TIN(s) of the Entity and the name, address, jurisdiction(s) of residence, TIN(s) and date and place of birth of each Controlling Person of the Entity that is a Reportable Person, as well as the role(s) by virtue of which each such Reportable Person is a Controlling Person of the Entity;

b) the name, address and identifying number (if any) of the Reporting Crypto-Asset Service Provider;

c) for each type of Relevant Crypto-Asset with respect to which the Reporting Crypto-Asset Service Provider has effectuated Relevant Transactions during the relevant calendar year or other appropriate reporting period:

   i) the full name of the type of Relevant Crypto-Asset;
   ii) the aggregate gross amount paid, the aggregate number of units and the number of Relevant Transactions in respect of acquisitions against Fiat Currency;
   iii) the aggregate gross amount received, the aggregate number of units and the number of Relevant Transactions in respect of disposals against Fiat Currency;
   iv) the aggregate fair market value, the aggregate number of units and the number of Relevant Transactions in respect of acquisitions against other Relevant Crypto-Assets;
   v) the aggregate fair market value, the aggregate number of units and the number of Relevant Transactions in respect of disposals against other Relevant Crypto-Assets;
   vi) the aggregate fair market value, the aggregate number of units and the number of Reportable Retail Payment Transactions;
   vii) the aggregate fair market value, the aggregate number of units and the number of Relevant Transactions, and subdivided by transfer type where known by the Reporting Crypto-Asset Service Provider, in respect of Transfers to the Reportable User not covered by subparagraphs c)(ii) and (iv);
   viii) the aggregate fair market value, the aggregate number of units and the number of Relevant Transactions, and subdivided by transfer type where known by the Reporting Crypto-Asset Service Provider, in respect of Transfers by the Reportable User not covered by subparagraphs c)(iii), (v) and (vi); and
   ix) the aggregate fair market value, as well as the aggregate number of units in respect of Transfers by the Reportable User effectuated by the Reporting Crypto-Asset Service Provider to wallet addresses not known by the Reporting Crypto-Asset Service Provider to be associated with a virtual asset service provider or financial institution.

SECTION 3

Time and Manner of Exchange of Information

1. With respect to paragraph 3 of Section 2, and subject to the notification procedure set out in Section 7, including the dates specified therein, information is to be exchanged commencing from the year specified in the notification pursuant to subparagraph 1a) of Section 7 within nine months after the end of the calendar year to which the information relates. Notwithstanding the foregoing sentence, information is only required to be exchanged with respect to a calendar year if both Jurisdictions have legislation in place

to give effect to the Crypto-Asset Reporting Framework that requires reporting with respect to such calendar year that is consistent with the scope of exchange provided for in Section 2 and the reporting and due diligence procedures contained in the Crypto-Asset Reporting Framework.

2. The Competent Authorities will automatically exchange the information described in Section 2 in a common schema.

3. The Competent Authorities will transmit the information through the OECD Common Transmission System and in compliance with the related encryption and file preparation standards, or through another transmission method specified in the notification pursuant to subparagraph 1d) of Section 7.

SECTION 4

Collaboration on Compliance and Enforcement

A Competent Authority will notify the other Competent Authority when the first-mentioned Competent Authority has reason to believe that an error may have led to incorrect or incomplete information reporting or there is non-compliance by a Reporting Crypto-Asset Service Provider with the applicable reporting requirements and due diligence procedures consistent with the Crypto-Asset Reporting Framework. The notified Competent Authority will take all appropriate measures available under its domestic law to address the errors or non-compliance described in the notice.

SECTION 5

Confidentiality and Data Safeguards

1. All information exchanged is subject to the confidentiality rules and other safeguards provided for in the amended or original Convention, as applicable, including the provisions limiting the use of the information exchanged and, to the extent needed to ensure the necessary level of protection of personal data, in accordance with the safeguards which may be specified by the supplying Competent Authority as required under its domestic law and as set out in the notification pursuant to subparagraph 1e) of Section 7.

2. A Competent Authority will notify the Co-ordinating Body Secretariat immediately regarding any breach of confidentiality or failure of safeguards and any sanctions and remedial actions consequently imposed. The Co-ordinating Body Secretariat will notify all Competent Authorities with respect to which this is an Agreement in effect with the first mentioned Competent Authority.

SECTION 6

Consultations and Amendments

1. If any difficulties in the implementation or interpretation of this Agreement arise, a Competent Authority may request consultations with one or more of the Competent Authorities to develop appropriate measures to ensure that this Agreement is fulfilled. The Competent Authority that requested the consultations shall ensure that the Co-ordinating Body Secretariat is notified of any appropriate measures that were developed and the Co-ordinating Body Secretariat will notify all Competent Authorities, even those that did not participate in the consultations, of any measures that were developed.

2. This Agreement may be amended by consensus by written agreement of all of the Competent Authorities. Unless otherwise agreed upon, such an amendment is effective on the first day of the month following the expiration of a period of one month after the date of the last signature of such written agreement.

SECTION 7

General Terms

1. A Competent Authority must provide, at the time of signature of this Agreement or as soon as possible thereafter, notifications to the Co-ordinating Body Secretariat:

a) confirming that its Jurisdiction has the necessary laws in place to give effect to the Crypto-Asset Reporting Framework and specifying the relevant effective dates, or any period of provisional application of the Agreement due to pending national legislative procedures (if any);
b) confirming whether the Jurisdiction is to be listed as a non-reciprocal Jurisdiction;
c) requesting consent from the other Competent Authorities to use the information received for the assessment, collection or recovery of, the enforcement or prosecution in respect of, or the determination of appeals in relation to taxes with respect to which its Jurisdiction made a reservation pursuant to subparagraph 1(a) of Article 30 of the Convention and, if so, specifying these taxes and confirming that the use will be in line with the terms of the Convention;
d) specifying one or more alternative methods, if any, for data transmission including encryption;
e) specifying safeguards, if any, for the protection of personal data;
f) confirming that it has in place adequate measures to ensure the required confidentiality and data safeguards standards are met; and
g) a list of the Jurisdictions of the Competent Authorities with respect to which it intends to have this Agreement in effect, following national legislative procedures for entry into force (if any).

Competent Authorities must notify the Co-ordinating Body Secretariat, promptly, of any subsequent change to be made to the above-mentioned notifications.

2. This Agreement will come into effect between two Competent Authorities on the date on which the second of the two Competent Authorities has provided notification to the Co-ordinating Body Secretariat under paragraph 1, of this Section, including listing the other Competent Authority's Jurisdiction pursuant to subparagraph 1g) of this Section.

3. The Co-ordinating Body Secretariat will maintain a list that will be published on the OECD website of the Competent Authorities that have signed the Agreement and between which Competent Authorities this is an Agreement in effect.

4. The Co-ordinating Body Secretariat will publish on the OECD website the information provided by Competent Authorities pursuant to subparagraphs 1a), b) and e) of this Section. The information provided pursuant to subparagraphs 1c), d), f) and g) of this Section will be made available to other signatories upon request in writing to the Co-ordinating Body Secretariat.

5. A Competent Authority may suspend the exchange of information under this Agreement by giving notice in writing to another Competent Authority that it has determined that there is or has been significant noncompliance by the second-mentioned Competent Authority with this Agreement. Such suspension will have immediate effect. For the purposes of this paragraph, significant non-compliance includes, but is not limited to, non-compliance with the confidentiality and data safeguard provisions of this Agreement and

the Convention, or a failure by the Competent Authority to provide timely or adequate information as required under this Agreement.

6. A Competent Authority may terminate its participation in this Agreement, or with respect to a particular Competent Authority, by giving notice of termination in writing to the Co-ordinating Body Secretariat. Unless specified otherwise by the Competent Authority, such termination will become effective on the first day of the month following the expiration of a period of 12 months after the date of the notice of termination. In the event of termination, all information previously received under this Agreement will remain confidential and subject to the terms of the Convention.

SECTION 8

Co-ordinating Body Secretariat

Unless otherwise provided for in the Agreement, the Co-ordinating Body Secretariat will notify all Competent Authorities of any notifications that it has received under this Agreement and will provide a notice to all signatories of the Agreement when a new Competent Authority signs the Agreement.

Done in English and French, both texts being equally authentic.

5 Commentary to the Multilateral Competent Authority Agreement

Introduction

1. In order to exchange information under the Crypto-Asset Reporting Framework (CARF), Jurisdictions must have a legal framework in place that allows for the automatic exchange of information with partner Jurisdictions. This legal framework should include both a legal basis for the information exchanges, as well as administrative agreements to determine the scope, timing and method of the information exchanges.

2. Jurisdictions can have a legal basis for tax information exchanges pursuant to the Convention on Mutual Administrative Assistance in Tax Matters (Convention). Pursuant to Article 6 of the Convention, two or more Parties to the Convention can mutually agree to automatically exchange predefined foreseeably relevant information in accordance with the procedures determined by the Parties by mutual agreement. In the context of the Common Reporting Standard, this multilateral approach has proven to be an efficient route to put in place widespread networks of exchange relationships as it allows Jurisdictions to efficiently activate bilateral exchange relationships.

3. To operationalise Article 6 of the Convention, Jurisdictions must also have in place administrative agreements to determine, in particular, the information to be automatically exchanged and the time and method of the exchanges. For the CARF, this Multilateral Competent Authority Agreement (CARF MCAA), which is based on Article 6 of the Convention, sets out the detailed modalities of the exchanges taking place every year on an automatic basis.

4. The CARF MCAA consists of:

- a declaration to be signed by the Competent Authority of the Jurisdiction or its designated representative to become a signatory of the CARF MCAA;
- a preamble which explains the purpose of the CARF MCAA and contains representations on domestic reporting and due diligence rules that underpin the exchange of information pursuant to the CARF MCAA. It also contains representations on confidentiality, data protection safeguards and the existence of the necessary infrastructure;
- eight sections containing the agreed provisions of the CARF MCAA: Section 1 deals with definitions, Section 2 covers the items of information to be exchanged, Section 3 the time and manner of the exchange, Section 4 collaboration on compliance and enforcement and Section 5 the confidentiality and data safeguards that must be respected. Consultations between the Competent Authorities, amendments to the CARF MCAA and the general terms of the CARF MCAA, including the activation of exchange relationships through the submission of notifications, the suspension, deactivation and termination, as well as the role of the Co-ordinating Body Secretariat are dealt with in Sections 6, 7 and 8.

- seven notifications required under Section 7(1) for the CARF MCAA to enter into effect for a Competent Authority.

5. The CARF MCAA is a multilateral agreement based on the principle that automatic exchange is reciprocal and that the exchange will be done on a bilateral basis. There may be instances where Competent Authorities wish to enter into a non-reciprocal bilateral exchange relationship (e.g. where one Jurisdiction does not have an income tax), as confirmed in a notification provided pursuant to Section 7(1)(b).

6. As an alternative to the CARF MCAA, Jurisdictions can also establish automatic exchange relationships through bilateral competent authority agreements based on bilateral double tax treaties or tax information exchange agreements that permit the automatic exchange of information, or the Convention on Mutual Administrative Assistance in Tax Matters. Jurisdictions could also enter into a self-standing intergovernmental agreement or rely on regional legislation covering both the reporting obligations and due diligence procedures coupled with the exchange of information modalities.

Commentary on the Declaration

1. To become a signatory of the CARF MCAA, the Competent Authority of the Jurisdiction or its designated representative must sign the Declaration and provide it, together with the text of the CARF MCAA, to the Coordinating Body Secretariat.

2. The CARF MCAA will only enter into effect with respect to another Competent Authority once both Competent Authorities have signed the Declaration, have submitted all associated notifications pursuant to Section 7(1) to the Coordinating Body Secretariat and have included each other on the list of intended exchange partners in the notification provided pursuant to subparagraph 1g) of Section 7.

Commentary on the Preamble

1. The preamble ("whereas clauses") provides relevant context, explains the purpose of the CARF MCAA and contains representations of the signatories.

2. The first clause contains a confirmation that the Jurisdictions of the signatories to the CARF MCAA are Parties to, or territories covered by the Convention, which is a condition for being able to sign the CARF MCAA.

3. The second and third clauses serve as an introduction and clarify that the purpose of the CARF MCAA is to tackle tax avoidance and evasion and to improve tax compliance.

4. The fourth clause sets out the representations by the Competent Authorities that the laws of their respective Jurisdictions require, or are expected to require, Reporting Crypto-Asset Service Providers to report information regarding Relevant Crypto-Assets, consistent with the scope of exchange contemplated by Section 2. The language used in the fourth clause allows Competent Authorities, that so wish, to sign the CARF MCAA before their Jurisdiction has the relevant rules on due diligence and reporting in place.

5. The fifth clause provides that future amendments to the Crypto-Asset Reporting Framework are expected to be reflected in the domestic legislation of the Jurisdictions and that once enacted by a Jurisdiction, any reference to the term Crypto-Asset Reporting Framework would be deemed to refer to the amended version in respect of that Jurisdiction.

6. The sixth clause sets out the legal basis that authorises the automatic exchange of information and allows the Competent Authorities to agree the procedures to be applied to such automatic exchanges. The scope agreed to is consistent with the scope of exchange contemplated by Section 2.

7. The seventh clause specifies that, whereas the Convention allows for two or more Parties to mutually agree to exchanging specified information automatically, the actual exchange of information would occur on a bilateral basis (i.e. from the sending Competent Authority to the receiving Competent Authority).

8. The eighth clause sets out the representations by the Competent Authorities that their Jurisdictions have in place (i) appropriate safeguards to ensure the confidentiality of the information received and (ii) an infrastructure that allows for an effective exchange relationship.

9. The ninth clause restates the purpose of the CARF MCAA to improve international tax compliance with respect to Relevant Crypto-Assets. It also clarifies that the application of the CARF MCAA may depend on the successful completion of national legislative procedures (e.g. Parliamentary approval and/or a referendum) and reiterates that the conclusion of the CARF MCAA is subject to the Parties' adherence to the confidentiality, data safeguards and other protections, including that the use of the information exchanged is limited to the extent prescribed under the Convention.

Commentary on Section 1 concerning definitions

Paragraph 1 – Definitions

1. Subparagraph 1a) defines the Jurisdictions of the Competent Authorities that have signed the CARF MCAA and refers to a country or a territory in respect of which the Convention is in force (original Convention) or in effect (in case of the amended Convention) either through ratification or territorial extension.

2. The definition of the term "Competent Authority" contained in subparagraph 1b) refers to the persons and authorities listed in Annex B of the Convention.

3. The definition of the term "Crypto-Asset Reporting Framework" in subparagraph 1c) refers to the international framework for the automatic exchange of information with respect to Crypto-Assets (which includes the Commentaries) developed by the OECD, with G20 countries.

4. It is possible that the CARF, including the IT modalities such as the XML schema, will be updated from time to time as more Jurisdictions implement, and obtain experience with, the CARF. Furthermore, in the context of the CARF MCAA, Competent Authorities may sign on different dates and because of the differing dates of signature the CARF may have been updated in the interim. In this respect, and to ensure that there is an understanding that all Jurisdictions would be expected to implement the most recent version of the CARF with respect to the Reporting Crypto-Asset Service Providers that are subject to due diligence and reporting requirements in their Jurisdiction, the fifth whereas-clause states that it is "expected that the laws of the Jurisdictions would be amended from time to time to reflect updates to the Crypto-Asset Reporting Framework and once such amendments are enacted by a Jurisdiction the definition of the term Crypto-Asset Reporting Framework would be deemed to refer to the updated version in respect of that Jurisdiction".

5. The definition of the term "Co-ordinating Body Secretariat" in subparagraph 1d) refers to the OECD Secretariat that, pursuant to paragraph 3 of Article 24 of the Convention, provides support to the Co-ordinating Body that is composed of representatives of the Competent Authorities of the Parties to the Convention.

6. In accordance with subparagraph 1e), the CARF MCAA is an "Agreement in effect" in respect to any two Competent Authorities, if they have included each other in their list of intended exchange partners (notification pursuant to subparagraph 1g) of Section 7) and have satisfied the other conditions set out in paragraph 2 of Section 7. A list of the Competent Authorities between which the CARF MCAA is in effect will be published on the OECD website.

Paragraph 2 – General rule of interpretation

7. Paragraph 2 sets out the general rule of interpretation. The first sentence of paragraph 2 makes clear that any capitalised terms used in the CARF MCAA but not defined therein are meant to be interpreted consistently with the meaning given to them in the CARF.

8. The second sentence of paragraph 2 provides that, unless the context otherwise requires or the Competent Authorities agree to a common meaning, any term not otherwise defined in the CARF MCAA or in the Crypto-Asset Reporting Framework has the meaning that it has at that time under the law of the Jurisdiction applying the CARF MCAA. In this respect any meaning under the applicable tax laws of that Jurisdiction will prevail over a meaning given to that term under other laws of that Jurisdiction. Further, when looking at the context, the Competent Authorities should consider the Commentary on the Crypto-Asset Reporting Framework.

Commentary on Section 2 concerning Exchange of Information with Respect to Reportable Persons

1. Paragraph 1 provides the legal basis for the exchange and sets out that the information will be exchanged on an annual basis. Information may also be exchanged more frequently than once a year. For example, when a Competent Authority receives corrected data from a Reporting Crypto-Asset Service Provider, that information would generally be sent to the other Competent Authority as soon as possible after it has been received. The information to be exchanged is the information obtained pursuant to Section II of the Crypto-Asset Reporting Framework and is further specified in paragraph 3.

2. Paragraph 1 also makes clear that the exchange of information is subject to the applicable reporting and due diligence rules of the Crypto-Asset Reporting Framework. Thus, where those rules do not require the reporting of, for instance, a TIN or place of birth with respect to a particular Reportable Person, there is also no obligation to exchange such information.

3. Paragraph 2 describes the requirements with respect to Jurisdictions that have indicated they are to be listed as non-reciprocal Jurisdictions on the basis of a notification pursuant to subparagraph 1b) of Section 7. These Jurisdictions will send, but not receive, information specified in paragraph 3. Conversely, Jurisdictions that are not listed as non-reciprocal Jurisdictions will receive the information specified in paragraph 3 from non-reciprocal Jurisdictions, but will not send such information to non-reciprocal Jurisdictions.

4. Paragraph 3 lists the information to be exchanged with respect to each Reportable Person of another Jurisdiction. For all reporting categories under Section 2 (3)(c)(ii) through (3)(c)(ix), the Crypto-Asset Reporting Framework requires the aggregation, i.e. summing up, of all Relevant Transactions attributable to each reporting category for each type of Relevant Crypto-Asset, as converted and valued pursuant to paragraphs D and E of Section II of the Crypto-Asset Reporting Framework and paragraphs 33-41 of the Commentary on Section II.

Commentary on Section 3 concerning Time and Manner of Exchange of Information

Paragraph 1 – Time of exchange of information

1. Paragraph 1 provides that the information under Section 2 must be exchanged within nine months after the calendar year to which the information relates. The first year with respect to which the information is exchanged is the year indicated by the signatory Competent Authority in its notification pursuant to subparagraph 1a) of Section 7, in which it confirms its Jurisdiction has in place the required implementing legislation. The nine-month timeline in paragraph 1 is a minimum standard and Jurisdictions are free to exchange prior to the prescribed timelines.

2. Paragraph 1 also provides that notwithstanding the year that the Competent Authorities have indicated in their notification pursuant to Section 7(1)(a) as the year in respect of which the first exchange will take place, information is only required to be exchanged with respect to a calendar year if both Jurisdictions have in place legislation to give effect to the Crypto-Asset Reporting Framework with respect to such calendar year. A Jurisdiction may, however, choose, subject to its domestic laws, to exchange the information with another Jurisdiction in respect of (earlier) years, if it has given effect to the Crypto-Asset Reporting Framework and has the CARF MCAA in effect with the Competent Authority of such Jurisdiction.

3. The following example illustrates the operation of the last sentence of paragraph 1. Jurisdictions A and B have signed the CARF MCAA. Jurisdiction A provides its notifications pursuant to Section 7(1) on 7 June 2025, indicating that it has legislation in effect that requires reporting with respect to 2026. Jurisdiction B provides its notifications on 1 November 2025, indicating that it has legislation in effect to provide reporting with respect to 2027. In this case the last sentence of paragraph 1 will operate such that Jurisdiction A does not have an obligation to exchange information in respect of 2026. Both Jurisdictions A and B will have an obligation to exchange information with respect to 2027. However, Jurisdiction A may choose, subject to its domestic laws, to send information to Jurisdiction B in respect of 2026 even though Jurisdiction A will not receive information in respect of 2026.

Paragraphs 2 and 3 – Information technology modalities

CARF schema and user guide

4. Paragraph 2 provides that the Competent Authorities will automatically exchange the information described in Section 2 in a common schema in Extensible Markup Language, the CARF XML Schema.

Data transmission including encryption

5. Paragraph 3 provides that the Competent Authorities will transmit the information through the OECD Common Transmission System, which is the commonly developed secure transmission system in use by Competent Authorities across the globe for the transmission of confidential tax information. The information must further be prepared and encrypted in line with the latest internationally-agreed standards.

6. Alternatively, Competent Authorities may use another method for data transmission, as specified by such Competent Authorities in their notification pursuant to subparagraph 1d) of Section 7. Any alternative transmission method should meet equivalent security, encryption and file preparation standards to those applicable to the OECD Common Transmission System in order to ensure the confidentiality and integrity of data throughout the transmission, as to ensure that the data is in no case made available or disclosed to unauthorised persons and is not modified or altered in an unauthorised manner.

7. One method of encryption in common use for exchange of information uses both a public and a private key. Public key cryptography has been in use for some decades and allows parties to exchange

encrypted data without communicating a shared secret key in advance. The sending party encrypts the data file with a public key, and only the receiving party holds the secure private key that allows the data to be decrypted. There are standards for the length of encryption keys in use internationally that are recognised as providing the appropriate level of security for personal financial data, both now and for the foreseeable future, such as advanced encryption standard (AES) 256.

Commentary on Section 4 concerning Collaboration on Compliance and Enforcement

1. Section 4 sets out the expectations in terms of the collaboration between the Competent Authorities on compliance and enforcement. It provides that if one Competent Authority has reason to believe that an error may have led to incorrect or incomplete information reporting or there is non-compliance by a Reporting Crypto-Asset Service Provider that Competent Authority should notify the other Competent Authority. The notified Competent Authority is then expected to take all appropriate measures available under its domestic law to address the errors or non-compliance described in the notice. This includes instances where a Reportable Person invokes data subject rights to have its incorrect data corrected or deleted. Prior to sending a formal notification, Competent Authorities should consider consulting informally on the errors or instances of non-compliance identified. See the Commentary on Section V of the Crypto-Asset Reporting Framework regarding the rules and administrative procedures that Jurisdictions must have in place to ensure that the Crypto-Asset Reporting Framework is effectively implemented.

2. Any notification under this Section must clearly set out the error or non-compliance and the reasons for the belief that such error or non-compliance has occurred. The notified Competent Authority should provide a response or an update as soon as possible and no later than 90 calendar days of having received the notification from the other Competent Authority. If the issue has not been resolved, the notified Competent Authority should provide the other Competent Authority with updates every 90 days. If, however, after reviewing and considering the notification in good faith, the notified Competent Authority does not agree that there is, or has been, an error or non-compliance it should, as soon as possible, advise the other Competent Authority in writing of such determination and explain the reasons for it.

Commentary on Section 5 concerning Confidentiality and Data Safeguards

1. Confidentiality of taxpayer information has always been a fundamental cornerstone of tax systems, as well as for the international exchange of tax information. Jurisdictions have a legal obligation to ensure that information exchanged remains confidential and is used only in accordance with the terms of the agreement under which it was exchanged. In order to have confidence in their tax systems and comply with their obligations under the law, taxpayers need to know that financial information is not disclosed inappropriately, whether intentionally or by accident. Taxpayers and governments will only trust international exchange if the information exchanged is used and disclosed only in accordance with the instrument on the basis of which it was exchanged. This is a matter of both the legal framework, but also of having systems and procedures in place to ensure that the legal framework is respected in practice and that there is no unauthorised disclosure or use of information. The ability to protect the confidentiality of tax information is also the result of a "culture of care" within a tax administration which includes the entire spectrum of systems, procedures and processes to ensure that the legal framework is respected in practice and information security and integrity is also maintained in the handling of information. As the sophistication of a tax administration increases, the confidentiality processes and practices must keep pace to ensure that information exchanged remains confidential and is used appropriately. In this respect, several

Jurisdictions have specific rules on the protection of personal data and data subject rights, which also apply to taxpayer information.

2. Section 5 together with Section 7 and the representations in the eighth whereas-clause of the preamble explicitly recognise the importance of confidentiality and data safeguards in connection with the automatic exchange of information under the CARF MCAA. The Commentary on this Section briefly discusses paragraphs 1 and 2 followed by a comprehensive description of the approach towards confidentiality and data safeguarding in connection with the Crypto-Asset Reporting Framework.

Paragraph 1 – Confidentiality and protection of personal data

3. All information exchanged under the CARF MCAA is subject to the confidentiality rules and other safeguards provided for in the Convention. This includes the limitations based on the purposes for which the information may be used and limits to whom the information may be disclosed. In particular, Article 22 of the Convention states that the information exchanged with a Party should only be disclosed to persons or authorities concerned with the assessment, collection or recovery of, the enforcement or prosecution in respect of, or the determination of appeals in relation to taxes of that Party and that the Party may use the information and only for such purposes.

4. Many Jurisdictions have specific rules on the protection of personal data and data subject rights which apply to taxpayer information. For example, special data protection rules apply to information exchanges by EU Member States (whether the exchange is made to another EU Member State or a third Jurisdiction).[1] These rules include, inter alia, the data subject's right to information, access, correction, redress and the existence of an oversight mechanism to protect the data subject's rights.

5. Paragraph 1 of Article 22 of the amended Convention provides that "any information obtained by a Party [...] shall be treated [...], to the extent needed to ensure the necessary level of protection of personal data, in accordance with the safeguards which may be specified by the supplying Party as required under its domestic law". In that light, paragraph 1 of Section 5 provides that the supplying Competent Authority may specify such safeguards in a notification provided pursuant to subparagraph 1e) of Section 7. The Competent Authority receiving the information confirms in its notification provided pursuant to subparagraph 1g) of Section 7 (intended exchange partners) that its Jurisdiction is compliant with the requirements specified by Competent Authorities that are selected as intended exchange partners. The Competent Authority receiving the information shall treat the information in compliance not only with its own domestic law, but also with additional safeguards that may be required to ensure data protection under the domestic law of the supplying Competent Authority. Such additional safeguards, as specified by the supplying Competent Authority, may for example relate to individual access to the data, correction, deletion, or the right to redress. The specification of the safeguards may not be necessary if the supplying Competent Authority is satisfied that the receiving Competent Authority ensures the necessary level of data protection with respect to the data being supplied. In any case, these safeguards should be limited to what is needed to ensure the protection of personal data without unduly preventing or delaying the effective exchange of information, in recognition of the significant public interest of the exchange of information in tax matters.

6. Exchange of information instruments, including Article 21 of the Convention, generally provide that information does not have to be supplied to another jurisdiction if the disclosure of the information would be contrary to the *ordre public* (public policy) of the jurisdiction supplying the information. While it is rare for this to apply in the context of information exchanges between Competent Authorities, certain jurisdictions may, for instance, require their Competent Authorities to specify that information they supply may not be used or disclosed in proceedings that could result in the imposition and execution of the death penalty or torture or other severe violations of human rights (such as for example when tax investigations are motivated by political, racial, or religious persecution) if such exchange would contravene the public policy of the supplying jurisdiction.

Paragraph 2 – Breach of confidentiality

7. Ensuring ongoing confidentiality of information received under the applicable legal instrument is critical. Paragraph 2 of Section 5 provides that in the event of any breach of confidentiality or failure of safeguards in the Jurisdiction (including the additional safeguards specified by the supplying Competent Authority) the Competent Authority of such Jurisdiction must immediately notify the Co-ordinating Body Secretariat of such breach or failure, including any sanctions or remedial actions consequently imposed. The content of any such notice must itself respect the confidentiality rules and must be in accordance with the domestic law of the Jurisdiction where the breach or failure occurred. Further, Section 7 explicitly provides that non-compliance with the confidentiality and data safeguard provisions (including the additional safeguards specified by the supplying Competent Authority) would be considered significant non-compliance and a justification for immediate suspension of the CARF MCAA.

Ensuring ongoing compliance with confidentiality and data safeguarding requirements

8. Three building blocks are essential in order to ensure appropriate safeguards are in place to protect the information exchanged automatically: (i) a legal framework that ensures the confidentiality and appropriate use of exchanged information in accordance with international legal instruments; (ii) an information security management (ISM) system that adheres to internationally recognised standards or best practices; and (iii) enforcement provisions and processes to address the occurrence of confidentiality breaches and misuse of information.

Legal framework

9. Jurisdictions' domestic legal framework should include provisions sufficient to protect the confidentiality of taxpayer information, including exchanged information, and provide only for specific and limited circumstances under which such information can be disclosed and used, such circumstances being consistent, in relation to exchanged information, with the terms of the applicable international exchange instrument (bilateral or multilateral) under which the information was exchanged.

Information Security Management (ISM) framework

10. Tax administrations that are authorised to access information exchanged in accordance with paragraph 2 of Article 22 of the Convention or equivalent provisions in other international exchange agreements (hereafter, 'relevant organisations') must have an ISM policy and systems to ensure that information can be used solely for intended purposes and to prevent disclosure to unauthorised persons. An ISM system is a set of governance arrangements, policies, procedures and practices concerned with information security risks, including IT-related risks. ISM systems must adhere to internationally recognised standards or best practices.

11. Internationally recognised standards or best practices refers to the "ISO/IEC 27000-series," published jointly by the International Organisation for Standardisation (ISO) and the International Electro-technical Commission (IEC), which provides best practices on information security management, risks, and controls within the context of an overall ISM system.

12. Relevant organisations must meet the ISM requirements in their overall ISM system, in their implementation of various security controls, and in their operational framework to test the effectiveness of these controls, as follows:

13. In respect of the overall ISM system, relevant organisations should:

- display a clear understanding of the lifecycle of exchanged information within the organisation, and be committed to safeguard its confidentiality and appropriate use;

- manage information security through the medium of a written information security policy that is part of an overarching security framework that clearly defines security roles and responsibilities, is owned by senior management and is kept up to date;
- address information security, including technology, through appropriate operational arrangements and as an integrated part of the management of relevant business processes;
- systematically manage their information security risks, taking account of the threats, vulnerabilities, and impacts; and
- have appropriate arrangements to manage and maintain business continuity.

14. In respect of human resources controls, relevant organisations should:

- ensure that security roles and responsibilities of employees and contractors are defined, documented, and clearly communicated in terms of engagement, and regularly reviewed in accordance with the information security policy (this should include confidentiality and non-disclosure agreements);
- undertake background checks with appropriate vetting of all candidates for employment, employees, and contractors, in accordance with accepted best practices and perceived risks;
- ensure that all employees and contractors receive regular and up to date security training and awareness, with employees and contractors in sensitive roles receiving additional guidance relevant to the handling of more sensitive material;
- ensure that employees apply security policies and procedures; and
- have human resources policies and processes relating to the termination of engagement that protect sensitive information.

15. In respect of physical and logical access controls, relevant organisations should:

- have a physical access control policy owned by senior management;
- adequately protect physical premises and have appropriately defined internal and external secure perimeters;
- have a logical access control policy owned by senior management and based on the 'need to know' and 'least privileged access' principles; and
- have policies, processes and procedures, owned by senior management and not solely the organisation's IT function, that govern logical access, and effective processes for the provisioning and auditing of logical access and for the identification and authentication of users.

16. In respect of IT system security, relevant organisations should:

- make security an integral part of providing technology services, have a security plan for applications, and harmonise their systems with security;
- deploy an appropriate range of security controls;
- adequately manage their assets;
- appropriately manage supplier service delivery; and
- assure the continuity of IT services based on service level agreements.

17. In respect of the protection of information, relevant organisations should:

- effectively manage information in accordance with a set of policies and procedures throughout the information management lifecycle (including document naming, classification, handling, storage, monitoring, auditing, and destruction; and including devices and media that hold information); and

- have processes in place for information received from other Competent Authorities to ensure that obligations under international exchange agreements are met, including to prevent comingling with other information.

18. In respect of the operations management framework, including incident management, change management, monitoring and audit, relevant organisations should:

- be aware of the controls that protect exchanged information and have appropriate plans in place to manage them;
- have appropriate monitoring and logging arrangements in place, including to detect unauthorised access, use or disclosure of information;
- analyse and act upon security risks;
- have processes and procedures for the identification and management of known vulnerabilities;
- have a change management process, with security integrated into it;
- have an incident management system that covers all types of security incidents; and
- have internal audit and external audit functions.

Enforcement provisions and processes to address confidentiality breaches

19. Jurisdictions must further have penalties and/or sanctions for non-compliance with the required confidentiality and data safeguards in their legal framework to ensure compliance. The legal and ISM frameworks must be reinforced by adequate administrative rules, resources and procedures such as the ability to deal with suspected or actual breaches and take remedial action. There should also be process modifications to mitigate risk and prevent future breaches.

20. In particular, Jurisdictions' domestic legal framework should enable the imposition of adequate and appropriate penalties and/or sanctions for improper disclosure or use of taxpayer information, including exchanged information, with an appropriate consideration of administrative, civil, and criminal penalties or sanctions.

21. Furthermore, Jurisdictions should:

- have processes to follow when there is suspected or actual unauthorised access, use or disclosure, which should ensure such issues are reported and investigated;
- with the support of adequate administrative resources, processes and procedures, ensure that remedial action is taken where actual issues have been identified, with appropriate penalties or sanctions applied in practice against employees, contractors and other persons who violate confidentiality rules, security policies or procedures, to deter others from engaging in similar violations;
- apply processes to notify other Competent Authorities of breaches of confidentiality or failure of safeguards, and of sanctions and remedial actions consequently imposed; and
- review the monitoring and enforcement processes in response to non-compliance, with senior management ensuring that recommendations for change are implemented in practice.

Commentary on Section 6 concerning Consultations and Amendments

Paragraph 1 – Consultations

1. This paragraph provides that if any difficulties in the implementation or interpretation of the CARF MCAA arise, either Competent Authority may request consultations to develop measures to ensure that

the CARF MCAA is fulfilled. Consultations may also be held to analyse the quality of the information received.

2. The Competent Authorities may communicate with each other for purposes of reaching an agreement on appropriate measures to ensure that the CARF MCAA is fulfilled. The Co-ordinating Body Secretariat will notify all Competent Authorities, including those that did not participate in the consultation, of any measures developed to ensure the CARF MCAA is fulfilled.

Paragraph 2 – Amendments

3. This paragraph clarifies that the CARF MCAA may be amended by written agreement of the Competent Authorities. Unless the Competent Authorities otherwise agree, such amendment is effective on the first day of the month following a period of one month after the date of the last signature of such written agreement.

Commentary on Section 7 concerning General Terms

Paragraph 1 – Notifications

1. Paragraph 1 describes the notifications that, at the time of signing the CARF MCAA or as soon as possible thereafter, a Competent Authority must provide to the Co-ordinating Body Secretariat before the CARF MCAA can take effect with respect to another Competent Authority:

- the notification under subparagraph 1a) is a confirmation that the Jurisdiction has the necessary laws in place to implement the Crypto-Asset Reporting Framework, as well as a specification of the relevant effective dates of such legislation. This could include the specification of any conditions in national legislative procedures that may necessitate the provisional application of the CARF MCAA during a limited period. When specifying such provisional application, the notification should set out the state of advancement of the national legislative procedures, the reasons for the provisional application, and the time period, which should in no case extend beyond the end of the first reportable period. This notification should provide assurances that the legislation of the Jurisdiction can ensure the due diligence and reporting requirements of the Crypto-Asset Reporting Framework will be fulfilled with respect to all Reporting Crypto-Asset Service Providers that are subject to such requirements in the Jurisdiction pursuant to Section I of the Crypto-Asset Reporting Framework, notably by including specific references to the underlying legislation that ensures such requirements can be fulfilled;
- the notification under subparagraph 1b) is confirming whether the Jurisdiction should be listed as a reciprocal Jurisdiction, or as a non-reciprocal Jurisdiction (e.g. because the jurisdiction does not have a direct tax system or because the Competent Authority of the Jurisdiction does not meet an appropriate level of confidentiality and data safeguards). While a non-reciprocal Jurisdiction would be required to send information foreseen under Section 2, it would not receive information from other Competent Authorities. A Competent Authority should file its notification of intention for non-reciprocity even if this is only temporary (e.g. pending an assessment of its confidentiality and data safeguards);
- the notification under subparagraph 1c) provides for a declaration by the Competent Authority requesting consent from the other Competent Authorities to use the information received under the CARF MCAA for the assessment, collection or recovery of, the enforcement or prosecution in respect of, or the determination of appeals in relation to taxes with respect to which its Jurisdiction made a reservation pursuant to subparagraph 1(a) of Article 30 of the Convention. The requesting Competent Authority should specify these taxes and confirm the use will be in line with the terms of the Convention. The other Competent Authority must explicitly agree with

such use as part of listing the requesting Competent Authority as an intended exchange partner in the notification provided pursuant to subparagraph 1g);

- in the fourth notification provided under subparagraph 1d), the Competent Authorities should indicate whether it wishes to rely on any transmission and encryption methods other than the OECD Common Transmission System and the related file preparation and encryption methods;
- the notification under subparagraph 1e) states that the Jurisdiction should specify any requirements for the protection of personal data that must be respected in the receiving Jurisdiction with respect to information it sends to Competent Authorities in such Jurisdictions, in addition to the confidentiality and use limitation requirements contained in Article 22 of the Convention. This allows the sending Competent Authority to condition the sending of any information on the confirmation of specified safeguards being in place in the receiving Jurisdiction. The other Competent Authority must explicitly agree with such safeguards as part of listing the sending Competent Authority as an intended exchange partner in the notification provided pursuant to subparagraph 1g). Alternatively, under this notification, a Competent Authority can also simply indicate that it does not wish to make any further specifications with respect to data protection safeguards;
- the notification under subparagraph 1f) requires that Jurisdictions confirm whether it has in place adequate measures to ensure the required confidentiality and data safeguards standards, as discussed in Section 5, are met. This can be confirmed by referring to the relevant Confidentiality and Data Safeguards Report for the Jurisdiction, as adopted by the Global Forum on Transparency and Exchange of Information for Tax Purposes;
- finally, in the notification under subparagraph 1g), the Competent Authority should include a list of the Jurisdictions of the Competent Authorities with respect to which it intends to have the CARF MCAA in effect, following national legislative procedures for entry into force (if any). When including a Jurisdiction on this list, it also agrees to comply with the data protection requirements as notified by the Competent Authority of such Jurisdiction pursuant to subparagraph 1e). In addition, where relevant, the Competent Authority can specify in this notification whether it agrees with the use of information it is exchanging with the Competent Authority of another Jurisdiction for the administration of enforcement of taxes set out in the notification under subparagraph 1c).

2. In addition to providing these notifications set out above, paragraph 1 clarifies that Competent Authorities must notify the Co-ordinating Body Secretariat, promptly, of any subsequent changes to be made to the above-mentioned notifications, once they have been lodged.

Paragraph 2 – Entry into effect

3. Paragraph 2 provides that a specific bilateral exchange relationship is activated and enters into effect on the date the second of the two Competent Authorities provides all notifications required under paragraph 1 to the Co-ordinating Body Secretariat and has listed the other Competent Authority's Jurisdiction pursuant to subparagraph 1g) of Section 7.

Paragraphs 3 and 4 – Role of Co-ordinating Body Secretariat

4. Paragraph 3 clarifies that the Co-ordinating Body Secretariat will maintain a list of the Competent Authorities that have signed the CARF MCAA, as well as between which Competent Authorities the CARF MCAA is in effect. This information is published on the OECD website.

5. Paragraph 4 further explains that the Co-ordinating Body Secretariat will also publish on the OECD website the notifications filed under subparagraph 1a) (confirming that the Jurisdiction has the necessary laws in place), subparagraph 1b) (confirming whether the Jurisdiction is to be listed as a non-reciprocal

Jurisdiction) and subparagraph 1e) (specifying data protection requirements) of Section 7. The Co-ordinating Body Secretariat will also maintain the information provided by Competent Authorities pursuant to subparagraphs 1c), 1d), 1f) and 1g) of Section 7. This information, however, will not be published on the OECD website and will only be made available to the signatories of the CARF MCAA.

Paragraph 5 – Suspension

6. Paragraph 5 provides details on the possibility for a Competent Authority to suspend the CARF MCAA in relation to another Competent Authority when it has determined that there is or has been significant non-compliance by that other Competent Authority. Where possible, the Competent Authorities should try to resolve any issues of non-compliance, even those of significant non-compliance, before issuing a notification to suspend the CARF MCAA between them.

7. To suspend the CARF MCAA, a Competent Authority must notify the other Competent Authority in writing that it intends to suspend the CARF MCAA with such other Competent Authority. The notification should, whenever possible, set out the reasons for the suspension and the steps (to be) taken to resolve the issue. The suspension will have immediate effect.

8. The notified Competent Authority should, as soon as possible, undertake the necessary steps to address the significant non-compliance. As soon as the non-compliance is resolved, the notified Competent Authority should advise the other Competent Authority. Following successful resolution of the issue, the Competent Authority that sent the suspension notification should confirm in writing to the notified Competent Authority that the CARF MCAA is no longer suspended and exchanges of information should recommence as soon as possible.

9. Paragraph 5 provides that significant non-compliance includes, but is not limited to:

- non-compliance with the confidentiality or data safeguard provisions of the CARF MCAA, for example information is used for purposes not authorised in the CARF MCAA or the Convention or domestic legislation is amended in such a way that the confidentiality of information is compromised; or
- a failure by the Competent Authority to provide timely or adequate information as required under the CARF MCAA.

10. During the period of any suspension all information previously received under the CARF MCAA will remain confidential and subject to the terms of Section 5 of the CARF MCAA, including any additional data safeguards specified by the supplying Competent Authority.

Paragraph 6 – Deactivation and termination

11. Pursuant to paragraph 6, a Competent Authority may either deactivate a particular exchange relationship under the CARF MCAA or entirely terminate its participation in the CARF MCAA. In both instances the Competent Authority must notify the Co-ordinating Body Secretariat in writing. A deactivation or termination will become effective on the first day of the month following the expiration of a period of 12 months after the date of the notification. In circumstances where this is necessary (e.g. due to national legislative procedures or a court judgement), the Competent Authority deactivating one or more exchange relationships under, or terminating its participation in, the CARF MCAA, may deviate from the default 12 month period and specify another period.

12. The termination of the participation of a Jurisdiction in the Convention would lead to the automatic termination of the CARF MCAA in respect of such Jurisdiction. Accordingly in such circumstances the CARF MCAA would not separately need to be terminated.

13. Paragraph 6 clarifies that in the event of a deactivation or termination, all information previously received under the CARF MCAA will remain confidential and subject to the terms of Section 5, including any additional data safeguards specified by the supplying Competent Authority.

Commentary on Section 8 concerning the Co-ordinating Body Secretariat

1. Section 8 clarifies that, unless otherwise provided for in the CARF MCAA, the Co-ordinating Body Secretariat will notify all Competent Authorities of any notifications that it has received under the CARF MCAA. Section 8 also clarifies that the Co-ordinating Body will notify all signatories of the CARF MCAA when a new Competent Authority signs the CARF MCAA.

Note

[1] See EU General Data Protection Regulation (GDPR) 2016/679 on the protection of natural persons with regards to the processing of personal data and on the free movement of such data: https://eur-lex.europa.eu/legal-content/EN/TXT/?uri=CELEX%3A02016R0679-20160504&qid=1532348683434

Part II Amendments to the Common Reporting Standard

1 Introduction

1. The CRS was designed to promote tax transparency with respect to financial accounts held abroad and requires the collection and automatic exchange of information of the identity of account holders, as well as the balance and the income paid or credited to the accounts. Since the CRS was adopted in 2014, over seven years have passed, in which over 100 jurisdictions have implemented the CRS.

2. As such, there is now solid experience with the CRS both by governments and Financial Institutions. The OECD has therefore conducted the first comprehensive review of the CRS, with the aim of improving the operation of the CRS. To that end, the OECD has taken on board input from jurisdictions that have implemented the CRS, as well as from Reporting Financial Institutions reporting under the CRS, in order to determine areas meriting a review. This has resulted in amendments in two key areas.

3. Firstly, new digital financial products are included in the scope of the CRS, as they may constitute a credible alternative to holding money or Financial Assets in an account that is currently subject to CRS reporting. In this regard, the CRS now covers Specified Electronic Money Products and Central Bank Digital Currencies. In light of the development of the CARF, changes are also made to the definitions of Financial Asset and Investment Entity, to ensure that derivatives that reference Crypto-Assets and are held in Custodial Accounts and Investment Entities investing in Crypto-Assets are covered by the CRS. The CRS now also contains provisions to ensure an efficient interaction between the CRS and the CARF, in particular to limit instances of duplicative reporting, while maintaining a maximum amount of operational flexibility of Reporting Financial Institutions that are also subject to obligations under the CARF.

4. Secondly, the amendments enhance the reporting outcomes under the CRS, including through the introduction of more detailed reporting requirements, the strengthening of the due diligence procedures, the introduction of a new, optional Non-Reporting Financial Institution category for Investment Entities that are genuine non-profit organisations and the creation of a new Excluded Account category for capital contribution accounts. In addition, further details have been included in the Commentary to the CRS in a number of locations to increase consistency in the application of the CRS and to incorporate previously released Frequently Asked Questions and interpretative guidance.

5. In order to accommodate the expanded reporting requirements under the amended CRS, an Addendum to the CRS MCAA has been developed that provides an updated legal basis for participating jurisdictions exchanging CRS information under the CRS MCAA.

Covering new digital financial products

Digital money products

6. Certain e-money products, as well as Central Bank Digital Currencies (CBDCs) representing a digital fiat currency issued by a Central Bank, can be considered functionally similar to a traditional bank account from the perspective of customers and may therefore entail tax compliance concerns similar to those associated with bank accounts currently covered by the CRS. To ensure a level-playing field between digital money products and traditional bank accounts and to ensure consistent reporting outcomes, the following amendments to the CRS have been made:

- the term Specified Electronic Money Product is introduced, covering digital representations of a single fiat currency that are issued on receipt of funds for the purpose of making payment transactions, that are represented by a claim on the issuer denominated in the same fiat currency, that are accepted by a natural or legal person other than the issuer; and that, by virtue of regulatory requirements to which the issuer is subject, are redeemable at par for the same fiat currency upon request of the holder of the product. A carve-out is included for products that are created solely to facilitate a funds transfer pursuant to instructions of a customer and that cannot be used to store value;
- the term Central Bank Digital Currency (CBDC) is introduced, covering any official currency of a jurisdiction, issued in digital form by a Central Bank;
- the definition of Depository Institution and the related Commentary are amended to include those e-money providers that are not already Depository Institutions under the current definition and that are relevant from a CRS perspective by virtue of holding Specified Electronic Money Products or CBDCs;
- the definition of Depository Account is amended to include accounts that represent the Specified Electronic Money Products and CBDCs held for customers;
- a new category of Excluded Account is added to bring out of scope low-risk digital money products that represent a low-risk in light of the limited monetary value stored, namely Specified Electronic Money Products whose rolling average 90-day end-of-day account balance or value does not exceed USD 10,000 in any consecutive 90 day period; and
- additional wording is included on the definition of Non-Reporting Financial Institution to clarify that a Central Bank is not considered a Non-Reporting Financial Institution when it holds CBDCs on behalf of Non-Financial Entities or individuals.

Coverage of derivatives referencing Crypto-Assets and Investment Entities investing in Crypto-Assets

7. In order to ensure consistency between derivatives referencing Crypto-Assets and derivatives referencing (other) Financial Assets, the latter of which are already covered under the CRS, derivative contracts referencing Crypto-Assets are included in the definition of Financial Assets, thereby allowing Reporting Financial Institutions to apply the same due diligence and reporting procedures to derivatives referencing different types of assets.

8. Beyond the direct transacting in and holding of Crypto-Assets, investors can alternatively invest in Crypto-Assets through funds and other wealth management vehicles, whose purpose is to acquire and hold Relevant Crypto-Assets for investment purposes. By doing so, investors can obtain exposure to price fluctuations of the fund's underlying Crypto-Assets, without directly owning any Crypto-Assets.

9. Interests in funds and wealth management vehicles are already subject to reporting under the CRS, either as Equity or Debt Interests in Investment Entities or as Financial Assets held in Custodial Accounts. However, the definition of Investment Entity does not currently contain Crypto-Assets as a category of eligible investments that would bring the Entity in scope of the CRS, as the definition presently only encompasses Financial Assets and money. The definition of Investment Entity is therefore expanded to include the activity of investing in Crypto-Assets.

Further amendments to improve CRS reporting

10. As set out above, a set of further amendments are made to the CRS and Commentary with a view to improving the quality and usability of CRS reporting. Each of the changes is briefly outlined below.

Expansion of the reporting requirements in respect of Account Holders, Controlling Persons and the Financial Accounts they own (Section I – Reporting requirements)

11. When the CRS was designed, the reporting requirements set out in Section I were primarily focused on the transmission of key identification items in respect of Account Holders and Controlling Persons, as well as on information related to the income realised and balances present on Financial Accounts.

12. At the same time, Reporting Financial Institutions may have knowledge of a set of other facts and circumstances surrounding the Account Holders, Controlling Persons and the Financial Accounts they own, which, if reported, allow tax administrations to better contextualise the information they receive under the CRS and to facilitate the use of the data for tax compliance purposes. The reporting requirements under the CRS are therefore expanded to cover the following:

- the role of Controlling Persons in relation to the Entity Account Holder and the role(s) of Equity Interest Holders in an Investment Entity – this ensures that tax administrations have visibility on the role(s) a Controlling Person/Equity Interest Holder plays with respect to the Entity, allowing a distinction between those Controlling Persons/Equity Interest Holders that have an interest through ownership, control or as beneficiaries, as opposed to those that have a managerial role (e.g. senior management officials, protectors, trustees);
- whether the account is a Preexisting Account or a New Account and whether a valid self-certification has been obtained – this information gives tax administrations visibility with respect to the due diligence procedures applied, and therewith gives insights into the reliability of the information;
- whether the account is a joint account, as well as the number of joint Account Holders – this information permits tax administrations to take the fact into account that the income and balance on joint accounts may not be attributable in full to each Account Holder, but would rather need to be apportioned, as appropriate, between the Account Holders; and
- the type of Financial Account – this distinction between Depository Accounts, Custodial Accounts, Equity and debt Interests and Cash Value Insurance Contracts allows tax administrations to better understand the financial investments held by their taxpayers.

Reliance on AML/KYC Procedures for determining Controlling Persons (Section VI – Due diligence requirements)

13. The conditions under which a Reporting Financial Institution can rely on AML/KYC Procedures to determine the Controlling Persons of a New Entity Account Holder have been moved into the text of the CRS itself. In particular, it is specified for New Entity Accounts that AML/KYC Procedures must be in line with 2012 FATF Recommendations. In addition, it is clarified that, if AML/KYC Procedures are not consistent with 2012 FATF Recommendations, the Reporting Financial Institution must apply substantially similar procedures.

Exceptional due diligence procedure for cases where a valid self-certification was not obtained, in order to ensure reporting with respect to such accounts (Sections II – VII – Due diligence requirements)

14. As the CRS requires Reporting Financial Institutions to obtain and validate self-certifications for all New Accounts, the CRS does not foresee any fall-back due diligence procedure to be applied in exceptional cases where a Reporting Financial Institution did not comply with the requirement to obtain a valid self-certification.

15. Reporting Financial Institutions are therefore required to temporarily determine the residence of the Account Holders and/or Controlling Persons on the basis of the due diligence procedures for Preexisting Accounts. It should be noted that this is not a standard procedure and is not an alternative to the requirement to obtain a valid self-certification.

Qualification of certain capital contribution accounts as Excluded Accounts (Section VIII(C)(17)(e) – Definition of Excluded Account)

16. So-called capital contribution accounts, the purpose of which is to block funds for a limited period of time in view of the incorporation of a new company or a pending capital increase, are now considered Excluded Accounts, provided that adequate safeguards are in place to avoid the misuse of such accounts. This is the case where such transactions are subject to regulation and, as a matter of law, are required to take place via a dedicated bank account, whereby the underlying funds are frozen until the capital contribution has taken place and, in the case of an incorporation, when the company has been legally established and registered in the jurisdiction's commercial register. As soon as the company is legally established and registered, the capital contribution account is then transformed into a regular Depository Account or the capital amount is transferred to a Depository Account and the initial capital contribution account is closed. On the contrary, if the company is not established, the contributions would be refunded to the subscriber(s).

17. In order to ensure that such accounts are only used for the completion of an imminent capital contribution transaction, such an account is treated as an Excluded Account only where the use of such accounts is prescribed by law and for a maximum period of 12 months.

Non-Reporting Financial Institution category for genuine charities

18. While most Active NFEs are not treated as Investment Entities even if they meet the Investment Entity definition, this carve-out does not apply to Entities that are Active NFEs by virtue of being a non-profit Entity as defined in subparagraph D(9)(h) of Section VIII. Representatives from the philanthropy sector have highlighted that this can lead to highly undesirable outcomes, requiring genuine public benefit foundations to apply due diligence procedures in respect of all beneficiaries of grant payments and report on grant payments to non-resident beneficiaries, such as for instance disadvantaged students receiving scholarships. At the same time, concerns have been expressed by governments that simply extending the carve out from the Investment Entity definition to all non-profit Entities described in Subparagraph D(9)(h) of Section VIII could give rise to situations where Investment Entities would circumvent their reporting obligations under the CRS by improperly claiming the status of non-profit Entities.

19. In light of these considerations, the CRS now contains an optional new Non-Reporting Financial Institution category for genuine Non-Profit Entities that (i) reflects the substantive conditions of Active NFEs pursuant to subparagraph D(9)(h) of Section VIII and (ii) makes the carve-out subject to adequate verification procedures by the tax administration of the jurisdiction in which the Entity is otherwise subject to reporting as an Investment Entity.

20. The Commentary language to Paragraph B of Section VIII now includes language outlining these conditions for excluding Qualified Non-Profit Entities from reporting obligations under the CRS. The Commentary also describes the confirmation a tax administration or other governmental authority would need to obtain before treating an Entity as a Qualified Non-Profit Entity.

Broadening of the scope of Depository Institution (Commentary to Depository Institution definition)

21. The Commentary on the term Depository Institution has been amended to expand the scope to include entities that are merely licensed to engage in certain banking activities but are not actually so engaged.

Notions of customer and business in the context of Investment Entities (Commentary to Investment Entity definition)

22. With respect to Investment Entities pursuant to subparagraph a of the definition, doubts have arisen as to the interpretation of the term "customer", as well as the condition that the activities listed in subparagraph must be conducted "as a business". This question is in particular relevant with respect to funds.

23. The scope of the definition is clarified via the terms "customer" and "business", by explicitly confirming in Commentary that investors of funds can be considered "customers" and the funds themselves can be considered to conduct activities "as a business". This is consistent with the interpretation of the definition of Financial Institution in the FATF Recommendations, on which subparagraph (a) is based.

Reporting in respect of dual-resident account-holders (paragraphs 4 and 7 to the Commentary on Section IV and VI, respectively)

24. The Commentary to the CRS acknowledges that an Entity or individual Account Holder may be resident for tax purposes in two or more jurisdictions. The Commentary also specifies that, in the context of the self-certification process, such dual-residents may rely on the tie-breaker rules contained in applicable tax conventions to determine their residence for tax purposes.

25. This may result in prematurely treating the Account Holder as tax resident in a single jurisdiction for the purposes of the CRS, leading to the CRS information with respect to the Account Holder not being reported to the other jurisdiction(s).

26. The Commentary is therefore revised in order to ensure that, in tiebreaker scenarios, all jurisdictions of tax residence should be self-certified by the Account Holder and the Account Holder should be treated as tax resident in all identified jurisdictions. The Commentary further clarifies that reliance on tiebreaker rules to determine the jurisdiction of residence for self-certification purposes is no longer permitted on a prospective basis, once the changes to the CRS have taken effect.

Reflecting Government Verification Services within the CRS due diligence procedures

27. At present, the CRS due diligence procedures are based on AML/KYC documentation, self-certifications and other account-related information collected by Reporting Financial Institutions. At the same time, technology is evolving in a direction that can potentially drastically simplify the documentation of taxpayers in a highly-reliable manner. Specifically, so-called Government Verification Services (GVS) may allow a third-party information provider, such as a Reporting Financial Institution, to obtain a direct confirmation in the form of an IT-token or other unique identifier from the tax administration of the jurisdiction of residence of the taxpayer in relation to their identity and tax residency.

28. Reporting Financial Institutions will be allowed to rely on a GVS procedure to document an Account Holder or Controlling Person in the CRS due diligence procedures, with the aim of making the CRS future-proof for future IT-developments. In this respect, the confirmation of an Account Holder's or Controlling Person's identity and tax residence via a GVS or similar IT-driven process is recognised as a functional equivalent to a TIN.

Look-through requirements in respect of Controlling Persons of publicly traded Entities (paragraphs 21 and 19 to the Commentary on Section V and VI, respectively)

29. The CRS due diligence procedures in respect of both Pre-existing and New Entity Accounts require Reporting Financial Institutions to look-through Passive NFEs to determine their Controlling Persons. In doing so, Reporting Financial Institutions may rely on information collected and maintained pursuant to AML/KYC Procedures. In this respect, the interpretative note to FATF Recommendation 10 (customer due diligence) provides that financial institutions are not required to request information on the beneficial owner(s) of publicly traded companies if such company is already otherwise subject to disclosure requirements ensuring adequate transparency of beneficial ownership information. This exclusion is now included in the CRS, in order to maintain alignment with the FATF Recommendations and in light of the limited utility of such information for tax risk assessment purposes.

Integrating CBI/RBI guidance within the CRS (paragraph 3bis to Commentary on Section VII)

30. In October 2018, the OECD released explanatory guidance for Reporting Financial Institutions aimed at addressing the misuse of certain citizenship and residence by investment (CBI/RBI) schemes, allowing foreign individuals to obtain citizenship or temporary or permanent residence rights on the basis of local investments or against a flat fee, to circumvent the CRS.

31. The explanatory guidance reiterates that a Reporting Financial Institution may not rely on a self-certification or Documentary Evidence where it knows or has reason to know, that it is incorrect or unreliable. In making this determination, Reporting Financial Institutions should take into account the information published by the OECD on potentially high-risk CBI/RBI schemes. The guidance also includes a number of additional questions that Reporting Financial Institutions may raise to determine the appropriate jurisdiction(s) of CRS reporting. The explanatory guidance is now included in the Commentary.

Incorporating FAQs

32. Since the CRS was adopted in 2014, the OECD has been regularly asked to provide guidance on the interpretation of the CRS. This has been typically done through the development of frequently-asked questions (FAQs) that are published on the OECD website. In order to reflect the substantive guidance given through the FAQs in the CRS itself, language has been added to the Commentary in several places. FAQs not explicitly incorporated into the Commentary still remain valuable guidance for interpreting the CRS.

2 Amendments to the Rules

Section I: General Reporting Requirements

A. Subject to paragraphs C through F, each Reporting Financial Institution must report the following information with respect to each Reportable Account of such Reporting Financial Institution:

1. the:

   a) name, address, jurisdiction(s) of residence, TIN(s) and date and place of birth (in the case of an individual) of each Reportable Person that is an Account Holder of the account *and whether the Account Holder has provided a valid self-certification*;

   b) in the case of any Entity that is an Account Holder and that, after application of the due diligence procedures consistent with Sections V, VI and VII, is identified as having one or more Controlling Persons that is a Reportable Person, the name, address, jurisdiction(s) of residence and TIN(s) of the Entity and the name, address, jurisdiction(s) of residence, TIN(s) and date, and place of birth of each Reportable Person, *as well as the role(s) by virtue of which each Reportable Person is a Controlling Person of the Entity and whether a valid self-certification has been provided for each Reportable Person; and*

   c) *whether the account is a joint account, including the number of joint Account Holders.*

2. the account number (or functional equivalent in the absence of an account number*), the type of account and whether the account is a Preexisting Account or a New Account*;

3. the name and identifying number (if any) of the Reporting Financial Institution;

4. the account balance or value (including, in the case of a Cash Value Insurance Contract or Annuity Contract, the Cash Value or surrender value) as of the end of the relevant calendar year or other appropriate reporting period or, if the account was closed during such year or period, the closure of the account;

5. in the case of any Custodial Account:

   a) the total gross amount of interest, the total gross amount of dividends, and the total gross amount of other income generated with respect to the assets held in the account, in each case paid or credited to the account (or with respect to the account) during the calendar year or other appropriate reporting period; and

   b) the total gross proceeds from the sale or redemption of Financial Assets paid or credited to the account during the calendar year or other appropriate reporting period with respect to which the Reporting Financial Institution acted as a custodian, broker, nominee, or otherwise as an agent for the Account Holder.

6. in the case of any Depository Account, the total gross amount of interest paid or credited to the account during the calendar year or other appropriate reporting period;

6bis. in the case of any Equity Interest held in an Investment Entity that is a legal arrangement, the role(s) by virtue of which the Reportable Person is an Equity Interest holder; and

7. in the case of any account not described in subparagraph A(5) or (6), the total gross amount paid or credited to the Account Holder with respect to the account during the calendar year or other appropriate reporting period with respect to which the Reporting Financial Institution is the obligor or debtor, including the aggregate amount of any redemption payments made to the Account Holder during the calendar year or other appropriate reporting period.

B. The information reported must identify the currency in which each amount is denominated.

C. Notwithstanding subparagraph A(1), with respect to each Reportable Account that is a Preexisting Account, the TIN(s) or date of birth is not required to be reported if such TIN(s) or date of birth is not in the records of the Reporting Financial Institution and is not otherwise required to be collected by such Reporting Financial Institution under domestic law. However, a Reporting Financial Institution is required to use reasonable efforts to obtain the TIN(s) and date of birth with respect to Preexisting Accounts by the end of the second calendar year following the year in which such Accounts were identified as Reportable Accounts *and whenever it is required to update the information relating to the Preexisting Account pursuant to domestic AML/KYC Procedures.*

D. Notwithstanding subparagraph A(1), the TIN is not required to be reported if (i) a TIN is not issued by the relevant Reportable Jurisdiction or (ii) the domestic law of the relevant Reportable Jurisdiction does not require the collection of the TIN issued by such Reportable Jurisdiction.

E. Notwithstanding subparagraph A(1), the place of birth is not required to be reported unless the Reporting Financial Institution is otherwise required to obtain and report it under domestic law and it is available in the electronically searchable data maintained by the Reporting Financial Institution.

F. Notwithstanding paragraph A, the information to be reported with respect to [xxxx] is the information described in such paragraph, except for gross proceeds described in subparagraph A(5)(b).

G. *Notwithstanding subparagraph A(5)(b) and unless the Reporting Financial Institution elects otherwise with respect to any clearly identified group of accounts, the gross proceeds from the sale or redemption of a Financial Asset are not required to be reported to the extent such gross proceeds from the sale or redemption of such Financial Asset are reported by the Reporting Financial Institution under the Crypto-Asset Reporting Framework.*

[…]

Section V: Due Diligence for Preexisting Entity Accounts

The following procedures apply for purposes of identifying Reportable Accounts among Preexisting Accounts.

[…]

D. Review Procedures for Identifying Entity Accounts With Respect to Which Reporting Is Required

[…]

2. Determine Whether the Entity is a Passive NFE with One or More Controlling Persons Who Are Reportable Persons

[…]

b) **Determining the Controlling Persons of an Account Holder.** For the purposes of determining the Controlling Persons of an Account Holder, a Reporting Financial Institution may rely on information collected and maintained pursuant to AML/KYC Procedures.

[…]

Section VI: Due Diligence for New Entity Accounts

The following procedures apply for purposes of identifying Reportable Accounts among New Entity Accounts.

[...]

A. Review Procedures for Identifying Entity Accounts With Respect to Which Reporting Is Required

[...]

2. Determine Whether the Entity is a Passive NFE with One or More Controlling Persons Who Are Reportable Persons

[...]

b) **Determining the Controlling Persons of an Account Holder**. For the purposes of determining the Controlling Persons of an Account Holder, a Reporting Financial Institution may rely on information collected and maintained pursuant to AML/KYC Procedures, *provided that such procedures are consistent with the 2012 FATF Recommendations. If the Reporting Financial Institution is not legally required to apply AML/KYC Procedures that are consistent with the 2012 FATF Recommendations, it must apply substantially similar procedures for the purpose of determining the Controlling Persons.*

[...]

Section VII: Special Due Diligence Rules

The following additional rules apply in implementing the due diligence procedures described above:

A. Reliance on Self-Certifications and Documentary Evidence

A Reporting Financial Institution may not rely on a self-certification or Documentary Evidence if the Reporting Financial Institution knows or has reason to know that the self-certification or Documentary Evidence is incorrect or unreliable.

A bis. Temporary lack of Self-Certification

In exceptional circumstances where a self-certification cannot be obtained by a Reporting Financial Institution in respect of a New Account in time to meet its due diligence and reporting obligations with respect to the reporting period during which the account was opened, the Reporting Financial Institution must apply the due diligence procedures for Preexisting Accounts, until such self-certification is obtained and validated.

[...]

Section VIII: Defined Terms

A. Reporting Financial Institution

[...]

5. The term **"Depository Institution"** means any Entity that:

   a) accepts deposits in the ordinary course of a banking or similar business*; or*

b) holds Specified Electronic Money Products or Central Bank Digital Currencies for the benefit of customers.

[...]

6. The term **"Investment Entity"** means any Entity:

a) that primarily conducts as a business one or more of the following activities or operations for or on behalf of a customer:

i. trading in money market instruments (cheques, bills, certificates of deposit, derivatives, etc.); foreign exchange; exchange, interest rate and index instruments; transferable securities; or commodity futures trading;

ii. individual and collective portfolio management; or

iii. otherwise investing, administering, or managing Financial Assets*,* ~~or~~ money *, or Relevant Crypto-Assets* on behalf of other persons; or

b) the gross income of which is primarily attributable to investing, reinvesting, or trading in *Financial Assets or Relevant Crypto-Assets, if the Entity is managed by another Entity that is a Depository Institution, a Custodial Institution*, a Specified Insurance Company, or an Investment Entity described in subparagraph A(6)(a).

An Entity is treated as primarily conducting as a business one or more of the activities described in subparagraph A(6)(a), or an Entity's gross income is primarily attributable to investing, reinvesting, or trading in Financial Assets *or Relevant Crypto-Assets* for purposes of subparagraph A(6)(b), if the Entity's gross income attributable to the relevant activities equals or exceeds 50% of the Entity's gross income during the shorter of: (i) the three-year period ending on 31 December of the year preceding the year in which the determination is made; or (ii) the period during which the Entity has been in existence. *For the purposes of subparagraph A(6)(a)(iii), the term "otherwise investing, administering, or managing Financial Assets, money, or Relevant Crypto-Assets on behalf of other persons" does not include the provision of services effectuating Exchange Transactions for or on behalf of customers*. The term "Investment Entity" does not include an Entity that is an Active NFE because it meets any of the criteria in subparagraphs D(9)(d) through (g).

This paragraph shall be interpreted in a manner consistent with similar language set forth in the definition of "financial institution" in the Financial Action Task Force Recommendations.

[...]

7. The term **"Financial Asset"** includes a security (for example, a share of stock in a corporation; partnership or beneficial ownership interest in a widely held or publicly traded partnership or trust; note, bond, debenture, or other evidence of indebtedness), partnership interest, commodity, swap (for example, interest rate swaps, currency swaps, basis swaps, interest rate caps, interest rate floors, commodity swaps, equity swaps, equity index swaps, and similar agreements), Insurance Contract or Annuity Contract, or any interest (including a futures or forward contract or option) in a security*, Relevant Crypto-Asset*, partnership interest, commodity, swap, Insurance Contract, or Annuity Contract. The term "Financial Asset" does not include a non-debt, direct interest in real property.

[...]

*9. The term **"Specified Electronic Money Product"** means any product that is:*

a) a digital representation of a single Fiat Currency;

b) issued on receipt of funds for the purpose of making payment transactions;

c) represented by a claim on the issuer denominated in the same Fiat Currency;

d) accepted in payment by a natural or legal person other than the issuer; and

e) by virtue of regulatory requirements to which the issuer is subject, redeemable at any time and at par value for the same Fiat Currency upon request of the holder of the product.

The term "Specified Electronic Money Product" does not include a product created for the sole purpose of facilitating the transfer of funds from a customer to another person pursuant to instructions of the customer. A product is not created for the sole purpose of facilitating the transfer of funds if, in the ordinary course of business of the transferring Entity, either the funds connected with such product are held longer than 60 days after receipt of instructions to facilitate the transfer, or, if no instructions are received, the funds connected with such product are held longer than 60 days after receipt of the funds.

*10. The term **"Central Bank Digital Currency"** means any digital Fiat Currency issued by a Central Bank.*

*11. The term **"Fiat Currency"*** means the official currency of a jurisdiction, issued by a jurisdiction or by a jurisdiction's designated Central Bank or monetary authority, as represented by physical banknotes or coins or by money in different digital forms, including bank reserves and Central Bank Digital Currencies. The term also includes commercial bank money and electronic money products (including Specified Electronic Money Products).

*12. The term **"Crypto-Asset"** means a digital representation of value that relies on a cryptographically secured distributed ledger or a similar technology to validate and secure transactions.*

*13. The term **"Relevant Crypto-Asset"** means any Crypto-Asset that is not a Central Bank Digital Currency, a Specified Electronic Money Product or any Crypto-Asset for which the Reporting Crypto-Asset Service Provider has adequately determined that it cannot be used for payment or investment purposes.*

*14. The term **"Exchange Transaction"** means any:*

a) exchange between Relevant Crypto-Assets and Fiat Currencies; and

b) exchange between one or more forms of Relevant Crypto-Assets.

[…]

B. Non-Reporting Financial Institution

1. The term **"Non-Reporting Financial Institution"** means any Financial Institution that is:

a) a Governmental Entity, International Organisation or Central Bank, other than:

i) with respect to a payment that is derived from an obligation held in connection with a commercial financial activity of a type *engaged in by a Specified Insurance Company, Custodial Institution, or Depository Institution; or*

ii) with respect to the activity of maintaining Central Bank Digital Currencies for Account Holders which are not Financial Institutions, Governmental Entities, International Organisations or Central Banks.

[…]

C. Financial Account

[…]

2. The term "**Depository Account**" includes any commercial, checking, savings, time, or thrift account, or an account that is evidenced by a certificate of deposit, thrift certificate, investment certificate, certificate of indebtedness, or other similar instrument maintained by a *Depository Institution* ~~Financial Institution in the ordinary course of a banking or similar business~~. A Depository Account also includes:

a) an amount held by an insurance company pursuant to a guaranteed investment contract or similar agreement to pay or credit interest therein;

b) an account or notional account that represents all Specified Electronic Money Products held for the benefit of a customer; and

c) an account that holds one or more Central Bank Digital Currencies for the benefit of a customer.

[...]

9. The term **"Preexisting Account"** means a Financial Account maintained by a Reporting Financial Institution as of [xx/xx/xxxx] *or, if the account is treated as a Financial Account solely by virtue of the amendments to the Common Reporting Standard, as of [effective date of the revised CRS-1 day].*

10. The term **"New Account"** means a Financial Account maintained by a Reporting Financial Institution opened on or after [xx/xx/xx] *or, if the account is treated as a Financial Account solely by virtue of the amendments to the Common Reporting Standard, on or after [effective date of the revised CRS].*

[...]

17. The term **"Excluded Account"** means any of the following accounts:

[...]

e) an account established in connection with any of the following:

[...]

v) a foundation or capital increase of a company provided that the account satisfies the following requirements:

i) the account is used exclusively to deposit capital that is to be used for the purpose of the foundation or capital increase of a company, as prescribed by law;

ii) any amounts held in the account are blocked until the Reporting Financial Institution obtains an independent confirmation regarding the foundation or capital increase;

iii) the account is closed or transformed into an account in the name of the company after the foundation or capital increase;

iv) any repayments resulting from a failed foundation or capital increase, net of service provider and similar fees, are made solely to the persons who contributed the amounts; and

v) the account has not been established more than 12 months ago.

ebis) A Depository Account that represents all Specified Electronic Money Products held for the benefit of a customer, if the rolling average 90 day end-of-day aggregate account balance or value during any period of 90 consecutive days did not exceed USD 10,000 at any day during the calendar year or other appropriate reporting period.

D. Reportable Account

[...]

2. The term **"Reportable Person"** means a Reportable Jurisdiction Person other than (i) ~~a corporation~~ *an Entity* the stock of which is regularly traded on one or more established securities markets; (ii) any ~~corporation~~ *Entity* that is a Related Entity of a*n Entity* described in clause (i)...

[...]

E. Miscellaneous

[…]

*7. The term **"Government Verification Service"** is an electronic process made available by a Reportable Jurisdiction to a Reporting Financial Institution for the purposes of ascertaining the identity and tax residence of an Account Holder or Controlling Person.*

[…]

Section X: Transitional Measures

A. The amendments to the Common Reporting Standard are effective as of [effective date of the revised CRS].

B. Notwithstanding paragraph A, under subparagraph A(1)(b) and A(6)(bis) of Section I, with respect to each Reportable Account that is maintained by a Reporting Financial Institution as of [effective date of the revised CRS-1 day] and for reporting periods ending by the second calendar year following such date, information with respect to the role(s) by virtue of which each Reportable Person is a Controlling Person or Equity Interest holder of the Entity is only required to be reported if such information is available in the electronically searchable data maintained by the Reporting Financial Institution.

3 Amendments to the Commentary to the Rules

Commentary on Section I

[...]

Paragraph A – Information to be reported

3. Pursuant to paragraph A, each Reporting Financial Institution must report the following information with respect to each Reportable Account of such Reporting Financial Institution:

a) in the case of any individual that is an Account Holder and a Reportable Person: the name, address, jurisdiction(s) of residence, TIN(s) and date and place of birth, *whether the Account Holder has provided a valid self-certification and whether the account is a joint account, including the number of joint Account Holders*;

b) in the case of any Entity that is an Account Holder and a Reportable Person: the name, address, jurisdiction(s) of residence and TIN(s), *whether the Account Holder has provided a valid self-certification and whether the account is a joint account, including the number of joint Account Holders*;

c) in the case of any Entity that is an Account Holder and that is identified as having one or more Controlling Persons that is a Reportable Person:

1. the name, address, jurisdiction(s) of residence and TIN(s) of the Entity; and
2. the name, address, jurisdiction(s) of residence, TIN(s), date and place of birth of each Controlling Person that is a Reportable Person, *as well as the role(s) by virtue of which the Reportable Person is a Controlling Person of the Entity and whether a valid self-certification has been provided for such Reportable Person;*

d) the account number (or functional equivalent in the absence of an account number) and *the type of account and whether the account is a Preexisting Account or a New Account*;

e) the name and identifying number (if any) of the Reporting Financial Institution; and

f) the account balance or value (including, in the case of a Cash Value Insurance Contract or Annuity Contract, the Cash Value or surrender value) as of the end of the relevant calendar year or other appropriate reporting period or, if the account was closed during such year or period, the closure of the account.

4. In addition, the following information must be reported:

[...]

bbis) in the case of any Equity Interest held in an Investment Entity that is a legal arrangement, the role(s) by virtue of which the Reportable Person is an Equity Interest holder.

[...]

Subparagraph A(1) – Role(s) of the Controlling Person

7bis. The role(s) of each Reportable Person that is a Controlling Person in respect of an Entity is required to be reported. The requirements to identify Controlling Persons, as well as their roles with respect to the Entity, are governed by AML/KYC Procedures, as set out in paragraphs 132 et seq. of the Commentary to Section VIII. Where a Reportable Person is a Controlling Person by virtue of more than one role in respect of an Entity other than a trust or a similar legal arrangement, the Reporting Financial Institution must report according to the hierarchy of roles indicated in paragraph 133 of the Commentary to Section VIII (i.e. ownership interests, control through other means, senior managing official), provided the identification of the role is required by AML/KYC Procedures. This is illustrated by the following example:

- *Example: A Reporting Financial Institution maintains a Financial Account on behalf of an Entity Account Holder that is a corporation. The Reporting Financial Institution identifies that a Reportable Person is a Controlling Person of such Entity Account Holder by virtue of owning 51% of the ownership and voting interests in such Entity, as well as by being a senior managing official of such Entity. The Reporting Financial Institution is only required to indicate that the Reportable Person is a Controlling Person by virtue of its ownership interests, as this role comes first in the hierarchy specified in paragraph 7bis of Commentary to Section I.*

7ter. Where a Reportable Person is a Controlling Person of a trust or a similar legal arrangement by virtue of more than one role, the Reporting Financial Institution must report each role, provided the identification of the roles is required by AML/KYC Procedures. This requirement also applies with respect to the identification of the roles of Equity Interest holders, pursuant to subparagraph A(6bis), of a trust or a similar legal arrangement.

[...]

Subparagraph A(2) – Account number, type of account, Preexisting or New Account

8bis. The Reporting Financial Institution must also report whether an account is a Preexisting Account or a New Account as defined under subparagraphs C(9) and C(10) of Section VIII, respectively.

8ter. The account type to be reported with respect to an account is the type of Financial Account maintained by the Reporting Financial Institution for the Account Holder, as described under subparagraph C(1) of Section VIII.

[...]

Subparagraph A(4) – Account balance or value

[...]

14. In the case of an account closure, the Reporting Financial Institution has no obligation to report the account balance or value before or at closure, but must report that the account was closed. In determining when an account is "closed", reference must be made to the applicable law in a particular jurisdiction. If the applicable law does not address closure of accounts, an account will be considered to be closed according to the normal operating procedures of the Reporting Financial Institution that are consistently applied for all accounts maintained by such institution. For example, an equity or debt interest in a Financial Institution would generally be considered to be closed upon termination, transfer, surrender, redemption, cancellation, or liquidation. An account with a balance or value equal to zero or that is negative will not be a closed account solely by reason of such balance or value. *Similarly, if a discretionary beneficiary of a trust that is a Financial Institution receives a distribution from the trust in a given year, but not in a following*

year, the absence of a distribution does not constitute an account closure, as long as the beneficiary is not permanently excluded from receiving future distributions from the trust.

[...]

Subparagraph A(5)(b) – Gross proceeds

17. In the case of a Custodial Account, information to be reported includes the total gross proceeds from the sale or redemption of Financial Assets paid or credited to *or with respect to* the account during the calendar year or other appropriate reporting period with respect to which the Reporting Financial Institution acted as a custodian, broker, nominee, or otherwise as an agent for the Account Holder. The term "sale or redemption" means any sale or redemption of Financial Assets, determined without regard to whether the owner of such Financial Assets is subject to tax with respect to such sale or redemption.

[...]

19. With respect to a sale that is effected by a broker that results in a payment of gross proceeds, the date the gross proceeds are considered paid is the date that the proceeds of such sale are credited to *or with respect to* the account of or otherwise made available to the person entitled to the payment.

20. The total gross proceeds from a sale or redemption means the total amount realised as a result of a sale or redemption of Financial Assets. In the case of a sale effected by a broker, the total gross proceeds from a sale or redemption means the total amount paid or credited to *or with respect to* the account of the person entitled to the payment increased by any amount not so paid by reason of the repayment of margin loans; the broker may (but is not required to) take commissions with respect to the sale into account in determining the total gross proceeds. In the case of a sale of an interest bearing debt obligation, gross proceeds includes any interest accrued between interest payment dates.

[...]

Paragraph C through G - Exceptions

Taxpayer Identification Number and date of birth

[...]

25. Paragraph C contains an exception applicable to Preexisting Accounts: the TIN or date of birth is not required to be reported if (i) such TIN or date of birth is not in the records of the Reporting Financial Institution, and (ii) there is not otherwise a requirement for such TIN or date of birth to be collected by such Reporting Financial Institution under domestic law. Thus, the TIN or date of birth is required to be reported if either:

- the TIN or date of birth is in the records of the Reporting Financial Institution (whether or not there is an obligation to have it in the records); or
- the TIN or date of birth is not in the records of the Reporting Financial Institution, but it is otherwise required to be collected by such Reporting Financial Institution under domestic law (e.g. AML/KYC Procedures).

26. The "records" of a Reporting Financial Institution include the customer master file and electronically searchable information (see paragraph 34 below). A "customer master file" includes the primary files of a Reporting Financial Institution for maintaining account holder information, such as information used for contacting account holders and for satisfying AML/KYC Procedures. Reporting Financial Institutions would generally have a two-year period to complete the review procedures for identifying Reportable Accounts among Lower Value Accounts (see paragraph 51 of the Commentary on Section III) and, thus, could first

review their electronic records (or obtain TIN or date of birth from the Account Holder) and then review their paper records.

27. In addition, even where a Reporting Financial Institution does not have the TIN or date of birth for a Preexisting Account in its records and is not otherwise required to collect such information under domestic law, the Reporting Financial Institution is required to use reasonable efforts to obtain the TIN and date of birth with respect to Preexisting Accounts by the end of the second calendar year following the year in which such Accounts were identified as Reportable Accounts *and whenever it is required to update the information relating to the Preexisting Account pursuant to domestic AML/KYC Procedures*, unless one of the exceptions in paragraph D applies with respect to the TIN and it is not required to be reported.

28. "Reasonable efforts" means genuine attempts to acquire the TIN and date of birth of the Account Holder of a Reportable Account. Such efforts must be made, at least once a year, during the period between the identification of the Preexisting Account as a Reportable Account and the end of the second calendar year following the year of that identification *and whenever it is required to update the information relating to the Preexisting Account pursuant to domestic AML/KYC Procedures*. Examples of reasonable efforts include contacting the Account Holder (e.g. by mail, in-person or by phone), including a request made as part of other documentation or electronically (e.g. by facsimile or by e-mail); and reviewing electronically searchable information maintained by a Related Entity of the Reporting Financial Institution, in accordance with the aggregation principles set forth in paragraph C of Section VII. However, reasonable efforts do not necessarily require closing, blocking, or transferring the account, nor conditioning or otherwise limiting its use. Notwithstanding the foregoing, reasonable efforts may continue to be made ~~after the abovementioned period~~ *at any time.*

[...]

Financial Assets subject to reporting under Crypto-Asset Reporting Framework

36. Paragraph G contains an optional exception for reporting by Reporting Financial Institutions with respect to the gross proceeds from the sale or redemption of a Financial Asset, to the extent such gross proceeds from the sale or redemption of such Financial Asset are reported by the Reporting Financial Institution under the Crypto-Asset Reporting Framework, as illustrated by the following example:

An individual, A, holds a Custodial Account with C, a custodial Crypto-Asset exchange that is a Reporting Financial Institution. At the beginning of the year, A holds 5 units of security token X in the Custodial Account with C. Throughout the year, A acquires an additional 3 units of security token X and disposes of 2 units. C reports the account balance of the Custodial Account under subparagraph A(4). C reports the disposals and acquisitions of security token X under the Crypto-Asset Reporting Framework and is therefore not required to report the gross proceeds from the disposals of security token X under subparagraph A(5)(b).

[...]

Commentary on Section IV

1. This Section contains the due diligence procedures for New Individual Accounts and provides for the collection of a self-certification (and confirmation of its reasonableness).

2. According to paragraph A, upon account opening, the Reporting Financial Institution must:

- obtain a self-certification, which may be part of the account opening documentation, that allows the Reporting Financial Institution to determine the Account Holder's residence(s) for tax purposes; and

- confirm the reasonableness of such self-certification based on the information obtained by the Reporting Financial Institution in connection with the opening of the account, including any documentation collected pursuant to AML/KYC Procedures.

2bis. While as a general rule a self-certification must be obtained on the day of the account opening, there may be a limited number of circumstances, where due to the specificities of a business sector it is not possible to obtain a self-certification on 'day one' of the account opening process. For example, this may be the case where an insurance contract has been assigned from one person to another, where an account holder changes as a result of a court order, where a newly created company is in the process of obtaining a TIN or where an investor acquires shares in an investment trust on the secondary market. In addition, it is acknowledged that, even where a self-certification is obtained at account opening, validation of the self-certification may not always be completed on the day of the account opening (e.g. in circumstances where validation is a process undertaken by a back-office function within the Reporting Financial Institution). In these circumstances, the self-certification must be both obtained and validated by the Reporting Financial Institution as quickly as feasible, and in any case within a period of 90 calendar days and in time to be able to meet its due diligence and reporting obligations with respect to the reporting period during which the account was opened. In this respect, it is expected that jurisdictions have strong measures in place to ensure that valid self-certifications are always obtained for New Accounts (as described in paragraph 18 to the Commentary on Section IX).

[…]

4. The self-certification must allow determining the Account Holder's residence(s) for tax purposes. Generally, an individual will only have one jurisdiction of residence. However, an individual may be resident for tax purposes in two or more jurisdictions under the domestic laws of such jurisdictions. *In those circumstances, the expectation is that all jurisdictions of residence are to be declared in a self-certification and that the Reporting Financial Institution must treat the account as a Reportable Account in respect of each Reportable Jurisdiction.* The domestic laws of the various jurisdictions lay down the conditions under which an individual is to be treated as fiscally 'resident'. They cover various forms of attachment to a jurisdiction which, in the domestic taxation laws, form the basis of a comprehensive taxation (full liability to tax). They also cover cases where an individual is deemed, according to the taxation laws of a jurisdiction, to be resident of that jurisdiction (e.g. diplomats or other persons in government service). ~~To solve cases of double residence, tax conventions contain special rules which give the attachment to one jurisdiction a preference over the attachment of the other jurisdiction for purposes of these conventions. Generally, an individual will be resident for tax purposes in a jurisdiction if, under the laws of that jurisdiction (including tax conventions), he pays or should be paying tax therein by reason of his domicile, residence or any other criterion of a similar nature, and not only from sources in that jurisdiction.~~ Dual resident individuals may rely on the tiebreaker rules contained in tax conventions (if applicable) to solve cases of double residence for determining their residence for tax purposes (see paragraph 23 below), *until [effective date of the amended CRS]. Following [effective date of the amended CRS], dual resident individuals that are (re-) documented may not rely on tiebreaker rules and will be expected to declare all their jurisdictions of residence.*

[…]

Requirements for validity of self-certification

7. A "self-certification" is a certification by the Account Holder that provides the Account Holder's ~~or~~ status and any other information that may be reasonably requested by the Reporting Financial Institution to fulfil its reporting and due diligence obligations, such as whether the Account Holder is resident for tax purposes in a Reportable Jurisdiction. With respect to New Individual Accounts, a self-certification is valid only if it is signed (or otherwise positively affirmed) by the Account Holder, it is dated at the latest at the date of receipt, and it contains the Account Holder's:

a) name;

b) residence address;

c) jurisdiction(s) of residence for tax purposes;

d) TIN with respect to each Reportable Jurisdiction (see paragraph 8 below); and

e) date of birth (see paragraph 8 below).

The self-certification may be pre-populated by the Reporting Financial Institution to include the Account Holder's information, except for the jurisdiction(s) of residence for tax purposes, to the extent already available in its records.

[...]

11. A self-certification may be signed (or otherwise positively affirmed) by any person authorised to sign on behalf of the Account Holder under domestic law. A person authorised to sign a self-certification generally includes an executor of an estate, any equivalent of the former title, and any other person that has been provided written authorisation by the Account Holder to sign documentation on such person's behalf.

11bis. A self-certification is otherwise positively affirmed if the person making the self-certification provides the Reporting Financial Institution with an unambiguous acknowledgement that they agree with the representations made through the self-certification. In all cases, the positive affirmation is expected to be captured by the Reporting Financial Institution in a manner such that it can credibly demonstrate that the self-certification was positively affirmed (e.g. voice recording, digital footprint, etc.). The approach taken by the Reporting Financial Institution in obtaining the self-certification is expected to be in a manner consistent with the procedures followed by the Reporting Financial Institution for the opening of the account. The Reporting Financial Institution will need to maintain a record of this process for audit purposes, in addition to the self-certification itself.

[...]

Reasonableness of self-certifications

[...]

25. In the case of a self-certification that would otherwise fail the reasonableness test, it is expected that in the course of the account opening procedures the Reporting Financial Institution would obtain either (i) a valid self-certification, or (ii) a reasonable explanation and documentation (as appropriate) supporting the reasonableness of the self-certification (and retain a copy or a notation of such explanation and documentation). Examples of such "reasonable explanation" include a statement by the individual that he or she (1) is a student at an educational institution in the relevant jurisdiction and holds the appropriate visa (if applicable); (2) is a teacher, trainee, or intern at an educational institution in the relevant jurisdiction or a participant in an educational or cultural exchange visitor program, and holds the appropriate visa (if applicable); (3) is a foreign individual assigned to a diplomatic post or a position in a consulate or embassy in the relevant jurisdiction; or (4) is a frontier worker or employee working on a truck or train travelling between jurisdictions. The following example illustrates the application of this paragraph: A Reporting Financial Institution obtains a self-certification for the Account Holder upon account opening. The jurisdiction of residence for tax purposes contained in the self-certification conflicts with the residence address contained in the documentation collected pursuant to AML/KYC Procedures. The Account Holder explains that she is a diplomat from a particular jurisdiction and that, as a consequence, she is resident in such jurisdiction; she also presents her diplomatic passport. Because the Reporting Financial Institution obtained a reasonable explanation and documentation supporting the reasonableness of the self-certification, the self-certification passes the reasonableness test.

25bis. Similarly, where an individual Account Holder indicates on a self-certification that he or she does not have a residence for tax purposes, the Reporting Financial Institution is required to confirm the reasonableness of the self-certification on the basis of other documentation, including any documentation collected pursuant to AML/KYC Procedures that is at its disposal. For instance, the fact that the self-certification indicates that the Account Holder has no residence for tax purposes but the other documentation on file contains an address constitutes a reason to doubt the validity of the self-certification. In such cases, the Reporting Financial Institution must ensure that it obtains a reasonable explanation and documentation, as appropriate, that supports the reasonableness of the self-certification. If the Reporting Financial Institution does not obtain a reasonable explanation as to the reasonableness of the self-certification, the Reporting Financial Institution may not rely on the self-certification and must obtain a new, valid self-certification from the Account Holder.

[...]

Commentary on Section V

[...]

Paragraph D – Review procedures

[...]

Subparagraph D2 – Review procedure for Controlling Persons

[...]

20. For purposes of determining whether the Account Holder is a Passive NFE, according to subparagraph D(2)(a), the Reporting Financial Institution must obtain a self-certification from the Account Holder to establish its status, unless it has information in its possession or that is publicly available (see paragraph 12 above), based on which it can reasonably determine that the Account Holder is an Active NFE or a Financial Institution other than a non-participating professionally managed investment entity (i.e. an Investment Entity described in subparagraph A(6)(b) of Section VIII that is not a Participating Jurisdiction Financial Institution). For example, a Reporting Financial Institution could reasonably determine that the Account Holder is an Active NFE where the Account Holder is legally prohibited from conducting activities or operations, or holding assets, for the production of passive income (see paragraph 126 of the Commentary on Section VIII). The self-certification to establish the Account Holder's status must comply with the requirements for the validity of self-certification with respect to Preexisting Entity Accounts (see paragraphs 13-17 above). A Reporting Financial Institution that cannot determine the status of the Account Holder as an Active NFE or a Financial Institution other than non-participating professionally managed investment entity must presume that it is a Passive NFE.

21. For the purposes of determining the Controlling Persons of an Account Holder, according to subparagraph D(2)(b), a Reporting Financial Institution may rely on information collected and maintained pursuant to AML/KYC Procedures *consistent with FATF Recommendation 10, where a publicly listed company exercises control over an Account Holder that is a Passive NFE there is no requirement to determine the Controlling Persons of such company, if such company is already subject to disclosure requirements ensuring adequate transparency of beneficial ownership information.*

[...]

Commentary on Section VI

[...]

4bis. In a limited number of circumstances where a self-certification cannot be obtained or validated upon account opening, the self-certification must be both obtained and validated by the Reporting Financial Institution as quickly as feasible and in any case within a period of 90 calendar days and in time to be able to meet its due diligence and reporting obligations with respect to the reporting period during which the account was opened (see paragraph 2bis of the Commentary on Section IV).

[...]

7. The self-certification must allow determining the Account Holder's residence(s) for tax purposes. It may be rare in practice for an Entity to be subject to tax as a resident in more than one jurisdiction, but it is, of course, possible. *In those circumstances, the expectation is that all jurisdictions of residence are to be declared in a self-certification and that the Reporting Financial Institution must treat the account as a Reportable Account in respect of each Reportable Jurisdiction.* The domestic laws of the various jurisdictions lay down the conditions under which an Entity is to be treated as fiscally 'resident'. They cover various forms of attachment to a jurisdiction which, in the domestic taxation laws, form the basis of a comprehensive taxation (full tax liability). To solve cases of double residence, tax conventions contain special rules which give the attachment to one jurisdiction a preference over the attachment of the other jurisdiction for purposes of those conventions. Generally, an Entity will be resident for tax purposes in a jurisdiction if, under the laws of that jurisdiction (including tax conventions), it pays or should be paying tax therein by reason of its domicile, residence, place of management or incorporation, or any other criterion of a similar nature, and not only from sources in that jurisdiction. Dual resident Entities may rely on the tiebreaker rules contained in tax conventions (if applicable) to solve cases of double residence for determining their residence for tax purposes (see paragraph 13 below), *until [effective date of the amended CRS]. Following [effective date of the amended CRS], dual resident Entities that are (re-)documented may not rely on tiebreaker rules and will be expected to declare all their jurisdictions of residence.*

[...]

Paragraph A(2) – Review procedure for Controlling Persons

[...]

19. For the purposes of determining the Controlling Persons of an Account Holder, according to subparagraph A(2)(b), a Reporting Financial Institution may rely on information collected and maintained pursuant to AML/KYC Procedures, *provided that such AML/KYC Procedures are consistent with FATF Recommendations 10 and 25 (as adopted in February 2012). If the Reporting Financial Institution is not legally required to apply AML/KYC Procedures that are consistent with the 2012 FATF Recommendations, it must apply substantially similar procedures for the purpose of determining the Controlling Persons. Consistent with FATF Recommendation 10, where a publicly listed company exercises control over an Account Holder that is a Passive NFE, there is no requirement to determine the Controlling Persons of such company, if such company is already subject to disclosure requirements ensuring adequate transparency of beneficial ownership information.*

[...]

Commentary on Section VII

[...]

Paragraph A – Reliance on Self-Certification and Documentary Evidence

2. Paragraph A contains the standards of knowledge applicable to a self-certification or Documentary Evidence. It provides that a Reporting Financial Institution may not rely on a self-certification or Documentary Evidence if the Reporting Financial Institution knows (i.e. has actual knowledge) or has reason to know that the self-certification or Documentary Evidence is incorrect or unreliable.

3. A Reporting Financial Institution has reason to know that a self-certification or Documentary Evidence is unreliable or incorrect if its knowledge of relevant facts or statements contained in the self-certification or other documentation, including the knowledge of the relevant relationship managers, if any (see paragraphs 38-42 and 50 of the Commentary on Section III), is such that a reasonably prudent person in the position of the Reporting Financial Institution would question the claim being made. A Reporting Financial Institution also has reason to know that a self-certification or Documentary Evidence is unreliable or incorrect if there is information in the documentation or in the Reporting Financial Institution's account files that conflicts with the person's claim regarding its status.

3bis. In confirming the reasonableness of a self-certification, Reporting Financial Institutions may be confronted with instances where an Account Holder or Controlling Person has provided documentation issued under a citizenship or residence by investment scheme (CBI/RBI scheme), which allows a foreign individual to obtain citizenship or temporary or permanent residence rights on the basis of local investments or against a flat fee. Certain high-risk CBI/RBI schemes may be potentially misused to circumvent reporting under the CRS. Such potentially high-risk CBI/RBI schemes are those that give a taxpayer access to a low personal income tax rate on offshore financial assets and do not require significant physical presence in the jurisdiction offering the CBI/RBI scheme. The OECD endeavours to publish information on such potentially high-risk CBI/RBI schemes on its website. It is expected that Reporting Financial Institutions rely on the OECD-published information in making the determination of whether they have a reason to know that the self-certification is incorrect or unreliable. In particular, where the Reporting Financial Institution has doubts as to the tax residency(ies) of an Account Holder or Controlling Person related to the fact that such person is claiming residence in a jurisdiction offering a potentially high-risk CBI/RBI scheme, the Reporting Financial Institution should not rely on such self-certification until it has taken further measures to ascertain the tax residency(ies) of such persons, including through raising further questions. Examples of such questions may include whether the Account Holder (1) has obtained residence rights under an CBI/RBI scheme; (2), holds residence rights in any other jurisdiction(s); and (3) has spent more than 90 days in any other jurisdiction(s) during the previous year, as well as (4) the jurisdictions in which the Account Holder has filed personal income tax returns during the previous year. The responses to these questions, accompanied by the relevant supporting documentation where applicable, should assist the Reporting Financial Institution in ascertaining whether the self-certification passes the reasonableness test.

Standards of knowledge applicable to self-certifications

4. A Reporting Financial Institution has reason to know that a self-certification provided by a person is unreliable or incorrect if the self-certification is incomplete with respect to any item on the self-certification that is relevant to the claims made by the person, the self-certification contains any information that is inconsistent with the person's claim, or the Reporting Financial Institution has other account information that is inconsistent with the person's claim. A Reporting Financial Institution that relies on a service provider to review and maintain a self-certification is considered to know or have reason to know the facts within the knowledge of the service provider.

4bis. A Reporting Financial Institution will have reason to know that a self-certification is unreliable or incorrect if the self-certification does not contain a TIN and the information disseminated by the OECD indicates that the Reportable Jurisdiction issues TINs to all tax residents. The Common Reporting Standard does not require a Reporting Financial Institution to confirm the format and other specifications of a TIN with the information disseminated by the OECD. However, Reporting Financial Institutions may nevertheless wish to do so in order to enhance the quality of the information collected and minimise the administrative burden associated with any follow up concerning reporting of an incorrect TIN. In this case, they may also use regional and national websites providing a TIN check module for the purpose of further verifying the accuracy of the TIN provided in the self-certification.

4ter. There may be instances where the AML/KYC Procedures to be applied by Reporting Financial Institutions change. In this respect, Section VIII(E)(2) provides that the term "AML/KYC Procedures" means the customer due diligence procedures of a Reporting Financial Institution pursuant to the anti-money laundering or similar requirements to which such a Reporting Financial Institution is subject. Consequently, for carrying out the due diligence procedures of Sections III-VII, the applicable AML/KYC Procedures are those to which a Reporting Financial Institution is subject at a given moment in time, as long as, for New Accounts, such procedures are consistent with the 2012 FATF Recommendations. Where there is an amendment to the applicable AML/KYC Procedures (e.g. upon a jurisdiction implementing new FATF Recommendations), Reporting Financial Institutions may be required to collect and maintain additional information for AML/KYC purposes in that jurisdiction. For the purposes of the due diligence procedures set out in Sections III-VII and in line with paragraph 17 of the Commentary on Section III, the additional information obtained under such amended AML/KYC Procedures must be used to determine whether there has been a change of circumstances in relation to the identity and/or reportable status of Account Holders and/or Controlling Persons. As explained in paragraph 4, above, if the additional information obtained is inconsistent with the claims made by a person in a self-certification, then there has been a change in circumstances and a Reporting Financial Institution will have a reason to know that a self-certification is unreliable or incorrect.

[...]

Paragraph Abis – Temporary lack of Self-Certification

10bis. Paragraph Abis contains the special due diligence procedure that must be temporarily applied in exceptional circumstances where a self-certification cannot be obtained and validated by a Reporting Financial Institution in respect of a New Account in time to meet its due diligence and reporting obligations with respect to the reporting period during which the account was opened. Where the self-certification cannot be obtained and validated in respect of a New Individual Account, the Reporting Financial Institution must temporarily apply the due diligence procedures for Preexisting Individual Accounts under Section III. Similarly, where a self-certification cannot be obtained and validated in respect of a New Entity Account, the Reporting Financial Institution must temporarily apply the due diligence procedures for Preexisting Entity Accounts under Section V.

10ter. Notwithstanding the above, for the purposes of subparagraph A(2) of Section I, such accounts should be reported upon as New Accounts.

[...]

Commentary on Section VIII

[...]

Paragraph A – Reporting Financial Institution

[...]

Subparagraph A(3) through (~~8~~11) – Financial Institution

[…]

Custodial Institution

9. Subparagraph A(4) defines the term "Custodial Institution" as any Entity that holds, as a substantial portion of its business, Financial Assets for the account of others.

10. It further establishes the 'substantial portion' test. An Entity holds Financial Assets for the account of others as a substantial portion of its business if the Entity's gross income attributable to the holding of Financial Assets and related financial services equals or exceeds 20% of the Entity's gross income during the shorter of:

- the three-year period that ends on 31 December (or the final day of a non-calendar year accounting period) prior to the year in which the determination is being made; or
- the period during which the Entity has been in existence.

'Income attributable to holding Financial Assets and related financial services' means custody, account maintenance, and transfer fees; commissions and fees earned from executing and pricing securities transactions with respect to Financial Assets held in custody; income earned from extending credit to customers with respect to Financial Assets held in custody (or acquired through such extension of credit); income earned on the bid-ask spread of Financial Assets held in custody; and fees for providing financial advice with respect to Financial Assets held in (or potentially to be held in) custody by the entity; and for clearance and settlement services.

10bis. Income attributable to related financial services also includes commissions and fees from holding, transferring and exchanging of Relevant Crypto-Assets held in custody.

10ter. For the purposes of the gross income test, all remuneration for the relevant activities of an Entity is to be taken into account, independent of whether that remuneration is paid directly to the Entity to which the test is applied or to another Entity. For example, in certain instances, a professional accounting or law firm sets up a trust for a client and, as part of that process, appoints a corporate trustee. The client then pays the accounting or law firm for all services rendered in relation to the set-up of the trust, including the appointment of the corporate trustee and other trustee services. As such, the corporate trustee itself does not receive a direct remuneration for its services as these are paid to the accounting or law firm as part of the overall package. This issue can also arise in the context of Entities that provide custodial services if the fees for such services are paid to another Entity. In both instances, such remuneration should be taken into account for the purposes of the gross income test.

11. Entities that safe keep Financial Assets for the account of others, such as custodian banks, brokers and central securities depositories, would generally be considered Custodial Institutions. Entities that do not hold Financial Assets for the account of others, such as insurance brokers, will not be Custodial Institutions.

11bis. For Financial Assets issued in the form of a Relevant Crypto-Asset, "safekeeping" is understood to also include the safekeeping or administration of instruments enabling control over such assets (for example, private keys), to the extent that the Entity has the ability to manage, trade or transfer to third parties the underlying Financial Assets on the user's behalf. Consequently, an Entity that solely offers storage or security services for private keys to such Financial Assets, would not be considered a Custodial Institution.

Depository Institution

12. Subparagraph A(5) defines the term "Depository Institution" as any Entity that *a)* accepts deposits in the ordinary course of a banking or similar business; *or b) holds Specified Electronic Money Products or Central Bank Digital Currencies for the benefit of customers.*

13. An Entity is considered to ~~be engaged in~~ *accept deposits in the ordinary course* of a 'banking or similar business' if, in the ordinary course of its business with customers, the Entity accepts deposits or other similar investments of funds and regularly engages in, *or is licenced to engage in*, one or more of the following activities:

a) mak*ing*~~es~~ personal, mortgage, industrial, or other loans or provid*ing*~~es~~ other extensions of credit;

b) purchas*ing*~~es~~, selli*ng*~~s~~, discount*ing*~~s~~, or negotiat*ing*~~es~~ accounts receivable, instalment obligations, notes, drafts, checks, bills of exchange, acceptances, or other evidences of indebtedness;

c) issu*ing*~~es~~ letters of credit and negotiat*ing*~~es~~ drafts drawn thereunder;

d) provid*ing*~~es~~ trust or fiduciary services;

e) financ*ing*~~es~~ foreign exchange transactions; or

f) enter*ing*~~s~~ into, purchas*ing*~~es~~, or dispos*ing*~~es~~ of finance leases or leased assets.

An Entity is not considered to ~~be engaged in~~ accept deposits in the ordinary course of a banking or similar business if the Entity solely accepts deposits from persons as a collateral or security pursuant to a sale or lease of property or pursuant to a similar financing arrangement between such Entity and the person holding the deposit with the Entity.

~~14. Savings banks, commercial banks, savings and loan associations, and credit unions would generally be considered Depository Institutions. However, whether an Entity conducts a banking or similar business is determined based upon the character of the actual activities of such Entity.~~

14. An Entity is also considered a Depository Institution if it holds Specified Electronic Money Products or Central Bank Digital Currencies for the benefit of customers. In most instances, such Entity will be the issuer of the Specified Electronic Money Products or Central Bank Digital Currencies. With respect to Specified Electronic Money Products issued in the form of a Crypto-Asset, the Depository Institution that holds such product will typically be a custodial Crypto-Asset exchange or wallet provider.

[…]

Investment Entity

[…]

16. Subparagraph A(6)(a) defines the first type of "Investment Entity" as any Entity that primarily conducts as a business one or more of the following activities or operations for or on behalf of a customer:

a) trading in money market instruments (cheques, bills, certificates of deposit, derivatives, etc.); foreign exchange; exchange, interest rate and index instruments; transferable securities; or commodity futures trading;

b) individual and collective portfolio management; or

c) otherwise investing, administering, or managing Financial Assets*,* ~~or~~ money *(including Central Bank Digital Currencies), or Relevant Crypto-Assets* on behalf of other persons.

Such activities or operations do not include rendering non-binding investment advice to a customer. For purposes of subparagraph A(6)(a), *the term "customer" includes the Equity Interest holder of a collective investment vehicle, whereby the collective investment vehicle is considered to conduct its activities or operations as a business. For purposes of subparagraph A(6)(a)(iii), the term "investing, administering, or trading" does not comprise the provision of services effectuating Exchange Transactions for or on behalf of customers.*

17. Subparagraph A(6)(b) defines the second type of "Investment Entity" as any Entity the gross income of which is primarily attributable to investing, reinvesting, or trading in Financial Assets *or Relevant Crypto-Assets,* if the Entity is managed by another Entity that is a Depository Institution, a Custodial Institution, a Specified Insurance Company, or an Investment Entity described in subparagraph A(6)(a). An Entity is 'managed by' another Entity if the managing Entity performs, either directly or through another service provider, any of the activities or operations described in subparagraph A(6)(a) on behalf of the managed Entity. However, an Entity does not manage another Entity if it does not have discretionary authority to manage the Entity's assets (in whole or part). Where an Entity is managed by a mix of Financial Institutions, NFEs or individuals, the Entity is considered to be managed by another Entity that is a Depository Institution, a Custodial Institution, a Specified Insurance Company, or an Investment Entity described in subparagraph A(6)(a), if any of the managing Entities is such another Entity. *For example, a private trust company that acts as a registered office or registered agent of a trust or performs administrative services unrelated to the Financial Assets, Relevant Crypto-Assets or money of the trust, does not conduct the activities and operations described in subparagraph (A)(6)(a) on behalf of the trust and thus the trust is not "managed by" the private trust company within the meaning of subparagraph (A)(6)(b). Also, an Entity that invests all or a portion of its assets in a mutual fund, exchange traded fund, or similar vehicle will not be considered "managed by" the mutual fund, exchange traded fund, or similar vehicle. In both of these examples, a further determination needs to be made as to whether the Entity is managed by another Entity for the purpose of ascertaining whether the first-mentioned Entity falls within the definition of Investment Entity, as set out in subparagraph (A)(6)(b).*

18. An Entity is treated as primarily conducting as a business one or more of the activities described in subparagraph A(6)(a), or an Entity's gross income is primarily attributable to investing, reinvesting, or trading in Financial Assets *or Relevant Crypto-Assets* for purposes of subparagraph A(6)(b), if the Entity's gross income attributable to the relevant activities equals or exceeds 50% of the Entity's gross income during the shorter of:

- the three-year period ending on 31 December of the year preceding the year in which the determination is made; or
- the period during which the Entity has been in existence.

As clarified in paragraph 10ter, above, for the purposes of the gross income test, all remuneration for the relevant activities of an Entity is to be taken into account, independent of whether that remuneration is paid directly to the Entity to which the test is applied or to another Entity.

19. The term "Investment Entity", as defined in subparagraph A(6), does not include an Entity that is an Active NFE because it meets any of the criteria in subparagraphs D(9)(d) through (g) (i.e. holding NFEs and treasury centres that are members of a nonfinancial group; start-up NFEs; and NFEs that are liquidating or emerging from bankruptcy).

20. An Entity would generally be considered an Investment Entity if it functions or holds itself out as a collective investment vehicle, mutual fund, exchange traded fund, private equity fund, hedge fund, venture capital fund, leveraged buy-out fund or any similar investment vehicle established with an investment strategy of investing, reinvesting, or trading in Financial Assets *or Relevant Crypto-Assets*. An Entity that primarily conducts as a business investing, administering, or managing non-debt, direct interests in real property on behalf of other persons, such as a type of real estate investment trust, will not be an Investment Entity.

[…]

Financial Asset

[...]

24. Within that context, subparagraph A(7) provides that the term "Financial Asset" includes a security (for example, a share of stock in a corporation; partnership or beneficial ownership interest in a widely held or publicly traded partnership or trust; note, bond, debenture, or other evidence of indebtedness), partnership interest, commodity, swap (for example, interest rate swaps, currency swaps, basis swaps, interest rate caps, interest rate floors, commodity swaps, equity swaps, equity index swaps, and similar agreements), Insurance Contract or Annuity Contract, or any interest (including a futures or forward contract or option) in a security, *Relevant Crypto-Asset,* partnership interest, commodity, swap, Insurance Contract, or Annuity Contract. However, the term "Financial Asset" does not include a non-debt, direct interest in real property; or a commodity that is a physical good, such as wheat.

[...]

25bis. In each case, the determination of whether an asset is a Financial Asset is independent from the form in which such asset is issued. Therefore, an asset issued in the form of a Crypto-Asset may simultaneously be a Financial Asset.

[...]

Specified Electronic Money Product

29bis. Subparagraph A(9) defines the term "Specified Electronic Money Product" as any product that is:

a) a digital representation of a single Fiat Currency;

b) issued on receipt of funds for the purpose of making payment transactions;

c) represented by a claim on the issuer denominated in the same Fiat Currency;

d) accepted in payment by a natural or legal person other than the issuer; and

e) by virtue of regulatory requirements to which the issuer is subject, redeemable at any time and at par value for the same Fiat Currency upon request of the holder of the product.

The term "Specified Electronic Money Product" does not include a product created for the sole purpose of facilitating the transfer of funds from a customer to another person pursuant to instructions of the customer. A product is not created for the sole purpose of facilitating the transfer of funds if, in the ordinary course of business of the transferring Entity, either the funds connected with such product are held longer than 60 days after receipt of instructions to facilitate the transfer, or, if no instructions are received, the funds connected with such product are held longer than 60 days after receipt of the funds.

29ter. Subparagraph A(9)(a) requires that a product must be a digital representation of a single Fiat Currency, in order to be a Specified Electronic Money Product. A product will be considered to digitally represent and reflect the value of the Fiat Currency that it is denominated in. Consequently, a product that reflects the value of multiple currencies or assets is not a Specified Electronic Money Product.

29quater. Subparagraph A(9)(b) provides that the product must be issued on receipt of funds. This part of the definition means that a Specified Electronic Money Products is a prepaid product. The act of "issuing" is interpreted broadly to include the activity of making available pre-paid stored value and means of payment in exchange for funds. In this respect, both electronically and magnetically stored products may be "issued", including online payment accounts and physical cards using magnetic stripe technology. In addition, this subparagraph provides that the product must be issued for the purpose of making payment transactions.

29quinquies. Subparagraph A(9)(c) requires that, in order to be a Specified Electronic Money Product, a product must be represented by a claim on the issuer denominated in the same Fiat Currency. In this respect, a "claim" includes any monetary claim against the issuer, reflecting the value of the Fiat Currency represented by the electronic money product issued to the customer.

29sexies. Under subparagraph A(9)(d), a product must be accepted by a natural or legal person other than the issuer in order to be a Specified Electronic Money Product, whereby such third parties must accept the electronic money product as a means of payment. Consequently, monetary value stored on specific pre-paid instruments, designed to address precise needs that can be used only in a limited way, because they allow the electronic money holder to purchase goods or services only in the premises of the electronic money issuer or within a limited network of service providers under direct commercial agreement with a professional issuer, or because they can be used only to acquire a limited range of goods or services, are not considered Specified Electronic Money Products.

29septies. Subparagraph A(9)(e) provides that the issuer of the product must be subject to supervision to ensure the product is redeemable at any time and at par value for the same Fiat Currency upon request of the holder of the product, in order to be a Specified Electronic Money Product. In this respect, the "same" Fiat Currency refers to the Fiat Currency that the electronic money product is a digital representation of. When proceeding to a redemption, it is acknowledged that the issuer can deduct from the redemption amount any fees or transaction costs.

29octies. The definition excludes those products that are created solely to facilitate a funds transfer pursuant to instructions of a customer and that cannot be used to store value. For example, such products may be used to enable an employer to transfer the monthly wages to its employees or to enable a migrant worker to transfer funds to relatives living in another country. A product is not created for the sole purpose of facilitating the transfer of funds if, in the ordinary course of business of the transferring Entity, either the funds connected with such product are held longer than 60 days after receipt of instructions to facilitate the transfer, or, if no instructions are received, the funds connected with such product are held longer than 60 days after receipt of the funds.

Central Bank Digital Currency, Fiat Currency, Crypto-Asset, Relevant Crypto-Asset, and Exchange Transaction

The terms "Central Bank Digital Currency", "Fiat Currency", "Crypto-Asset", "Relevant Crypto-Asset", and "Exchange Transaction" should be interpreted consistently with the Commentary of the Crypto-Asset Reporting Framework.

[...]

Paragraph B – Non-Reporting Financial Institution

[...]

Subparagraph B(1) – In general

30. Subparagraph B(1) sets out the various categories of Non-Reporting Financial Institutions (i.e. Financial Institutions that are excluded from reporting). "Non-Reporting Financial Institution" means any Financial Institution that is:

a) a Governmental Entity, International Organisation or Central Bank, other than:

   i. with respect to a payment that is derived from an obligation held in connection with a commercial financial activity of a type engaged in by a Specified Insurance Company, Custodial Institution, or Depository Institution; *or*

ii. *with respect to the activity of maintaining Central Bank Digital Currencies for Account Holders which are not Financial Institutions, Governmental Entities, International Organisations or Central Banks.*

[...]

Subparagraphs B(2) through (4) – Governmental Entity, International Organisation and Central Bank

31. ~~A Financial Institution that is a Governmental Entity, International Organisation or Central Bank is a Non-Reporting Financial Institution, according to subparagraph B(1)(a), other than with respect to a payment that is derived from an obligation held in connection with a commercial activity of a type engaged in by a Specified Insurance Company, Custodial Institution, or Depository Institution.~~ *According to subparagraph B(1)(a), a Financial Institution that is a Governmental Entity, International Organisation or Central Bank is a Non-Reporting Financial Institution. However, under subparagraph B(1)(a)(i), the exclusion does not apply with respect to a payment that is derived from an obligation held in connection with a financial activity of a type engaged in by a Specified Insurance Company, Custodial Institution, or Depository Institution. Equally, under subparagraph B(1)(a)(ii), the exclusion does not apply with respect to the activity of maintaining Central Bank Digital Currencies for Account Holders which are not Financial Institutions, Governmental Entities, International Organisations or Central Banks.* Thus, for example, a Central Bank that conducts a financial activity, such as acting as an intermediary on behalf of persons other than in the bank's capacity as a Central Bank, is not a Non-Reporting Financial Institution under subparagraph B(1)(a)(i) with respect to payments received in connection with an account held in connection with such activity. *Equally, under subparagraph B(1)(a)(ii), maintaining Central Bank Digital Currencies for Account Holders which are not Financial Institutions, Governmental Entities, International Organisations or Central Banks, is also an activity in respect of which a Central Bank is not a Non-Reporting Financial Institution*.

[...]

Subparagraphs B(5) through (7) - Funds

36. Subparagraph B(5) defines the term "Broad Participation Retirement Fund" as a fund established to provide retirement, disability, or death benefits, or any combination thereof, to beneficiaries that are current or former employees (or persons designated by such employees) of one or more employers in consideration for services rendered, provided that the fund:

a) does not have a single beneficiary with a right to more than 5% of the fund's assets;
b) is subject to regulation and provides information reporting to the tax authorities; and
c) satisfies at least one of the four requirements listed in subparagraph B(5)(c) (i.e. the fund is tax-favoured; most contributions are received from sponsoring employers; distributions or withdrawals are only allowed upon the occurrence of specified events; and contributions by employees are limited by amount).

36bis. Section VIII(B)(5)(a) requires that, in order for a Financial Institution to be able to qualify as a Non-Reporting Financial Institution under the Broad Participation Retirement Fund category, the Financial Institution needs, inter alia, to ensure that it has no single beneficiary with a right to more than 5% of the fund's assets. In case the fund is compartmentalised into sub-funds that are in practice working as separated pension products, including through the segregation of the assets, risks and income attributed to such sub-funds, the test of whether a single beneficiary has a right to more than 5% of the fund's assets is to be applied at the level of each sub-fund.

Qualified Non-Profit Entity

36ter. Subparagraphs B(2) through B(9) contain the categories of Non-Reporting Financial Institutions: "Governmental Entity", "International Organisation", "Central Bank", "Broad Participation Retirement Fund", "Narrow Participation Retirement Fund", "Pension Fund of a Governmental Entity, International Organisation or Central Bank", "Qualified Credit Card Issuer" and "Exempt Collective Investment Vehicle".

36quater. In addition to these categories, jurisdictions may wish to also treat Qualified Non-Profit Entities as Non-Reporting Financial Institutions. Any jurisdiction adopting this optional provision must have in place appropriate legal and administration mechanisms to ensure that any Entity claiming the status of a Qualified Non-Profit Entity is confirmed to fulfil the conditions of subparagraph D(9)(h) of Section VIII before such Entity is treated as a Non-Reporting Financial Institution.

36quinquies. Examples of appropriate mechanisms include a detailed regulatory regime that indicates the conditions pursuant to which an Entity can be treated as a Qualified Non-Profit Entity, where such Entities are verified by a governmental authority as meeting such conditions. A mechanism could also be appropriate if a Qualified Non-Profit Entity would need to obtain a favourable ruling from a governmental or judicial authority on whether the Entity is a Qualified Non-Profit Entity. Similarly, a listing mechanism whereby Qualified Non-Profit Entities must request to be included on a state-run registry (e.g. in the framework of obtaining a domestic qualification as a tax-exempt entity or to confirm the tax deductibility of donations made to the charity), could be an appropriate mechanism. In any event, confirmation pursuant to such a mechanism that an Entity fulfils the conditions of subparagraph D(9)(h) of Section VIII must be obtained before such Entity can be considered a Qualified Non-Profit Entity and, hence, a Non-Reporting Financial Institution.

36sexies. Provided the implementing jurisdiction wishes to include the Qualified Non-Profit Entity category and has, or expects to have, the required appropriate legal and administrative verification mechanisms in place, such jurisdiction may modify the section on Non-Reporting Financial Institutions by adding an additional term, "Qualified Non-Profit Entity", in subparagraphs B(1)(f) and B(10), that either contains a list of the categories of domestic entities that meet the conditions of subparagraph B(10) or that generically spells out the conditions, as follows:

> B. Non-Reporting Financial Institution
>
> 1. The term "Non-Reporting Financial Institution" means any Financial Institution that is:
>
> […]
>
> f) a Qualified Non-Profit Entity.
>
> […]
>
> 10. The term "Qualified Non-Profit Entity" means an Entity resident in [Jurisdiction] that has obtained confirmation by the tax administration [or other governmental authority] of [Jurisdiction] that such Entity meets all of the following conditions:
>
> i) it is established and operated in [Jurisdiction] exclusively for religious, charitable, scientific, artistic, cultural, athletic, or educational purposes; or it is established and operated in [Jurisdiction] and it is a professional organisation, business league, chamber of commerce, labour organisation, agricultural or horticultural organisation, civic league or an organisation operated exclusively for the promotion of social welfare;
>
> ii) it is exempt from income tax in [Jurisdiction];
>
> iii) it has no shareholders or members who have a proprietary or beneficial interest in its income or assets;

iv) the applicable laws of [Jurisdiction] or the Entity's formation documents do not permit any income or assets of the Entity to be distributed to, or applied for the benefit of, a private person or a noncharitable Entity other than pursuant to the conduct of the Entity's charitable activities, or as payment of reasonable compensation for services rendered, or as payment representing the fair market value of property which the Entity has purchased; and

v) the applicable laws of [Jurisdiction] or the Entity's formation documents require that, upon the Entity's liquidation or dissolution, all of its assets be distributed to a Governmental Entity or other Entity that meets the conditions set out in i) to v), or escheat to the government of [Jurisdiction] or any political subdivision thereof.

Paragraph C – Financial Account

[…]

Subparagraph C(2) – Depository Account

66. The term "Depository Account"[…] includes any commercial, checking, savings, time, or thrift account, or an account that is evidenced by a certificate of deposit, thrift certificate, investment certificate, certificate of indebtedness, or other similar instrument maintained by a *Depository Institution* ~~Financial Institution in the ordinary course of a banking or similar business.~~ A Depository Account also includes:

a) an amount held by an insurance company pursuant to a guaranteed investment contract or similar agreement to pay or credit interest therein*;*

b) an account or notional account that represents all Specified Electronic Money Products held for the benefit of a customer; and

c) an account that holds one or more Central Bank Digital Currencies for the benefit of a customer.

[…]

67bis. All Specified Electronic Money Products an Entity holds for the benefit of a customer are together considered a Depository Account of that customer. For the purposes of determining the value of such Depository Account, a Reporting Financial Institution is required to aggregate the value of all Specified Electronic Money Products the Account Holder holds with the Reporting Financial Institution. Similarly, any arrangement through which the Entity holds Central Bank Digital Currency for the benefit of a customer will be regarded as a Depository Account. In cases where a Specified Electronic Money Product or Central Bank Digital Currency has been issued as a Crypto-Asset, an Entity is considered to hold such asset for the benefit of a customer to the extent it safekeeps or administers the instruments enabling control over the asset (for example, private keys) and the Entity has the ability to manage, trade or transfer to third parties the underlying asset on behalf of such customer.

[…]

Subparagraph C(3) – Custodial Account

68. Subparagraph C(3) defines the term "Custodial Account" as an account (other than an Insurance Contract or Annuity Contract) for the benefit of another person that holds one or more Financial Assets.

68bis. An arrangement to safe keep or administer the instrument enabling control over one or more Financial Assets issued in the form of a Crypto-Asset for the benefit of another person is also a Custodial Account, to the extent that the Entity has the ability to manage, trade or transfer to third parties the underlying Financial Assets on the person's behalf.

Subparagraph C(4) – Equity Interest

69. The definition of the term "Equity Interest" specifically addresses interests in partnerships and trusts. In the case of a partnership that is a Financial Institution, the term "Equity Interest" means a capital or profits interest in the partnership. In the case of a trust that is a Financial Institution, an "Equity Interest" is considered to be held by any person treated as a settlor or beneficiary of all or a portion of the trust, or any other natural person exercising ultimate effective control over the trust. The same as for a trust that is a Financial Institution is applicable for a legal arrangement that is equivalent or similar to a trust, or foundation that is a Financial Institution.

70. Under subparagraph C(4), a Reportable Person will be treated as being a beneficiary of a trust if such Reportable Person has the right to receive, directly or indirectly (for example, through a nominee), a mandatory distribution or may receive, directly or indirectly, a discretionary distribution from the trust. *Indirect distributions by a trust may arise when the trust makes payments to a third party for the benefit of another person. For example, instances where a trust pays the tuition fees or repays a loan taken up by another person are to be considered indirect distributions by the trust. Indirect distributions also include cases where the trust grants a loan free of interest or at an interest rate lower than the market interest rate or at other non-arm's length conditions. In addition, the write-off of a loan granted by a trust to its beneficiary constitutes an indirect distribution in the year the loan is written-off. In all of the above cases the Reportable Person will be person that is the beneficiary of the trust receiving the indirect distribution (i.e. in the above examples, the debtor of the tuition fees or the recipient of the favourable loan conditions).* ~~For these purposes, a~~ *A* beneficiary who may receive a discretionary distribution from the trust only will be treated as a beneficiary of a trust if such person receives a distribution in the calendar year or other appropriate reporting period (i.e. either the distribution has been paid or made payable). The same is applicable with respect to the treatment of a Reportable Person as a beneficiary of a legal arrangement that is equivalent or similar to a trust, or foundation.

71. Where Equity Interests are held through a Custodial Institution, the Custodial Institution is responsible for reporting, not the Investment Entity. The following example illustrates how such reporting must be done: Reportable Person A holds shares in investment fund L. A holds the shares in custody with custodian Y. Investment fund L is an Investment Entity and, from its perspective, its shares are Financial Accounts (i.e. Equity Interests in an Investment Entity). L must treat custodian Y as its Account Holder. As Y is a Financial Institution (i.e. a Custodial Institution) and Financial Institutions are not Reportable Persons, such shares are not object of reporting by investment fund L. For custodian Y, the shares held for A are Financial Assets held in a Custodial Account. As a Custodial Institution, Y is responsible for reporting the shares it is holding on behalf of A.

[...]

Subparagraphs C(9) through (16) – Preexisting and New, Individual and Entity Accounts

81. Subparagraphs C(9) through (16) contain the various categories of Financial Accounts classified by reference to date of opening, Account Holder and balance or value: "Preexisting Account", "New Account", "Preexisting Individual Account", "New Individual Account", "Preexisting Entity Account", "Lower Value Account", "High Value Account" and "New Entity Account".

82. First, a Financial Account is classified depending on the date of opening. Thus, a Financial Account can be either a "Preexisting Account" or a "New Account". Subparagraphs C(9) and (10) define those terms as a Financial Account maintained by a Reporting Financial Institution as of [xx/xx/xxxx], and opened on or after [xx/xx/xxxx] *or if the account is treated as a Financial Account solely by virtue of the amendments to the Common Reporting Standard, as of [effective date of the revised CRS-1 day] or opened on or after [effective date of the revised CRS],* respectively. However, when implementing the Common Reporting

Standard, jurisdictions are free to modify subparagraph C(9) in order to also include certain new accounts of preexisting customers. In such a case, subparagraph C(9) should be replaced by the following:

9. The term "Preexisting Account" means:

- *a) a Financial Account maintained by a Reporting Financial Institution as of [xx/xx/xxxx] or, if the account is treated as a Financial Account solely by virtue of the amendments to the Common Reporting Standard, as of [effective date of the revised CRS-1 day];*
- *b) any Financial Account of an Account Holder, regardless of the date such Financial Account was opened, if:*
  - *i. the Account Holder also holds with the Reporting Financial Institution (or with a Related Entity within the same jurisdiction as the Reporting Financial Institution) a Financial Account that is a Preexisting Account under subparagraph C(9)(a);*
  - *ii. the Reporting Financial Institution (and, as applicable, the Related Entity within the same jurisdiction as the Reporting Financial Institution) treats both of the aforementioned Financial Accounts, and any other Financial Accounts of the Account Holder that are treated as Preexisting Accounts under this subparagraph C(9)(b), as a single Financial Account for purposes of satisfying the standards of knowledge requirements set forth in paragraph A of Section VII, and for purposes of determining the balance or value of any of the Financial Accounts when applying any of the account thresholds;*
  - *iii. with respect to a Financial Account that is subject to AML/KYC Procedures, the Reporting Financial Institution is permitted to satisfy such AML/KYC Procedures for the Financial Account by relying upon the AML/KYC Procedures performed for the Preexisting Account described in subparagraph C(9)(a); and*
  - *iv. the opening of the Financial Account does not require the provision of new, additional or amended customer information by the Account Holder other than for purposes of the Common Reporting Standard.*

Subparagraph C(17) – Excluded Account

86. Subparagraph C(17) contains the various categories of Excluded Accounts (i.e. accounts that are not Financial Accounts and are therefore excluded from reporting), which are:

a) retirement and pension accounts;

b) non-retirement tax-favoured accounts;

c) term life insurance contracts;

d) estate accounts;

e) escrow accounts;

ebis) low-value Specified Electronic Money Products

f) Depository Accounts due to not-returned overpayments; and

g) low-risk excluded accounts.

[…]

93. Subparagraph C(17)(e) generally refers to accounts where money is held ~~by a third party~~ on behalf of transacting parties (i.e. escrow accounts). The accounts can be Excluded Accounts where they are established in connection with any of the following:

[…]

e) a foundation or capital increase of a company provided that the account satisfies all the requirements listed in subparagraph C(17)(e)(v).

94. An Excluded Account, as described in subparagraph C(17)(e)(ii), must be established in connection with a sale, exchange, or lease of real or personal property. Defining the concept of real or personal property by reference to the laws of the jurisdiction where the account is maintained will help to avoid difficulties of interpretation over the question whether an asset or a right is to be regarded as real property (i.e. immovable property), personal property or neither of them.

94bis. An "independent confirmation" means for the purposes of subparagraph C(17)(e)(v)(ii) a written confirmation evidencing the company foundation or capital increase, such as an extract from the commercial register or confirmation from the lawyer, notary, or other service provider facilitating the transaction pursuant to the relevant law.

94ter. Subparagraph C(17)(e)(v)(iv) acknowledges that in some instances where the foundation of a company fails, an account established for this purpose may also be used to make payments to various service providers involved in the incorporation process. As a result, repayments made to persons who contributed the amounts may be made net of service provider and similar fees, which for the purposes of subparagraph C(17)(e)(v)(iv) includes amounts paid to lawyers, notaries, corporate registrars and other payments required to facilitate the incorporation or capital contribution.

Low-value Specified Electronic Money Products

94quater. Subparagraph C(17)(ebis) provides that a Depository Account representing all Specified Electronic Money Products of an Account Holder, with a rolling average 90 day end-of-day aggregate account balance or value during any period of 90 consecutive days that did not exceed USD 10,000 at any day during the calendar year or other appropriate reporting period is an Excluded Account. The rolling average 90 day end-of-day account balance or value during a period of 90 consecutive days must be determined for every day and is obtained on a particular day by adding the end-of-day account balance of each of the last 90 consecutive days and to then divide the sum obtained by 90, as illustrated by the following example:

- *A Depository Account representing all Specified Electronic Money Products of an Account Holder is created on 12 October of the year N. The end-of-day account balance or value is USD 10 over the last 81 days of the year N (i.e. 12 October to 31 December), and USD 100,000 over the first 9 days of the year N+1 (i.e. 1 January to 9 January), the rolling average 90 day end-of day account balance or value during a period of 90 consecutive days is (10*81)+(100,000*9)=900,810/90, i.e. USD 10,009. Therefore, the threshold is exceeded on 9 January N+1 and the Depository Account is not an Excluded Account as of that day. It will therefore be subject to CRS reporting in respect of the year N+1. The Depository Account is an Excluded Account in respect of the year N.*

[...]

Low-risk Excluded Accounts

[...]

103. The following examples illustrate the application of subparagraph C(17)(g):

[...]

- *Example 7 (Housing cooperative account): a type of account held by or on behalf of a group of owners or by the condominium company for the purpose of paying the expenses of the condominium or housing cooperative which meets the following requirements: (i) it is regulated in domestic law as a specific account for covering the costs of a condominium or housing cooperative, (ii) the account or the amounts contributed and/or kept in the account are tax-favoured, (iii) the amounts in the account may only be used to pay for the expenses of the condominium or housing cooperative and (iv) no single owner can annually contribute an amount that exceeds USD 50,000. Where some of the above requirements (such as the Financial Account being tax-favoured or contributions being limited to USD 50,000) are not met, substitute characteristics or restrictions that assure an equivalent level of low risk could be considered, taking into account domestic specificities. This may include features such as: (i) no more than 20% of the annual and total contributions due in the year being attributable to a single person, (ii) the account being operated by an independent professional, (iii) the amounts of the contributions and the use of the money being decided by agreement of owners in accordance with the condominium's or housing cooperative's constituting documents or (iv) disallowing withdrawals from the account for purposes other than the expenses of the condominium or housing cooperative. Because there are overall, substitute requirements that provide equivalent assurance that the account presents a low-risk of tax evasion, this type of account could be defined in domestic law as an Excluded Account.*

Paragraph D – Reportable Account

[…]

Subparagraph D(2) and (3) – Reportable Person and Reportable Jurisdiction Person

[…]

Reportable Person

[…]

111. Subparagraph D(2) defines the term "Reportable Person" as a Reportable Jurisdiction Person other than:

a) an *Entity* ~~corporation~~ the stock of which is regularly traded on one or more established securities markets;

b) any *Entity* that is a Related Entity of a*n Entity* ~~corporation~~ described previously;

[…]

112. Whether a*n Entity that is a* corporation that is a Reportable Jurisdiction Person is a Reportable Person, as described in subparagraph D(2)(i), can depend on the stock of that corporation being regularly traded on one or more established securities markets. Stock is "regularly traded" if there is a meaningful volume of trading with respect to the stock on an on-going basis, and an "established securities market" means an exchange that is officially recognised and supervised by a governmental authority in which the market is located and that has a meaningful annual value of shares traded on the exchange.

113. With respect to each class of stock of the corporation, there is a "meaningful volume of trading on an on-going basis" if (i) trades in each such class are effected, other than in de minimis quantities, on one or more established securities markets on at least 60 business days during the prior calendar year; and (ii) the aggregate number of shares in each such class that are traded on such market or markets during the prior year are at least 10% of the average number of shares outstanding in that class during the prior calendar year. *For the purposes of the Standard, "each share class of the stock of the corporation" means one or more classes of the stock of the corporation that (i) were listed on one or more established securities markets during the prior calendar year and (ii), in aggregate, represent more than 50% of (a) the total combined voting power of all class of stock of such corporation entitled to vote and (b) the total value of the stock of such corporation.*

[…]

Subparagraphs D(6) through (9) – NFE and Controlling Persons

[...]

125. Subparagraph D(9)(a) describes the criterion to qualify for the Active NFE status for "active NFEs by reason of income and assets" as follows: less than 50% of the NFE's gross income for the preceding calendar year or other appropriate reporting period is passive income and less than 50% of the assets held by the NFE during the preceding calendar year or other appropriate reporting period are assets that produce or are held for the production of passive income. *The test of whether an asset is held for the production of passive income does not require that passive income is actually produced in the period concerned. Instead, the asset must be of the type that produces or could produce passive income. For example, cash should be viewed as producing or being held for the production of passive income (interest) even if it does not actually produce such income.*

126. In determining what is meant by "passive income", reference must be made to each jurisdiction's particular rules. Passive income would generally be considered to include the portion of gross income that consists of:

a) dividends;

b) interest;

c) income equivalent to interest or dividends;

d) rents and royalties, other than rents and royalties derived in the active conduct of a business conducted, at least in part, by employees of the NFE;

e) annuities;

f) income derived from Relevant Crypto-Assets;

~~*f*~~*g*) the excess of gains over losses from the sale or exchange of Financial Assets *or Relevant Crypto-Assets*;

~~*g*~~*h*) the excess of gains over losses from transactions (including futures, forwards, options, and similar transactions) in any Financial Assets *or Relevant Crypto-Assets*;

~~*h*~~*i*) the excess of foreign currency gains over foreign currency losses;

~~*i*~~*j*) net income from swaps; or

~~*j*~~*k*) amounts received under Cash Value Insurance Contracts.

Notwithstanding the foregoing, passive income will not include, in the case of a NFE that regularly acts as a dealer in Financial Assets *or Relevant Crypto-Assets*, any income from any transaction entered into in the ordinary course of such dealer's business as such a dealer. Further, income received on assets to invest the capital of an insurance business can be treated as active income.

126bis. To facilitate effective implementation of the Standard, a jurisdiction's definition of passive income should in substance be consistent with the list provided in paragraph 126. Each jurisdiction may define in its particular rules the items contained in the list of passive income (such as, income equivalent to interest and dividends) consistent with domestic rules.

[...]

Paragraph E – Miscellaneous

Subparagraph E(1) – Account Holder

140. With respect to a jointly held account, each joint holder is treated as an Account Holder for purposes of determining whether the account is a Reportable Account. Thus, an account is a Reportable Account if any of the Account Holders is a Reportable Person or a Passive NFE with one or more Controlling Persons

who are Reportable Persons. When more than one Reportable Person is a joint holder, each Reportable Person is treated as an Account Holder and is attributed the entire balance of the jointly held account, including for purposes of applying the aggregation rules set forth in subparagraphs C(1) through (3) of Section VII. *In the case of an account for which ownership rights are split between the bare owner and a usufructuary, both the bare owner and the usufructuary may be considered as joint Account Holders or as Controlling Persons of a trust for due diligence and reporting purposes.*

141. In the case of a Cash Value Insurance Contract or an Annuity Contract, the Account Holder is any person entitled to access the Cash Value or change the beneficiary of the contract. If no person can access the Cash Value or change the beneficiary, the Account Holder is any person named as the owner in the contract and any person with a vested entitlement to payment under the terms of the contract. Upon the maturity of a Cash Value Insurance Contract or an Annuity Contract (i.e. when obligation to pay an amount under the contract becomes fixed), each person entitled to receive a payment under the contract is treated as an Account Holder. *Persons that have the right to access the Cash Value or the right to change the beneficiaries of the contract are to be considered Account Holders with respect to the Cash Value Insurance Contract in all instances, unless they have finally, fully and irrevocably renounced both the right to access the Cash Value and the right to change the beneficiaries of the Cash Value Insurance Contract.*

142. The following examples illustrate the application of subparagraph E(1):

- Example 1 (Account held by agent): F holds a power of attorney from U, a Reportable Person, that authorises F to open, hold, and make deposits and withdrawals with respect to a Depository Account on behalf of U. The balance of the account for the calendar year is USD 100 000. F is listed as the holder of the Depository Account at a Reporting Financial Institution, but because F holds the account as an agent for the benefit of U, F is not ultimately entitled to the funds in the account. Because the Depository Account is treated as held by U, a Reportable Person, the account is a Reportable Account.
- Example 2 (Jointly held accounts): U, a Reportable Person, holds a Depository Account in a Reporting Financial Institution. The balance of the account for the calendar year is USD 100,000. The account is jointly held with A, an individual who is not a Reportable Person. Because one of the joint holders is a Reportable Person, the account is a Reportable Account.
- Example 3 (Jointly held accounts): U and Q, both Reportable Persons, hold a Depository Account in a Reporting Financial Institution. The balance of the account for the calendar year is USD 100,000. The account is a Reportable Account and both U and Q are treated as Account Holders of the account.

[...]

Subparagraphs E(3) and (4) – Entity and Related Entity

144. Subparagraph E(3) defines the term "Entity" as a legal person or a legal arrangement. This term is intended to cover any person other than an individual (i.e. a natural person), in addition to any legal arrangement. Thus, e.g. a corporation, partnership, trust, fideicomiso, foundation (fondation, Stiftung), company, co-operative, association, or asociación en participación, falls within the meaning of the term "Entity".

145. An Entity is a "Related Entity" of another Entity, as defined in subparagraph E(4), if either Entity controls the other Entity, or the two Entities are under common control. For this purpose control includes direct or indirect ownership of more than 50% of the vote and value in an Entity. *In this respect, Entities are considered Related Entities if these Entities are connected through one or more chains of ownership by a common parent Entity and if the common parent Entity directly owns more than 50% of the stock or other equity interest in at least one of the other Entities. A chain of ownership is to be understood as the*

ownership by one or more Entities of more than 50% of the total voting power of the stock of an Entity and more than 50% of the total value of the stock of an Entity, as illustrated by the following example:

Entity A owns 51% of the total voting power and 51% of the total value of the stock of Entity B. Entity B on its turn owns 51% of the total voting power and 51% of the total value of the stock of Entity C. Entities A and C are considered "Related Entities" pursuant to subparagraph E(4) of Section VIII because Entity A has a direct ownership of more than 50% of the total voting power of the stock and more than 50%of total value of the stock of Entity B, and because Entity B has a direct ownership of more than 50% of the total voting power of the stock and more than 50% of total value of the stock of Entity C. Entities A and C are, hence, connected through chains of ownership. Notwithstanding the fact that Entity A proportionally only owns 26% of the total value of the stock and voting rights of Entity C, Entity A and Entity C are Related Entities.

Whether an Entity is a Related Entity of another Entity is relevant for the account balance aggregation rules set forth in paragraph C of Section VII, the scope of the term " Reportable Person" described in subparagraph D(2)(ii), and the criterion described in subparagraph D(9)(b) that an NFE can meet to be an Active NFE.

Subparagraph E(5) – Taxpayer Identification Number

146. According to subparagraph E(5), the term "TIN" means Taxpayer Identification Number (or functional equivalent in the absence of a Taxpayer Identification Number). A Taxpayer Identification Number is a unique combination of letters or numbers, however described, assigned by a jurisdiction to an individual or an Entity and used to identify the individual or Entity for purposes of administering the tax laws of such jurisdiction.

147. TINs are also useful for identifying taxpayers who invest in other jurisdictions. TIN specifications (i.e. structure, syntax, etc.) are set by each jurisdiction's tax administrations. Some jurisdictions even have a different TIN structure for different taxes or different categories of taxpayers (e.g. residents and non-residents).

148. While many jurisdictions utilise a TIN for personal or corporate taxation purposes, some jurisdictions do not issue a TIN. However, these jurisdictions often utilise some other high integrity number with an equivalent level of identification (a "functional equivalent"). Examples of that type of number include, for individuals, a social security/insurance number, citizen/personal identification/service code/number, and resident registration number; and for Entities, a business/company registration code/number. *In addition, some jurisdictions may also offer Government Verification Services for the purpose of ascertaining the identity and tax residence of an Account Holder or Controlling Person. In this respect, a unique reference number, code or other confirmation received by a Reporting Financial Institution in respect of an Account Holder or Controlling Person via a Government Verification Service is also a functional equivalent to a TIN.*

149. Participating Jurisdictions are expected to provide Reporting Financial Institutions with information with respect to the issuance, collection and, to the extent possible and practical, the structure and other specifications of taxpayer identification numbers *and their functional equivalents for the purposes of the CRS.* The OECD will endeavour to facilitate its dissemination. Such information will facilitate the collection of accurate TINs by Reporting Financial Institutions.

[...]

Subparagraph E(7) – Government Verification Service

163. Subparagraph E(7) defines a "Government Verification Service" as an electronic process made available by a Reportable Jurisdiction to a Reporting Financial Institution for the purposes of ascertaining the identity and tax residence of an Account Holder or Controlling Person.

164. Such services may include the use of Application Programming Interfaces (APIs) and any other government-authorised solutions that allow Reporting Financial Institutions to confirm the identity and tax residence of an Account Holder or Controlling Person.

165. Where a tax administration opts for identification of Account Holders or Controlling Persons based on an API solution, it would normally make an API portal accessible to Reporting Financial Institutions. Subsequently, if the Account Holder's or Controlling Person's self-certification indicates residence in that jurisdiction, the Reporting Financial Institution can direct the Account Holder or Controlling Person to the API portal which would allow the jurisdiction to identify the Account Holder or Controlling Person based on its domestic taxpayer identification requirements (for example a government ID or username). Upon successful identification of the Account Holder or Controlling Person as a taxpayer of that jurisdiction, the jurisdiction, via the API portal, would provide the Reporting Financial Institution with a unique reference number or code allowing the jurisdiction to match the Account Holder or Controlling Person to a taxpayer within its database. Where the Reporting Financial Institution subsequently reports information concerning that Account Holder or Controlling Person, it would include the unique reference number or code to allow the jurisdiction receiving the information to enable matching of the Account Holder or Controlling Person.

166. For the purposes of subparagraph E(5), a unique reference number, code or other confirmation received by a Reporting Financial Institution in respect of an Account Holder or Controlling Person via a Government Verification Service is equivalent to a TIN.

167. Participating Jurisdictions are expected to provide Reporting Financial Institutions with information with respect to any Government Verification Services such jurisdictions have made available. The OECD will endeavour to facilitate its dissemination.

Commentary on Section IX

[...]

2. Under Section IX, a jurisdiction must have rules and administrative procedures in place to ensure the effective implementation of, and compliance with, the reporting and due diligence procedures set out in the Common Reporting Standard. The Standard will not be considered effectively implemented unless it is adopted in good faith with consideration to its Commentary which seeks to promote its consistent application across jurisdictions. *It is therefore acknowledged that effective implementation of the Common Reporting Standard may in some instances also necessitate reflecting parts of the Commentary in binding rules*. Since the application of the CRS requires that it be translated into domestic law, there may be differences in domestic implementation. Therefore, in the cross-border context, reference needs to be made to the law of the implementing jurisdiction. For example, the question may arise whether a particular Entity that is resident in a Participating Jurisdiction and has a Financial Account in another Participating Jurisdiction, meets the definition of "Financial Institution". The Entity may meet the "substantial portion" test to be a Custodial Institution in one Participating Jurisdiction, but different measurement techniques for gross income may mean that the Entity does not meet such test in another Participating Jurisdiction. In such a case, the classification of the Entity ought to be resolved under the law of the Participating Jurisdiction in which the Entity is resident. *If an Entity is resident in a jurisdiction that has not implemented the Common Reporting Standard, the rules of the jurisdiction in which the account is maintained determine the Entity's status as a Reporting Financial Institution or NFE since there are no other rules available. Further, when determining an Entity's status as an Active or Passive NFE, the rules of the jurisdiction in which the account is maintained determine the Entity's status. However, a jurisdiction in which the account is maintained may permit (e.g. in its domestic implementation guidance) an Entity to determine its status as an Active or Passive NFE under the rules of the jurisdiction in which the Entity is resident provided that the jurisdiction in which the Entity is resident has implemented the Common Reporting Standard.*

[...]

18. Subparagraph A(5) requires that a jurisdiction must have effective enforcement provisions to address non-compliance. In some cases, the anti-avoidance rule described in Subparagraph A(1) may be broad enough to cover enforcement. In other cases, there may be separate or more specific rules that address certain enforcement issues on a narrower basis. For example, a jurisdiction may have rules that provide for the imposition of fines or other penalties where a person does not provide information requested by the tax authority. Further, given that obtaining a self-certification for New Accounts is a critical aspect of ensuring that the CRS is effective, it is expected that jurisdictions have strong measures in place to ensure that valid self-certifications are always obtained for New Accounts, *including New Accounts documented on the basis of paragraph A bis of Section VII. What will constitute a "strong measure" in in this context may vary from jurisdiction to jurisdiction and should be evaluated in light of the actual results of the measure. The crucial test for determining what measures can qualify as "strong measures" is whether the measures have a strong enough impact on Account Holders and/or Reporting Financial Institutions to effectively ensure that self-certifications are obtained and validated in accordance with the rules set out in the Common Reporting Standard.* An effective way to achieve this outcome would be to introduce legislation making the opening of a New Account conditional upon the receipt of a valid self-certification in the course of account opening procedures. Other jurisdictions may choose different methods, taking into account their domestic law. This could include, for example, imposing significant penalties on Account Holders that fail to provide a self-certification, or on Reporting Financial Institutions that do not take appropriate measures to obtain a self-certification upon account opening, or closing or freezing of the account after the expiry of 90 days.

Commentary on Section X

1. Paragraph A of Section X contains the general effective date in respect of the amendments to the Common Reporting Standard, i.e. [xx/xx/xxxx].

2. Paragraph B contains a limited exception to the general effective date for reporting on the role(s) by virtue of which each Reportable Person is a Controlling Person or Equity Interest holder of the Entity with respect to Financial Accounts opened prior to the effective date of the revised Common Reporting Standard: in respect of reporting periods ending by the second calendar year following the effective date of the revised CRS the Reporting Financial Institution is only required to report such information if it is available in its electronically searchable data.

4 Addendum to the Multilateral Competent Authority Agreement on Automatic Exchange of Financial Account Information

DECLARATION

I, [NAME and TITLE], [on behalf of] the Competent Authority of [JURISDICTION], declare that it hereby agrees to comply with the provisions of the

Addendum to the Multilateral Competent Authority Agreement on Automatic Exchange of Financial Account Information

hereafter referred to as the "Addendum" and attached to this Declaration.

By means of the present Declaration, the Competent Authority of [JURISDICTION] is to be considered a signatory of the Addendum as of [DATE]. The Addendum will come into effect in respect of the Competent Authority of [JURISDICTION] in accordance with paragraph 1 of Section 2 thereof.

Signed in [PLACE] on [DATE]

ADDENDUM TO THE MULTILATERAL COMPETENT AUTHORITY AGREEMENT ON AUTOMATIC EXCHANGE OF FINANCIAL ACCOUNT INFORMATION

Whereas, the Competent Authorities are signatories to the Multilateral Competent Authority Agreement on Automatic Exchange of Financial Account Information (the "CRS MCAA");

Whereas, the Competent Authorities intend to continuously improve international tax compliance by further building on their relationship with respect to mutual assistance in tax matters, as reflected in the existing automatic exchanges of information under the CRS MCAA;

Whereas, the CRS MCAA provides that the laws of the Jurisdictions would be amended from time to time to reflect updates to the Common Reporting Standard and, once such changes to the Common Reporting Standard are enacted by a Jurisdiction, the CRS MCAA would be deemed to refer to the updated version in respect of that Jurisdiction;

Whereas, the Common Reporting Standard has been updated in 2023 to amend its scope and enhance the reporting requirements and due diligence procedures;

Whereas, the present Addendum seeks to add certain information items to be exchanged under the CRS MCAA to reflect the additional reporting requirements introduced by the 2023 update to the Common Reporting Standard;

Now, therefore, the Competent Authorities have agreed as follows:

SECTION 1

Additions to the Information to be Exchanged with Respect to Reportable Accounts

Subject to the notification pursuant to subparagraph 2(a)(i) of Section 2 of this Addendum, the additional information to be exchanged pursuant to subparagraph 2 of Section 2 of the CRS MCAA, with respect to each Reportable Account of another Jurisdiction, is:

1. whether a valid self-certification has been provided for each Account Holder;
2. the role(s) by virtue of which each Reportable Person that is a Controlling Person of an Entity Account Holder is a Controlling Person of the Entity and whether a valid self-certification has been provided for each such Reportable Person;
3. the type of account, whether the account is a Preexisting Account or a New Account and whether the account is a joint account, including the number of joint Account Holders; and
4. in the case of any Equity Interest held in an Investment Entity that is a legal arrangement, the role(s) by virtue of which the Reportable Person is an Equity Interest holder.

SECTION 2

General Terms

1. This Addendum will be in effect with respect to Competent Authorities that are also signatories to the Addendum. It will be an integral part of the CRS MCAA and the provisions of the CRS MCAA will be applied mutatis mutandis to this Addendum.

2. A Competent Authority must provide to the Co-ordinating Body Secretariat at the time of signature of this Addendum or as soon as possible thereafter:

a) an updated notification pursuant to subparagraph 1(a) of Section 7 of the CRS MCAA:

   i) confirming that its Jurisdiction has the necessary laws in place to implement the 2023 update to the Common Reporting Standard and specifying the relevant effective dates with respect to Section 1 of this Addendum and the application or completion of the enhanced reporting and due diligence procedures, or any period of provisional application of this Addendum due to pending national legislative procedures (if any); or

   ii) indicating that its Jurisdiction does not yet have the necessary laws in place to implement the 2023 update to the Common Reporting Standard and, therefore, requesting consent to continue sending information without the application or completion of the enhanced reporting and due diligence procedures of the 2023 update to the Common Reporting Standard during a specified transitional period; and

b) an updated notification pursuant to subparagraph 1(f) of Section 7 of the CRS MCAA, specifying the Jurisdictions of the Competent Authorities for which it accepts their request specified in the notification provided pursuant to subparagraph 2(a)(ii) of this Addendum.

Done in English and French, both texts being equally authentic.

5 Commentary to Addendum

1. The Addendum to the Multilateral Competent Authority Agreement on Automatic Exchange of Financial Account Information (the "Addendum") consists of:

- a declaration to be signed by the signatories of the CRS MCAA, therewith indicating their intention to implement the amended CRS and to exchange based on the expanded reporting requirements. To become a signatory of the Addendum, the Competent Authority of the Jurisdiction or its designated representative must sign the Declaration and provide it, together with the text of the Addendum, to the Coordinating Body Secretariat.
- a preamble, which explains the purpose of the Addendum; and
- two sections containing the agreed provisions of the Addendum. Section 1 specifies the additional information items to be exchanged that result from the amended CRS. The first paragraph of Section 2 clarifies that the Addendum will be in effect amongst signatories of the Addendum; that it will be an integral part of the CRS MCAA and that the provisions of the CRS MCAA apply mutatis mutandis to the Addendum. The second paragraph of Section 2 provides the notification procedure for Competent Authorities under the Addendum, which is further set out hereafter.

2. Subparagraph 2(a)(i) foresees a notification through which the Competent Authorities inform each other that their respective Jurisdictions have in place the necessary laws to implement the Addendum, i.e. by lodging an updated notification pursuant to subparagraph 1(a) of Section 7 of the CRS MCAA at the time of signature of this Addendum or as soon as possible thereafter, and specifying the relevant effective dates. This could also include the specification of any conditions in national legislative procedures that may necessitate the provisional application of the Addendum during a limited period.

3. It is acknowledged that it may not be possible for some Jurisdictions, in particular those who have either recently implemented, or are in the process of implementing, the Common Reporting Standard, to give effect to the additional reporting requirements in Section 1 of the Addendum at the same date. In such instances, the notification pursuant to subparagraph 2(a)(ii) allows a Competent Authority to indicate that its Jurisdiction does not yet have the necessary laws in place to implement the 2023 update to the Common Reporting Standard and is, therefore; requesting consent to continue sending information without the application or completion of the enhanced reporting and due diligence procedures of the 2023 update to the Common Reporting Standard during a specified transitional period. As the counterpart to the notification pursuant to subparagraph 2(a)(ii), the notification pursuant to subparagraph 2(b) then allows Competent Authorities to accept requests from other Competent Authorities for transitional periods specified in their notifications provided pursuant to subparagraph 2(a)(ii) by providing an updated notification pursuant to subparagraph 1(f) of Section 7 of the CRS MCAA.

4. In instances where consent for a transitional period in accordance with the above mechanism is not provided or where such period has expired, the Competent Authority whose Jurisdiction has the necessary laws in place to implement the 2023 update to the Common Reporting Standard may, as appropriate and in application of paragraph 1 of Section 2 of this Addendum, rely on the existing provisions pursuant to paragraph 3 of Section 3, and paragraphs 3 and 4 of Section 7 of the CRS MCAA, to no longer send the information or to suspend or deactivate the exchange relationship with another Competent Authority that has not implemented the 2023 update to the Common Reporting Standard.

Annex A. Revised Recommendation of the Council on the International Standards for Automatic Exchange of Information in Tax Matters[1] (Adopted on 8 June 2023)

THE COUNCIL,

HAVING REGARD to Article 5 b) of the Convention on the Organisation for Economic Co-operation and Development of 14 December 1960;

HAVING REGARD to the standards developed by the OECD in the areas of mutual administrative assistance in tax matters, automatic exchange of information in tax matters, tax avoidance and evasion, the use of tax identification numbers in an international context, and the undertaking of simultaneous tax examinations;

HAVING REGARD to the significant progress achieved by the Global Forum on Transparency and Exchange of Information for Tax Purposes (GFTEI) in ensuring that the international standard of transparency and exchange of information on request and the Standard for Automatic Exchange of Financial Account Information in Tax Matters are fully implemented around the globe;

CONSIDERING that international co-operation is critical in the fight against tax fraud and tax evasion and in ensuring tax compliance, and that a key aspect of such co-operation is effective exchange of information on an automatic basis subject to appropriate safeguards;

CONSIDERING that the implementation of the international Standard for Automatic Exchange of Financial Account Information in Tax Matters has avoided the proliferation of different domestic or regional standards which would have increased complexity and costs for both governments and financial institutions;

CONSIDERING that implementation of international standards by all jurisdictions of relevance on a reciprocal basis serves to ensure a level playing field, noting that they can rely on either multilateral or bilateral agreements to give effect to such standards;

CONSIDERING the need to encourage consistent application and interpretation of international standards across countries;

RECOGNISING the need to review the Standard for Automatic Exchange of Financial Account Information in Tax Matters in light of the experience gained, the evolution and digitalisation of financial markets and the rise of new investment and payment practices, including with respect to crypto-assets;

CONSIDERING that crypto-asset markets are of a global nature and it is therefore appropriate to ensure the widespread and consistent implementation of the Crypto-Asset Reporting Framework as an international standard by all jurisdictions hosting crypto-asset service providers;

CONSIDERING that the International Standards for Automatic Exchange of Information in Tax Matters, are composed of i) the Common Reporting Standard, the Model Competent Authority Agreement, the associated Commentaries, as well as guidance on common technical solutions; and ii) the Crypto-Asset

Reporting Framework, the Multilateral Competent Authority Agreement (or bilateral competent authority agreements or arrangements), the associated Commentaries, as well as guidance on common technical solutions, and that they may be modified as appropriate by the Committee on Fiscal Affairs;

On the proposal of the Committee on Fiscal Affairs:

I. **RECOMMENDS** that Members and non-Members having adhered to this Recommendation (hereafter the "Adherents") swiftly implement on a reciprocal basis the International Standards for Automatic Exchange of Information in Tax Matters.

To this effect, Adherents should:

a) transpose the International Standards for Automatic Exchange of Information in Tax Matters into domestic law, as may be amended from time to time;

b) follow the latest Commentaries when applying and interpreting the relevant domestic law provisions; and

c) ensure that appropriate safeguards are in place to protect the confidentiality of information exchanged and comply with the requirement that information may be used only for the purposes foreseen by the legal instrument pursuant to which the information is exchanged.

II. **INVITES** Adherents and the Secretary-General to disseminate this Recommendation.

III. **INVITES** non-Members to implement the International Standards for Automatic Exchange of Information in Tax Matters.

IV. **INVITES** Adherents to support efforts for capacity building and assistance to developing countries so that they may be able to fully participate in and reap the benefits of this form of co-operation.

V. **INVITES** the GFTEI to:

a) continue to monitor the implementation of the International Standards for Automatic Exchange of Information in Tax Matters; and

b) identify jurisdictions to which crypto-asset service providers have nexus as relevant for the widespread and consistent implementation of the Crypto-Asset Reporting Framework, and define interested appropriate jurisdictions for receiving information under the Crypto-Asset Reporting Framework amongst Adherents, with the primary objective for receiving such information to be the administration of taxes and with due regard for the requirements in relation to confidentiality and data safeguards.

VI. **INSTRUCTS** the Committee on Fiscal Affairs to:

a) review the International Standards for Automatic Exchange of Information in Tax Matters in the light of experience gained by Adherents and in consultation with stakeholders; and

b) update the International Standards for Automatic Exchange of Information in Tax Matters over time to ensure that they remain relevant.

Note

[1] The OECD Recommendation on the International Standards for Automatic Exchange of Information in Tax Matters [OECD/LEGAL/0407] was adopted by the OECD Council on 15 July 2014 and revised on 8 June 2023. For access to the official and up-to-date text of the Recommendation, as well as other related information, please consult the Compendium of OECD Legal Instruments at http://legalinstruments.oecd.org.

www.ingramcontent.com/pod-product-compliance
Ingram Content Group UK Ltd.
Pitfield, Milton Keynes, MK11 3LW, UK
UKHW051505290926
15471UKWH00008B/1432

9 789264 410619